ROY

)CCAN FEMINISMS

:rspectives

MOROCCAN FEMINISMS

New Perspectives

Edited by

Moha Ennaji, Fatima Sadiqi, and Karen Vintges

AWP

AFRICA WORLD PRESS

TRENTON | LONDON | CAPE TOWN | NAIROBI | ADDIS ABABA | ASMARA | IBADAN | NEW DELHI

AFRICA WORLD PRESS
541 West Ingham Avenue | Suite B
Trenton, New Jersey 08638

Cover design by Joshua Porter
Book Typeset by SpiralUp Solutions Pvt. Ltd.

Library of Congress Cataloging-in-Publication Data

Names: Ennaji, Moha, editor. | Sadiqi, Fatima, editor. | Vintges, Karen, editor.
Title: Moroccan feminisms : new perspectives / edited by Moha Ennaji, Fatima Sadiqi, and Karen Vintges.
Description: 1 Edition. | Trenton : The Red Sea Press, 2016. | Includes bibliographical references and index.
Identifiers: LCCN 2016004644| ISBN 9781569024744 (pb : alk. paper) | ISBN 9781569024737 (hb : alk. paper)
Subjects: LCSH: Women--Political activity--Morocco. | Feminism--Morocco. | Women--Legal status, laws, etc.--Morocco. | Women--Morocco--Social conditions.
Classification: LCC HQ1236.5.M8 M67 2016 | DDC 305.40964--dc23
LC record available at http://lccn.loc.gov/2016004644

To the Memory of Fatema Mernissi

CONTENTS

INTRODUCTION

Moha Ennaji, Fatima Sadiqi,
and Karen Vintges

Feminist activism in Morocco, where Islam is the prevailing religion, has been growing since the 1980s. The last three decades have witnessed the emergence of numerous women's organizations in Morocco, with a considerable national and regional impact, such as among others, the well-known women's associations: Association Démocratique des Femmes Marocaines, Union de l'Action Féminine, and Josour. However, Moroccan feminism, thus far, has not received the attention of many researchers. This book aims to fill this gap and to promote academic debates about the interplay between women's movements and corresponding counter movements in the Middle East and North Africa (MENA). It discusses the various strands of Moroccan feminism and women's organizations which strive for the empowerment of Moroccan women. Its main focus is the various practices of female Moroccan activists and the vocabularies they use to underpin their struggle for women's emancipation, political participation, and legal rights. The book adopts a comparative approach to underscore women's agency in various political and socio-economic contexts, and highlight the fact that agency can be appreciated only within a specific context.

Contemporary Moroccan women today openly challenge the disparities in the legal treatment of women and other practices which have long been understood as Islamic, and formulate their own interpretations of Islamic sources and local traditions concerning the position of women. Moroccan Muslim women both individually and through organized efforts, claim various forms of full citizenship and identity (religious, national, ethnic) by appropriating cultural and / or religious traditions. Other strands of the Moroccan women's movement are frankly secular in character or secularist in that they criticize any religious base for women's organizations. Thus, feminism in Morocco, which is becoming polyvocal in character, necessitates the use of the plural form "Moroccan feminisms" rather than "Moroccan feminism."

The present volume aims to take stock of these feminisms as constitutive of Morocco's situation, and as an aspect that qualifies the country as an important player in the Middle East and North Africa. Morocco is characterized by its linguistic and cultural diversity. Along its multilingual character – the languages being used include Berber, Arabic, French, and Spanish – its multiculture consists among others of deeply committed Arab-Muslim and Berber identities. The multilingual and multicultural aspects of the country obviously color Moroccan feminisms as well. However, Moroccan feminisms succeeded in the past in overcoming these differences in their struggle for women's rights.

They namely played a central role in the struggle for democratization and women's rights, and made a vital contribution to important societal changes such as the reform of the Family Code in 2004 (Sadiqi and Ennaji 2006). Secular women's groups rallied with the progressive and democratic forces, while Islamist feminists joined the Islamist Parti de la Justice et du Développement (PJD), and later obtained important social and political gains (new seats in parliament and decision-making positions in the government (Moghadam 2012, Jaquette 2001). The Consultative Council of Human Rights and the Equity and Reconciliation Commission, created in 2003, are major signs of reconciliation within Moroccan society that reinforce democratization. Women's movements have contributed to a dialogue between secular strands and Islamists and managed to find a balance or compromise between these two poles. Likewise, the feminist movement has democratized public space and transformed the political history of Morocco. The reformed Family Code, which gives more rights to women and ensures gender equality before the law, has affected a country so deeply religious and patriarchal, to the extent that the Code has become an integral part and a constitutive component of the process of democratization and modernization.

Most currents of the Moroccan feminist movement negotiate Morocco's cultural heritages and display an outspoken commitment to gender equality and justice, which has been established as an international norm since 1981 as defined by the Convention on the Elimination of All Forms of Discrimination Against Women (CEDAW) and brought into force by the United Nations. Recent legal and institutional reforms in Morocco, particularly the amended constitution of 2011, which guarantees gender equality and women's political participation, along with the reform of the Family Code in 2004, have significantly impacted democracy and the modernization in Moroccan society.

Unlike Libya and Egypt, Morocco did not experience a revolution. Yet, it did not escape the tumult of the so-called Arab spring. Thousands of protesters took to the streets in a dozen of cities led by the February 20 Movement, which demanded the end of corruption and the right to social justice and democracy. This social movement displayed strong disgruntlement with the prevailing authoritarian political system. Women were strongly represented in these protests for democracy; they came from different religious and political backgrounds and marched alongside the men, demanding social and political change. On March 9th, 2011 King Mohammed VI responded by promising several political and social reforms. He amended the constitution which guaranteed gender equality, human rights, women's political participation, and the division of powers. In the November 2011 elections, the moderate Islamist party (PJD) won a majority of seats, beating the traditional *Istiqlal* (independence) party, the Party for Authenticity and Modernity and the socialist party which all have strong ties to the monarchy.

This peaceful transition was marked by the government's attempts to send an image of a modern and moderate Islam through the respect for women's rights. The government has committed to implement the new constitution through women's increased political participation. Yet, Prime Minister Abdelilah Benkirane's first ministerial cabinet comprised only one female minister, Bassima Hakkaoui. In the amended government of 2012, more women joined the cabinet, mostly as deputy ministers or as ministers in charge of specific departments. Bassima Hakkaoui kept the Ministry of Solidarity, Women, Family, and Social Development. Soumiya Benkhaldoun became "Ministre Déléguée" for Higher Education, and three liberal unveiled women took the reins of the Ministries of Foreign Affairs, Mines and Environment, respectively; but they were all "Ministres Déléguées", which is equivalent to Deputy Ministers. By contrast, the government prior to the Arab Spring included a total of seven women ministers from 2007 to 2011. This decrease in the number of women in government has caused unease amongst secular-liberal activists who viewed it as a regression. By contrast, more women joined parliament through the quota system for women and youth. Thus, a total of sixty eight women reached parliament after the 2011 legislative elections. The 2011 constitution reserved ten per cent of seats for women and ten percent for youth, in the hope of encouraging their political participation and their representation in parliament and government (Ennaji forthcoming).

This move, however modest it may appear, is an indicator of the new opportunities created for women by the Arab Spring: the state would simply not have authorized such a large number of women to enter parliament had it not been put under strain to democratize (El Haitami 2013).

Moroccan Feminism: an exemplary case?

Despite the positive changes in Morocco and the growing emancipation of women in all domains, there are still hurdles that hinder their emancipation and participation in public life such as illiteracy (50 percent), lack of education and information, lack of technical and professional training, weak resources available to them, difficult access to loans, and weak or lack of representation in decision and policy-making (Ennaji 2008).

More women than men suffer from social exclusion; their poverty is noticeable in the rural areas and in the poor urban districts, as well as in the growing number of beggars amongst women (generally widows, divorced, sick, or women with many children). Furthermore, cultural hurdles and patriarchal traditions, illiteracy, and lack of information prevent women from invoking their rights or reporting crimes against them, such as rape, child abuse, sexual exploitation and domestic violence. Concerning such cases, lawyers do not often make legal arguments based on international human rights treaties.

Women's organizations and civil society in general today do play a major role in sensitizing women, families, and social actors as to the importance of integrating women in economic, social, and cultural development. Further steps in favor of protecting women's rights are badly needed to ensure their strong contribution to sustainable development. Likewise, education and training are so important for women to enable them to meet the new challenges, and to help them safeguard their rights and interests. The development of society cannot be achieved without the integration of women in the process of growth and democratization.

Whereas recent political developments tend to undo the new coalitions that have arisen in the past, the Moroccan case in our view remains an interesting exemplar, in that internal factors played a significant role in shaping women's activism and political participation, including their capacity to influence political and social change. Has there been a spirit of cooperation in the past between the several strands of feminism, that might inspire future coalitions, in Morocco and elsewhere? What could such a future polyvocal feminism look like in the Middle East and North Africa?

Along the lines of Moghadam (2012), linking democratization and women's rights is of paramount importance because women in North Africa are the main advocates of development and social justice, including civil liberties as well as political participation. Across the region, women's organizations are characterized as democratic as well as feminist, often advocating and campaigning for gender equality, inclusion, and rights.

In the case of the Middle East and North Africa, emphasis ought to be put on women's participation, and on feminist non-government organizations (NGOs). Thus, the major proposal derived from the debate between feminist theory and democracy theory is that issues related to democratization and to women's rights cannot be separated, as they are closely linked and reciprocally inter-reliant. In the Arab-Muslim world, demands for democratization and women's legal rights have recently surfaced concomitantly, and it is of paramount significance not to split them up, or to regard them as two separate projects with different goals, structures, and results (Moghadam 2012).

Today, North African Women are no longer absent from the public sphere. They are activists "claiming equal rights and full citizenship" (Arfaoui 2012). Women's organizations in the region have made demands of their respective governments and put pressure on their parliaments or on the United Nations Commission on the Status of Women for radical changes in gender roles. Feminist activists continue the fight against all forms of violence and discrimination against women. They articulate diverse struggles to expand women's rights and for their societies' transition into the direction of pluralist democracy.

The Chapters

The chapters of this volume address these issues from various but inter-related perspectives: secular, Islamic, grassroot, etc., sometimes using a specific feminist female figure to make a point. Taken together, the chapters tell the story of feminisms born and developing in Morocco, a Muslim and emerging country where women's and gender issues are increasingly becoming central to the new actors on the political scene. As such, the chapters of the volume carry hope for future academic research on Moroccan feminist voices and discourses. Hence, in her chapter "Women and the Politics of Reform in Morocco", Souad Eddouada centers the 1990s reforms which capitalize on progressive representations of women and their political participation as individual citizens to highlight the pivotal role of Moroccan women's demands not only for the secularization of the Moroccan legal system, but also in the family and penal codes of this country. Women's call for the adoption of equal rights in legal reforms and in the campaign for the amendment of the penal code served Morocco's overall trend towards more democratization. For the author, the main challenges to the feminists claims are rural areas, which led her to discuss an alternative ideology of gender justice predating the aforementioned reforms.

Along the same line of thought, Moha Ennaji's chapter "Secular and Islamic Feminist Movements in Morocco: Contentions, Achievements, and Challenges" argues that the locus of women's movement in Morocco resides in its political nature, which allowed it to reach a compromise with the Islamic feminist organizations. In this chapter, the political nature of the Moroccan feminist movement is contextualized in the various secular and religious debates over the status of women and the challenges posed by the contemporary political history of the country. A milestone in the rapprochement between the secular and Islamist feminist trends is the legal status of women and Moroccan women's agency, reflected in their vibrant activism for legal rights and political participation. More specifically, the chapter reveals the positive role that secular Moroccan women have been playing in the struggle for social change. It also shows that women's gains are irrevocable and that the future of the country is significantly linked to the fate of women's movements and women's emancipation from their oppressed positions.

As for Fatima Sadiqi's chapter "An Assessment of Today's Moroccan Feminist Movements (1946–2014)," it retraces the journey of the Moroccan feminist voices, which started as secular voices and developed into diverse, polyvocal and complex expressions. In her assessment of these voices, Sadiqi underlines the fact that, although they may converge for political reasons, the philosophical and ideological concepts on which secular and Islamic feminisms in Morocco are inherently divergent. Being based on an Islamist ideology where religion is foregrounded, Islamic feminism cannot converge with secular feminism, based on a (leftist) progressive ideology where religion is backgrounded. For the author, with the advent of the twenty-first century and especially in the aftermath of the so-called Arab Spring, the "secular/Islamic" paradigm is becoming too narrow a space as it does not encompass the growing and poorly understood feminist voices where concepts like diversity, online synergy, Berber and rural are gaining momentum across the boundaries of gender and class. Although still in the making, these developments are real. In order to give as clear a view of the various feminist voices in Morocco as possible, Sadiqi's chapter focuses on contextualizing the main trends, secular and Islamic, comparing them, assessing their achievements and failures, and gauging the new feminist nuances where the Berber element is looming in the horizon.

Beyond the secular/Islamic paradigm, Susan Schaefer Davis and Amina Yabis' chapter "Moroccan Feminism at the Grassroots Level" underlines the importance of grassroots NGOs in promoting feminism in Morocco. Using an in-depth interview with an "average" woman who grew up in a working class family in the Fes medina and is currently married to a school teacher and living in a middle class neighborhood of a small town, the authors address the ways in which middle and working class Moroccan women view the larger project of feminism. For the authors, the fact that their informant founded a women's cooperative, and was nominated for Morocco's prestigious Khamisa Award as a woman leader, shows that the woman's upbringing, education, and current work place her among other women at a grassroots level rather than at the level of feminist activists – although she works to benefit women. The authors explores how this "average" woman became involved in her work with women, and how she sees feminism in Morocco.

Turning to another aspect of Moroccan feminism, "Islamic feminism in Morocco: Concepts and Perspectives" by Meriem Yafout looks at Moroccan women's engagement in the "male" subject of *Ijtihad* (the interpretation of the sacred texts: Qur'an and Sunnah – the Prophet's Sayings). The author ties the roots of this endeavor in women's frustration with men's interpretations of religious texts which they see as misogynistic, exclusive and patriarchal. The first such endeavors appeared in the late 1980s and aimed at empowering women through focus on the liberating spirit of Islam. Developing jurisprudence from a female perspective has ever since attracted more and more women. The author develops her ideas by considering the thoughts of some figures of Islamic feminism in Morocco.

In the same vein, Sara Borrillo's "Islamic feminism in Morocco: the Discourse and the Experience of Asma Lamrabet" identifies some of the most relevant aspects of the particular trajectory and discourse of Asma Lamrabet as an "Islamic feminist". Borrillo contextualizes Lamrabet's experience in the Moroccan women's movement and highlights the elements of continuity and innovation in her feminist approach. The author sees the Moroccan women's movement as consisting of various components that need to be singled out and distinguished according to the factors that orient women's different strategies, ideological identities and the forms in which they express protest or the practical outputs of their action.

Using the same broad approach, but tackling a different topic, Raja Rhouni uses her chapter "Decolonizing Feminism: a Look at Fatema Mernissi's Work and its Legacy" to highlight the scholarship and trajectories of an icon of Moroccan feminism: Fatema Mernissi. Rhouni offers a critique of Mernissi where she stresses the impor- tance of her work in understanding third world and/or postcolonial feminism in comparison with "Western feminism". At the same time the author states that although issues such as the validity of femi- nism's universalist claims and the colonial and imperial premises on Islam and Muslim societies lie at the heart of Mernissi's feminist thought, there are instances where this work inadvertently repro- duced some of those very premises, hence delaying decolonization. In other words, both the bright and the "less bright" aspects of Mernissi's contribution to the production of Moroccan feminism are critiqued. More specifically, this chapter questions the extent to which Mernissi's work achieved decolonization, allowing ordinary women's voices to emerge. The author underlines the importance of asking this question today especially that Mernissi has immensely contributed to draw a route for a number of feminists both in Morocco and around the globe. Rhouni's critical reading of Mernissi's work is a way of stressing its relevance for present research on Moroccan feminisms.

In "Deconstructing Female Identities within a Polyphony of Feminist Voices", Soumaya Belhabib uses the female identity as a theoretical paradigm where various social, economic, cultural, linguistic and ethnic criteria intersect. The author addresses women's multi-layered identities, often resulting from various competing socio-cultural models and influences which put women at the heart of the ongoing ideological, philosophical and religious ques- tioning that society goes through. By so doing Belhabib shows that the diversity in women's profiles cannot be represented by one single type of feminist leadership but that it necessarily gives rise to a polyphony of feminist stands with often diverging perceptions of gender equality and justice. Using the intersectionality theory, the author deconstructs women's identities and argues that the social cleavage between modernity and tradition has resulted in conservatism and modernity, giving way to two major feminist discourses: the progressive liberal discourse and the conservative Islamic one. The author adds that different types of feminism are emerging due to this very diverse society that we have today but also as a result of the multiple influences that globalization brings and the endless virtual possibilities that the new technologies have opened up. For the author, even if these 'feminisms' are not always on the same line, they nevertheless manage through opposing positions to advance women's rights and be in that difference truly representative of all identities.

As for Mohammed Yachoulti's "Women of February 20th Movement in Morocco: A New Feminist Consciousness", Moroccan women have managed in 2011 to forge a new political identity in the public arena. Through embracing the February 20th Movement's claims and strategies of activism and most importantly applying the principle of parity in all aspects of its uprisings that swept over the country, the new generation of women activists has drawn a new picture of feminist activism in Morocco. In fact, the dissatisfaction with previous forms of feminist activism and its elite nature not to mention their aspiration to put the whole society on the democracy track are but some of the triggers that pushed the new generation of Moroccan women to seize the Moroccan Spring moment to invest the public arena with new feminist beliefs and assumptions. This new shift is significant in terms of the future action of these actors, as well as in terms of democratic political practice.

In her chapter "Divas, Psychos and Action Chicks: Depictions of Women's Place and Space in Moroccan Cinema in the Age of Globalization", Valérie K. Orlando centers the contemporary film industry in Morocco to reflect on the sociopolitical and cultural transitions that have taken place in the country since 1999. The fact that the country's film industry has fully engaged with some of the most pressing issues of the era, encouraged by increased democratic transparency, men and women filmmakers have started to explore the sociocultural and political debates of their country; a nation, like others across the Arab world, undergoing huge sociocultural and political transitions. Hence, both male and female filmmakers have become more daring in how they depict women's bodies and sexual desires on screen. For the author, the degree to which sexual freedom is explored has, in part, been influenced by several monumental pieces of legislation enacted since 2000 that favor women's rights. These legal initiatives have helped to foster conceptual understandings of how heterosexual sex and sexuality are viewed in Islamic society at large. The positive reforms have, in turn, shaped what is shown on the screen. The 2004

Moudawwana (reform to the Moroccan family code) and the 2005 report handed in by the Instance d'Equité et Reconciliation (IER, Truth and Reconciliation Committee), which documented and made public egregious violations of human rights under Hassan II's near-forty-year regime, have greatly impacted women's lives, consequently opening the floodgates for the exposition of controversial subjects on film. Orlando underlines the fact that cinematic heroines in today's Morocco are at the heart of some of the most crucial socio-cultural dualisms that stratify discourse in Morocco; a discourse which is often most effectively transcribed on the screen. Women find themselves imbedded in scenarios which tackle secularism verses religiosity, Western verses Eastern, and French verses Arabic and/or Berber languages.

On the other hand, Aziza Ouguir's chapter "The Empowering Legacy of Women Saints: Venerators and Islamist Feminists" draws on the author's research for her doctoral thesis, which focuses on female religious agents in Morocco's past and present. More specifically, this chapter investigates historical women saints and their reception today by Moroccan women in general and by Moroccan feminist activists in particular. Despite the fact that women saints impacted their communities and marked Moroccan history with their legacy, little is known about them. Their lives, practices, and participation in their religious communities and society are rarely studied by social scientists. This chapter addresses women saints' construction of sainthood within the context of Islam as a religion and Sufism as the mystical dimension of that religion and the significance of this construction for broader discourses on gender and feminism in Morocco.

Finally, "The Implications of Having Drunk the Water of the Netherlands: Narrations on Agency and Communion in the Life Story of a Moroccan-Dutch Woman" by Marjo Buitelaar uses the story of Boushra, a 30 year-old Moroccan-Dutch medical specialist, to interrogate the term 'gastarbeider' as used by Moroccan migrants to describe their fathers, hence evoking the prototype of the rural migrant with little or no formal education and little knowledge about the country of settlement where he performed heavy and often dirty labor for very low wages. By thus characterizing their fathers, the children of migrants point to their fathers' great efforts to provide their families with a better future, as well as to the enormous social mobility that they themselves have accomplished in comparison to their parents. Boushra belongs to the category of first children of Moroccan background who entered the higher echelons of the Dutch educational system and labor market. Using a longitudinal research methodology, the author constructed a narrative of multiple identifications of highly educated women of Moroccan descent in the Netherlands. For the author, this narrative lends itself *par excellence* to reflect on the agency of female descendants of Moroccan background in the Netherlands. This final chapter moves Moroccan women's polyvocal feminisms beyond the country and opens up on the effect of migration on such feminisms.

Bibliography

Arfaoui, Khedija. 2012. "Women on the Move for Gender Equality in the Maghreb", In Di Marco, G. and C. Tabbush, (Eds.). *Feminisms, Democratization and Radical Democracy*, pp. 101–138 Buenos Aires: Universidad Nacional de San Martin Press.

El Haitami, Meryem. 2013. "Women in Morocco: political and religious power". In Open Democracy.net https://www.opendemocracy.net/5050/meriem-el-haitami/women-in-morocco-political-and-religious-power (accessed on March 21, 2014).

Ennaji, Moha. This volume. "Secular and Islamic Feminist Movements in Morocco: Contentions, Achievements, and Challenges".

Ennaji, Moha. 2008. "Steps to the Integration of Moroccan Women in Development", *The British Journal of Middle Eastern Studies* 35 (33), 339–348.

Jaquette, Jane. 2001. "Regional Differences and Contrasting Views", *Journal of Democracy*, Volume 12, N° 3, July 2001, pp. 11–125.

Moghadam, V. 2012. "Democracy and Women's Rights: Reflections on the Middle East and North Africa", In Di Marco, G. and C. Tabbush (Eds.). *Feminisms, Democratization and Radical Democracy*, pp. 46–60. Buenos Aires: Universidad Nacional de San Martin Press.

Sadiqi, Fatima and Ennaji, Moha, 2006. "The Feminization of Public Space: Women's Activism, the Family Law, and Social Change in Morocco", in *Journal of Middle East Women's Studies (JMEWS)*. Indiana: Indiana University Press.

This study was made possible with the financial support of The Netherlands Organization for Scientific Research

Chapter 1

WOMEN AND THE POLITICS OF REFORM IN MOROCCO

Souad Eddouada

Introduction

The purpose of this paper is to argue that given the particular and the complex issues that feminism as a framework of analysis and a project of social justice reform needs to address, it is difficult to assume that the path to gender equality can be designed and previously set up in a context that might not be receptive to a feminist approach. Within a context that is not receptive to a feminist perspective, addressing the issues that determine declared or implied closures becomes necessary.

While putting forward a context-based analysis the Algerian writer Maghnia Lazreg (1994) levels a critique against universal models of feminism. While distinguishing between eastern and western feminisms, Lazreg points out that within a western context, feminism is already established and normalized. Lazreg's advocacy for a feminist paradigm of difference is grounded on the failure of the western feminist model to produce in other places the emancipation it produced in the west[12].

For this reason, in Algeria and the Middle East, feminist projects evolve according to "external standards" since they operate within a "hostile context". Arguments using the universal feminist perspective can be misleading in the sense that they obscure the multiple systems of oppression in culturally, politically, socially and economically different contexts. While notions like the "East", the "West" or the Middle East are highly problematic in the sense that they reduce a heterogeneous and complex realities to one entity, still the notion of diversity of women's experiences within multiple systems is, in my contention, relevant to the understanding of particular local forms of oppression and already existing voices of women's resistance.[3].

The emancipatory aspirations of feminisms, although universal, are nevertheless confronted by additional dimensions of gender inequality in different contexts. These additional dimensions demand different frameworks of analysis within which women's struggle with gender-based oppression can be addressed. Although they all seek to determine and remedy inequality against women, feminisms as movements that evolved within different cultural and historical contexts of social change have different views depending on the agencies producing and reproducing inequality, which vary according to different contexts[4].

In 1999, the Moroccan newly created ministry of the family and women published the "Plan of Action of the Integration of Women into Development" (PAIWD). The publication of the PAIWD represents a case in point that is worth exploring here in order to show how an unexamined language on gender equality as it is produced in different contexts can culturally and socially alienate and, consequently constraints possibilities for a project for gender-based social justice.

The 1995 Beijing Declaration and Platform for Action adopted at the Fourth World Conference on Women identified the main impediments to women's rights improvement. It defined different objectives that called for action from the governments represented at the conference. Chief among these governmental actions is the adoption of gender-based policies which can be initiated by the elaboration of plans of action that translate "concretely" this United Nations' Women's Conference[5], which called for the establishment of an institutional mechanism with a decision making power that coordinates among ministerial departments and review policies and "equality programs". The publication of the 1995 United Nations Human Development Report which ranked Morocco 117th out of 147 countries, brought the issue of social inequality in Morocco to the forefront. As an issue dealt with in terms of the country's "international reputation", the urgency of change largely depended on international ranking produced from the perspective of Human Development Indicators[6]. This, in fact, confirms the impact of international feminist agenda on the visibility that gender-based reforms have acquired during the United Nations decade for women's rights.

The World Bank's report on Morocco officially initiated and put the reform on the agenda. The reform produced a political context favoring "change". The adoption of the World Bank's 1995 report as a reference for reform could be read as a background of the political decision implementing "change". The impact of such a report can be connected to the country's commitment as a State with a liberal system largely dictated by a heavily indebted economy (Khatibi 2002). For international liberalism, Morocco sees itself as a powerful State functioning with strategic flexibility, i.e. a reformist State committed to political and social reform[7]

This commitment to political and social reform has produced a political context more open to women's demands[8]. According to Belghazi and Madani:

> Many Social moblizations took advantage of the « Alernance » . . . Protest actions have largely benefited from the regime's dynamic open attitude offering space for tolerance and attention. As case in point, women's claims are received differently in the context of "Alternance" from the 1980's (2001: 19)

As a text produced within a context of reform receptive to women's demands, the PAIWD was also supported by the above-mentioned Beijing Conference recommendation. The distinction between the 80's and the 90's is mainly marked by a governmental recognition of the issue of gender through the creation of the *Secretariat d'Etat Chargé de la Femme et de la Famille* and the elaboration of a National Plan for Women's Integration into Development.

Le Plan d'action national pour L'intégration de la femme au Développement, a "Feminist" plan?

Even if the title *Intégration de la Femme au Développement* manifestly endorses the integrationist approach, namely that development is taking place and women are outside of it and must be integrated into it, the introductory part of the PANIFD suggests a certain distance from this premise and suggests that the international community's awareness of development and equality are the framework within which gender equality should be addressed. Development as well as its assumptions are framed from within an international agenda of development and equality: " Equality and development as tools provided by the international community in Nairobi (1985), Cairo (1994), Vienna (1993), Copenhaguen (1994) and Beijing (1995) combined with the convention for the elimination of all types of discrimination against women (CEDAW) are all phases in the achievement of the double objective of development and equality" (my translation from the text of the Plan of Action of Women's Integration into Development)

The nonexistence of "national" or "local" grounds for a development based on gender equality suggests that the project was mainly based on international conference recommendations. The Moroccan reservation with regard to the CEDAW is, however, mentioned without any comment. The Beijing Platform of Action was described as real 'normative' progress and standardization. The plan introduces itself to the reader as an attempt to put into practice a national strategy for women's improvement, an alternative to the previous government's policy failures. This is why, for future policies to be successful and for purposes of efficiency, the plan starts with an assessment of those policy constraints.

The main weakness of the public policies in the past was identified as the confinement of programs and actions targeting women to the social domain. Instead of effectively contributing to women's promotion, those policies contributed to the construction of "feminine identities" closely or exclusively bound to the family and social well-being .

Women's present status is described as not only the result of a cultural heritage but also the product of a State policy which reproduces daily practices that are never gender (or class) neutral. In this way, the State's institutions participate through a range of official and written rules (legal texts or decrees, school textbooks) and non-written conventions (norms and values) to fix and normalize manners that appear natural and unchangeable. Hence the necessity to change institutional practices so as to change unequal relationships (5).

Although it emerges as a plan with radical demands for women's rights since it questions the private/public dichotomy in the mainstream approach to gender[9], it does not lead to the identification of the reasons behind such a dichotomy. The PANIFD identifies the incoherent governmental policy and the dispersion along with the marginalization of women's concerns among insignificant ministerial departments. Its alternative is to organize and set up priorities which are identified as education, reproductive health, economic integration and empowerment.

Statistics on illiteracy among women show that 7 million women are illiterate (with a rate that reaches 67 % and 41 % among men). The first priority shows that illiteracy in the urban areas reaches 50 % and sometimes 100 % among rural women. This, in fact, illustrates the inadequacy of a national plan that aims at integrating 'woman' into development, since assumptions about women as a uniform group are undercut by factors like class or urban/rural divide, which are acknowledged by the plan as elements that question the accuracy of seeing women as a uniform category[10].

Furthermore, the PANIFD mentions that during a national inquiry in 1990–1991, the rate of illiteracy was not exact because only one person answered for all household members, which implies that the rate of illiteracy of women (and men) might be higher than expected. No explanation was given and no analysis was provided for the fact that one member of the family could speak, and his version could be adopted by official statistics; neither is there any analysis of this very obvious illustration of the way androcentrism functions within development ideology.

The section dedicated to reproductive rights is introduced by the argument that any development policy in a country with limited resources needs to focus on mastering population growth. Women's notion of reproductive rights seems to be abstract since it is not correlated with women's inability to exercise basic rights (Obyermer 1990: 19) . The PANIFD also glosses over the question of "autonomy" of choice and its incompatibility with the officially endorsed vision of woman in the family. The PANIFD includes women's individual human rights in the Family Code. Autonomy is in contradiction with the Family Code's gender discriminating principles of tutorship (the fact that women must be represented by their male guardian tutor in order to marry)[11], obedience to the husband[12], and the male's exclusive right of repudiation and marriage dissolution[13].

This suggests a complex relationship between demography and the cultural context. Fecundity is not only a biological but also a social and cultural phenomenon and, therefore, cannot be exclusively approached from a technical perspective. According the statistics citied by the PANIFD, the structure of contraceptive usage is dominated by the use of pills (70 %). Other methods do not go beyond 17.5 %, including traditional methods (12.5%). The latter two types are identified as weak in the program and are provided without comment, which implies an avoidance of the discussion of strategies to involve both men and women and of the cultural resistance that could impede this particular strategy and family planning in general. No explanation of the traditional versus modern dichotomy is given. Despite the cultural and social dimensions of women's and men's present connection to procreation as well as the cultural resistance that the State's family planning policies produce, the PANIFD deals with the questions in purely technical terms and exclusively targets women for contraceptive use.

Another priority is women's integration into development. The PANIFD underlines women's participation within an invisible economy that maintains fundamental relationships within the patriarchal family. Women's education, urbanization and development of manual work have all begun a process; however, it is not complete since it is not quite recognized.

By reducing women's issues to human development questions, the PANIFD reproduces what it criticizes for it gives only a partial view that confines the issue to technical interventions without questioning the mainstream development system. Women are said to suffer from poverty and social marginalization more than men. Statistics show that 52 % households headed by women are vulnerable. No connection is made to the conditions that explain this, namely divorce and widowhood as the main reasons behind the emergence of women as heads of poor households.

The main priority for the PANIFD is identified in terms of women's empowerment. Starting with a description of the Moroccan legal system's ambivalence, the PANIFD"s argument suggests a duality between a private space subject to "Muslim" law and public space dominated by a "modern" law inspired by Western values.

Women's legal status in Morocco shows an ambivalent judicial system. The Private sphere is entirely covered by Muslim law, while public space is inspired and dominated by western modern law (my translation PANIFD p 67)

In doing so, the PANIFD upholds two dichotomies it should challenge: an essentially Muslim misogynist law in contrast to an emancipating "Western model", and a private familial space as opposed to a public space. Not only does it maintain these dichotomies but identifies the duality "modernity" and "universality" versus "tradition" and "specificity" as the main issue for women.

By producing descriptions which maintain instead of questioning the existence of such a cultural duality between "spiritual and Muslim morality" as opposed to "materialistic modernity", the PANIFD rehearses stereotypes about feminism as an alien concept with no social support and thus, the PANIFD's "feminist" thesis maintains what it needs to problematize. In addition to endorsing existing androcentric assumptions, the PANIFD's abstract language does not build a case for the relevance of a feminist egalitarian project. Instead, it advocates the universal model as the only path to gender equality.

In trying to identify the PANIFD's pitfalls, my objective is neither to promote distrust of the sincerity of the intentions behind its implementation nor to seek true development that will benefit women. Rather I claim that, despite the text's desire to be an alternative model to previous development programs and their limitations, it shares some basic premises about "development" and "women" with those very programs. Implicitly, the PANIFD assumes that a linear, rational and pragmatic view is not imposed from above. Without showing how education, wealth, and access to power are denied to women just because of a biological difference from men, its integrationist approach fails to challenge the basic premises underlying the andocentric view.

In failing to show that feminism, as an analytical framework, can be supported by unfair expectations about women and men, the PANIFD indirectly endorsed the argument that the path to gender equality rests on an uncritical appropriation of abstract concepts with no local footholds. By reducing the diverse reasons that explain women's subordinate status, the text of the PANIFD erases all the complexities and "realities of women's lives. By ignoring the class dimension and its effect on women's different conditions (urban/rural discrepancy is either ignored or provided in terms of neutral statistics) "women" is constructed as a coherent group with the same interests. As Mohantly (1997) rightly points out, "the homogeneity of women as a group is produced not on the basis of biological essentials but rather on the basis of secondary sociological and anthropological universals." (1997:18) The essentialist developmentalist discourse on women reinforces the sexist discourse that labels them as a powerless group. The identification of women as a homogenous group is misleading, for as Mohanty maintains:

> Practices, which characterize women's status and roles, vary according to class. Women are constituted as women through the complex interaction between class, culture, religion and other ideological institutions and frameworks. They are not 'women' -as a coherent group- solely on the basis of a particular economic system or policy. (1997:83)

Mohanty sees the assumption that women can be homogenized into an isolated and uniform group target for a planned policy as problematic and reductionist. While women suffer from an oppressive Family Code and detrimental socioeconomic conditions, their experiences with gender inequality are neither identical nor separate from the impact of class and area of residence. (Rural women might share more conditions with rural men than with middle class, educated urban women).

The "Islamist"Anti-Thesis

By glossing over local cultural impediments to a linear view of development and gender equality, the PANIFD could not anticipate the resistance it raised in the name of an oppressed "Muslim identity". The PANIFD is attacked for its "anti-Islamist" thesis, that is, the materialist view of society and family and the uncritical adoption of international principles of gender equality, which overlook over the Moroccan reservations such as the Moroccan government's refusal to be part of the convention that stipulates men/women's equality in rights and duties during both marriage and its dissolution, as such a principle contradicts the "complementarity" of roles within the family where role divisions adhere to "biology" and "nature".

The fundamentalist anti-thesis to the PANIFD published by the fundamentalist organization *"Harakat Ataouhid Wa Ilislah"*

(The movement of Unity and Reform), in a pamphlet called *"Notre position"*, argues for female and male role divisions within the "Muslim family" that are disregarded by the PANIFD. These roles are mainly characterized as follows: the man is leader of the family, the woman is not supposed to contribute financially to the household expenses. Man's preeminence is due to his financial responsibility, which fits within the context of role divisions[14].

According to *"Notre position"*, the assumption of "roles' complementarity" is subverted by the gender approach. Through adopting a gender approach, the PANIFD, according to this position, undermines the Islamic view of the family as an institution based on compassion and turns it into a conflictual and tense set of relationships. By obstructing the gender specificity as it is determined by Islamic values, the PANIFD is at odds with family and society as structured by Islam. Gender is explained as a "reversal" of male and female "natural" roles, which undermines the value of "maternity" and "paternity". These social roles, as they are valued and determined in a Muslim family, are undermined by the gender approach since they are said to be only names of roles and notions without the values they imply.[15]Such values are targeted by Neo-colonial Western projects that aim to "disintegrate the Muslim's religious and cultural integrity"[16].

The mobilizing discourse of the fundamentalists[17] rests upon the anti-neo-colonial thesis that defines gender hierarchy and fixed gender roles within a patriarchal family as the foundations of cultural resistance (Yassine 190–274). Moreover, "woman status" is a central point for the fundamentalists' mobilizing strategies[18]. Their plan to maintain a political distinction as a powerful, constructive opposition is centered on strategic issues such as women and education (Tozy 1999: 257). As a political movement which strategically stands in opposition to the feminist egalitarian perspective, fundamentalism highlights the political foundation of gender issues that needs to be advocated on multiple and indigenous grounds by political, feminist and autonomous movements. While fundamentalism is mainly founded on a radical enmity to any feminist egalitarian thesis, it is now emerging as one of the major movements of political and social automation.

This automation is based on an affirmation of a collective Muslim identity threatened by "Western influence". As Zakia Daoud (1993) contends, women's status would usually undergo the risks of an imposed modernization taking place in the name of either colonization or reform (*IBID:* 9). Daoud further maintains that the "nativist" reaction to modernization, as it was introduced by the colonial experience and furthered by the requirements of the integration into an international order, is one of the main foundations upon which "anti-colonial" resistance was built. To this effect, resistance to both colonial and neo-colonial orders is founded on a basic social cell, the family, where women hold a central position (Daoud: 1993:12). Centrality is, however, deployed to maintain the stability of a sociocultural order through endorsing a fixed meaning to a produced and reproduced category of "woman", whose given and "natural" identity and role set the ground for her "specificity". To hinder the translation of an adopted liberal economic system into liberal social relationships, family structure and woman's fixed identity are crucial in maintaining the "coherence" of the patriarchal family.

Having been neither assimilated nor annihilated, the ex-colonized societies or "*sociétés colonisables*" have, according to Daoud who quotes Laroui, developed a powerful sense of identity which is simultaneously a sign of fragility engendering passivity (Daoud 1993:9 In this sense, identity depends on a continuous negation of what is labeled as colonial, "neo-colonial" and/or "western". This, in fact, can explain the mobilizing power of a negative identity-based discourse. While I argue for the limitations of such a monolithic and essentialist identity discourse, I contend that such a perspective is not empty of resistance to a neo-colonial status imposed by dependence on "development" and "modernization" as they are determined by international funding institutions. Yet, this does not mean withdrawing into identity-based defensive attacks against a "homogenizing" neo-colonialism. Historically, women have usually been used as the pillars of a nativist claim for defense of "cultural specificity"; against the hegemony of both colonialism and neo-colonialism.

In her "Engendering Development", Geeta Chowdhry's reading of Western representation of Third World women suggests how the colonial vision of colonized women is surviving within international development agencies. She describes the World Bank's policies as an updated colonial data in the sense that it relies on the presumption of a "developed" and "modernized" "West" as the measure to produce an "underdeveloped", "traditional" orient". She further suggests that "[t]he colonial State has been replaced by Women In Development projects and the World Bank" (p.29). Arguments for integration into development need to question and rethink development itself. The adoption of concepts as they are produced elsewhere creates the need to work with assumptions about women and impedes women's views of better life conditions from affecting the linearity of "development".

My critique of the PANIFD is not to downgrade its value as a text with the potential to start a process where gender could find a path to the government agenda. Rather my critique is based on its lack of a critical stance needed for a project that claims to be an alternative to a gender-blind development ideology. In so doing, I maintain that a feminist[19] alternative to gender-blind development[20] needs to challenge the claims of "universal truths" embedded in prescribed paths to "development" and "equality". On the other hand, this feminist alternative must simultaneously deal with the fundamentalist's thesis for the "Islamization" of the country, which systematically downgrades supporters of human and women's rights by associating women's rights activism with Western hegemonic schemes meant to destroy "national integrity" and Muslim traditions. Feminists are, according to this view, identified as "servants of imperialist agenda" (Mayer 1998: 370) The challenge for an egalitarian thesis lies in asserting through politically-subversive feminist activism demands for egalitarianism. Feminist activism to become a mobilizing power must turn the multiple social aspects of gender oppression into an engine of social mobilization and political action.

Conclusion

This chapter's attempt to focus on a textual analysis of the PANIFD is due to the fact it represents a historical turning point for gender issues in contemporary Morocco. The implementation of the PANIFD rather than its cancelation could have disintegrated the issue from identity-based rhetoric of either universal feminism or Muslim identity. The absence of a coherent governmental policy to gender-based reforms is furthered by a persistent polarization of the issue in terms of "private" versus "public" status, "secular" and "religious". Such a view assigns a private status to legal reform, which blocks an "emerging" "public" dimension with regard to the gradual integration of the issue into the government agenda. The dismissal of the 1998 Secretary of State, which was the first government institution for "women's issues", the cancellation of the PANIFD as well as the constitution of a committee made of a majority of Ulema and a minority of women and representatives of progressive readings of the scripture can be read in terms of the will to keep the "private" versus "public" dichotomy in the offical approach to the gender question. This dichotomy restrains a gender-based reform within the constraints of the Maliki doctrine of the Muslim State. The importance of framing the issue within the constraints of Muslim identity as it is suggested by the constitution of the committee of conservative "Ulema", indicates the official discourses' persistent conservative approach to gender despite its favorable reception of claims for gender equality within the Family Code. Being approached in terms of a "private issue" in isolation from "public issues", the government's policy towards gender is at a disjunct with women's differential needs.

This chapter is a critique of the constraints that reduce women's different subject positions and complex ways of negotiating with various levels of power relationships into a singular "woman" or a homogeneous group of women undergoing subordination. The essentialization of women can both emanate from gender biased and feminist representations of women. The constraints that the State's determination of women as the guardians of a religious and "cultural specificity" was contested by women's organization on the basis of the "universality of women's rights". The international economic and political pressures that pushed the State to integrate the "universality" in its determination of the Moroccan "specificity" have created space for women's organizations advocacy of gender equality. Yet the State's recognition of gender equality was not accompanied with a socio-economic redistribution. The current grassroots rural movement of women's land ownership (Soulaliyat) clearly indicates this lack and calls for an alternative approach to gender-based reform that goes beyond universal feminism or Muslim identity.

Notes

1 Lazreg (1994) recognizes the inadequacy of the terms West and East. These terms do not refer to ontological differences. Instead the West is for Lazreg a term denoting a geographical and cultural belonging called the "First World".

2 ibid

3 In an interview describing her career as a feminist scholar that she contends is epitomized by her novel *Dreams of Trespass*. Mernissi says:

> An autobiographical novel where I explain that the west is not the home of feminism. I explain that women who lived in harems, because they were encloistered, they could transcended the harem's ties through their transgressive dreams of (*Le Maghreb Littéraire* 100).

4 See the Penguin Dictionary of Critical Theory.

5 According the Beijing Platform of action set for 2000:

> The Platform for Action establishes a set of actions that should lead to fundamental change. Immediate action and accountability are essential if the targets are to be met by the year 2000 ... At the national level, commitment at the highest political level is essential for the successful implementation of the platform. By the end of 1996, all Governments should have their own national strategies or plans of action. (ATTN : The United Nations Department of Public Information. 1995 http//www.fwcw/daw.htm).

6 As I have noted earlier, the United Nation Development Program uses Human Development Indicators such as access to health care, education and GNP per Capita for each resident to assess human development in each country. The 1995 report used a gender-specific indicator which measured the socioeconomic gaps between men and women. This indicator ranked Morocco 85th.

7 The coming to power of the old Opposition is part of this strategy; it brought to the scene a new elite with new ways of work. Socialism as a distinguishing aspect of this new elite constitutes a political tendency *since L'Union Socialiste des Forces Populaires*, the leader of this new government, is the main socialist party in the country. With a social program that is also dictated not only by the ideological orientations of the new government but also by the devastating impacts of Structural Adjustment Programs, "women issues" appeared among the social issues in the government's reform agenda.

8 The 1998 newly designed Prime Minister received women's organization delegates and asked them to cancel their scheduled "Marche Féminine". Instead, the Prime Minister promised a gender-based policy through a government mechanism for women's issues in addition to the reform of the Family Code.

9

10 Although the PANIFD acknowledges differences at least between rural and urban women, it does not go beyond the neutral presentation of numbers without an interpretation and a possible intervention that responds to these differences.

11 This clause is amended by the present draft Code which redefines tutorship as a woman's right: " Entitle the woman who has come of age to guardianship as a right, if she so chooses or if it serves her interest." (http//www.map.co.ma)

12 Obedience in conformity with conventions (Mudawana Article 36/2).

13 Repudiation is the dissolution of marriage pronounced by the husband (my translation) (Mudawana, Article 44)

14 Harakat Attaouhid was Isllah . Notre Position._Casablanca: Editions Alforkane, 1999.
15 Harakat Attaouhid was Isllah . Notre Position._Casablanca: Editions Alforkane, 1999.
16 Harakat Attaouhid was Isllah . Notre Position._Casablanca: Editions Alforkane, 1999.
17 There are different trends within the fundamentalist movement. For example, the radical Islamists like Jamaat El Adl Wa Ilhassan is different from the moderate Party of Justice and Development.
18 *"Le Journal Hebdomadaire"* organized and published a debate called "Face á Face: Islamistes et Progressistes" where Nadia Yassine the daughter of Abdsselam Yassine, the leader of El Adl wa l'Ihsane declared with regard the anti- plan march organized by the fundamentalists that "Nous sommes d'accord avec les féministes. Il y'a énormément de choses positives dans le Plan. Si nous sommes descendues le 12 mars, c'était essentiellement un message politique."
19 In addition to the fact that the PANIFD is identified to be an alternative to the mainstream development approach to gender, it is elaborated by an elite of politicians and active members in either political parties or women's organizations standing for advocates of women's' rights and gender equality.
20 In its introduction, the PANIFD identifies the limitations of gender blind development policies based on a male vision that disregards the gender approach in main policy orientations, which confines the issue to isolated projects within marginal ministry departments. (*Le Plan national de L'intégration de La femme au développement* 10–11–12–13) .

Bibliography

Association Démocratique des Femmes du Maroc. 2000. *Le harcèlement sexuel au Maroc: brisons le mur du silence*. Casablanca: Le Fennec.

Association Démocratique des Femmes du Maroc. 2001. *Les discriminations à l'égard des femmes dans la législation pénale Marocaine*. Casablanca: Le Fennec.

Association Démocratique des Femmes du Maroc. 2001. *Convention CEDAW : Rapport parallèle*. Rabat: ADFM.

Association Démocratique des Femmes du Maroc. 2001. *Rapport d'activités*. Rabat: ADFM.

Belghazi, Taieb, and Madani Mohammed. 2001. *L'action collective au Maroc : de la mobilisation à la prise de parole*. Rabat: Publications de la Faculté des Lettres et des Sciences Humaines.

Cheryl, Jhososn- odim. 1991. "Common Themes, Different Contexts, Third World Women and Feminism." In *Third World Women and the Politics of Feminism*, edited by Chandra Talpade Mohanty, Ann Russo and Lourdes Torres, 314–327. Bloomington and Indianapolis: Indiana University Press.

Chowdhry, Geeta. 1995. "Engendering Development." In *Feminism, Postmodernism Development*, edited by Marianne H. Marchand and Jane L. Parpat, 26–41. London and New York : Routledge.

Daoud, Zakia. 1993. *Féminisme et politique au Maghreb : Soixante ans de Lutte*. Casablanca : Editions Eddif.

Darif, Mohammed. 1998. *Alhakl Assiassi Almaghribi*. Casablanca: Almajala Almaghribia Liilm Alijtimaa Assiassi.

Direction de La Statistique. 1992. *Les Emplois du temps de la femme au Maroc: Enquête nationale sur le budget temps des femmes.* Vol 2.

Khatibi, Abdelkébir. 1998. *L'Alternance et les partis politiques.* Casablanca : Eddif.

Khatibi, Abdelkébir. 2002. "La sexualité selon Le coran." *Chemins de traverse essais de sociologie,* 237–258. Rabat : Université Mohammed V – Souissi Institut Universitaire de La Recherche scientifique.

Laroui, Abdallah. 1997. "Religion, société, culture." *Islamisme, modernisme libéralisme,* 145–170. Casablanca: Centre Culturel Arabe.

Lazreg, Marnia. 1994. "Decolonizing Feminism." *The Eloquence of Silence.* Routeldge, 6–19 New York-London.

Lazreg, Marnia. 1988. "Feminism and Difference: the Perils of Writing as a Woman on Women in Algeria." *Feminist Studies* 14, 81–105.

Majid, Anouar. 1998. "The Politics of Feminism in Islam." *Signs* 23, 2: 321–362.

Mayer, Ann Elizabeth. 1998. "Comment on Majid's The Politics of Feminism in Islam." *Signs* 23, 2: 369–377.

Mernissi, Fatema. 1998. Interview with Serge MENAGER. *Le Maghreb littéraire.* University of Natal, République d'Afrique du Sud. Vol 2,4: 97–119.

Ministère de La Prévision Economique et du Plan. 2000. *Plan De développement économique et social: La valorisation des resources humaines et le développement Social,* 248–252 Rabat.

Mohanty, Chandra Talpade. 1997. "Under Western Eyes: Feminist scholarship and Colonial discourses." In *The Women, Gender and Development Reader,* edited by Nalinin Visvanathan, Lynn Duggan, Laurie Nisonoff and Nan Wiegersma, 79–85. London and New Jersy: Zed Books.

M. Moudden, Abdelhay. 1996. "Cultural Struggles In Morocco." In Proceedings of the Conference *Cultural Studies, Interdisciplinarity, and The University,* edited by Mohamed Dahbi, Mohamed Ezroura and Lahcen Haddad, 135–145. Publications of the Faculty of Letters and Human Sciences: Rabat.

Mounib, Mohamed. 2002. Introduction. *Adahiir AlBarbari Akbar Okdouba Siassia Fi al Maghrib Almoaasir,* 11–34. Rabat: Daar Abi Rakrak.

Secrétariat d'Etat Chargé de La Protection Sociale, de La Famille et de l'Enfance. 1999. *Projet plan d'action national pour L'intégration de la femme au développement.* Rabat.

Chapter 2

SECULAR AND ISLAMIC FEMINIST MOVEMENTS IN MOROCCO

Contentions, Achievements, and Challenges

Moha Ennaji

Introduction

The chapter argues that women's movement in Morocco draws its strength from being political in nature, particularly in pushing for women's rights while trying to reach a compromise with the Islamic feminist organizations. The chapter contextualizes secular and religious debates over the feminist movement and the status of women in Morocco and their challenges in relation to the contemporary political history of the country. As an attempt to find a balance between the perspectives of the more conservative Islamic feminists and progressive women's groups, the new family code was established and significantly improved the legal status of women.

The major aim of this chapter is to highlight the agency of Moroccan women since independence. It focuses on their activism for legal rights and political participation. Issues related to these domains are considered from a broad comparative perspective. The chapter reveals the positive role that secular Moroccan women have been playing in the struggle for social change. It also shows that women's gains are irrevocable and that the future of the country is significantly linked to the fate of women's movements and women's emancipation from their oppressed positions.

To examine discrimination facing Moroccan women, it is useful to adopt intersectionality theory, which was first proposed by black feminist scholars to understand the interconnection of various forms of oppression faced by Black women in America (Collins 2008; Crenshaw et al. 1996). Intersectionality theory covers the concurrent and intertwined types of oppression based on variables such as gender, race, class, age, ethnicity, religion, citizenship, or appearance. These regular types of oppression may crisscross in individuals' lives, leading to complex impacts. For example, being a Muslim woman and being poor may correspond to overlapping types of oppression, which aggravate gender-based discrimination facing North African women in a male-dominated region (Collins 2008; Mullings 1996; Inhorn 2015).

This chapter is based on a larger research project among women activists which I carried out between 2011 and 2014. The findings are derived from semi-structured interviews of women and feminist leaders in Morocco and on my previous research and readings. The ethnographic interviews were conducted with 49 women from Morocco, most of whom were aged between 25 and 67.Interviews were conducted in either Colloquial Arabic, French, English, or a mixture of French/English and Arabic, depending upon the principal language and first choice of the interviewee.

Women's movements, activism and their achievements should be interpreted in a broader socio-political context. The emergence of women's movements is an answer to the crisis of the nation-state model form of governance. Such grassroots movements are treated as a way to ensure democracy and sustainable development. They create social dynamism through the mobilization and participation of the masses. They also decentralize governance in a more globalized world and locally contribute to the feminization and democratization of public space (Sadiqi and Ennaji 2006). Their modes of action raise new challenges for government development policies and open up new ways of thinking about the issues of sustainability.

To fully understand the significance of Moroccan women's activism, it is essential to relate it to the rise of Islamism in the region and to the role of human rights organizations which treat women's rights as human rights. The role of women's non-governmental Organizations (NGO's) in the struggle against gender inequalities is remarkable. It highlights their efforts to consolidate democracy and social justice and to challenge traditional thinking and practices of governance. While secular women's organizations struggle for a liberal societal project,

Islamic women's associations work within the framework of Islam and aim for the Islamization of the country. Secular activists participate in interreligious/interfaith dialogues and networks by reaching out to Islamist organizations and at times using their discourse to attain the masses, as we shall examine in the following section.

The secular women's movement

Moroccan secular feminism has been developing since independence. After the end of the French colonial period, a reactionary family law was established in 1957, which denied women a number of basic rights. However, when women had more access to education and to the labor market, these basic rights became vital to their struggle. In such a context, women's rights are closely linked to democratization and political liberalization (Sadiqi 2014). The greatest success of the Moroccan feminist movement (secular and Islamic) lies in the fact that it has brought a holy text (the *Mudawana*) to public debate. The movement's use of universal values and socially acceptable local strategies has succeeded in impacting the main political actors in the promulgation of the new family law enacted in 2004. The Moroccan feminist movement has managed to demystify the "holyness" of "Shariâ" (Islamic law), a fact that contributed to the democratization of the public sphere and to the practice of human rights in daily life.

However, there is still a long way to go before the new family law can be effectively implemented. Two mechanisms are needed: men and women should become sensitive to the significant changes achieved, and judges should leave prejudice aside and join in the implementation of the new law. Public debate of the Moroccan family private issues will help the Moroccan society to be prepared for the challenge facing the country's feminist movement, particularly the rise of radical Islamism and the role of religion in an ever more secular public space within a context in which women are acquiring new public visibility.

A historical background of the Family Law Reforms

The struggle to amend the family law occurred in a controversial sociopolitical context with a strong opposition, stemming from the organizing efforts of Islamist associations and factions. The conformist mentality and institutional environment were also unfavorable to lobbying for women's legal rights and reform of the family law. However, secular women's NGOs managed to draw the attention of decision-makers and civil society to the urgency of the reform. At the outset, liberal feminists used only secular arguments to advocate women's rights, but later on, under the pressure of Islamists, demanded reforms by appealing to Islamic arguments in combination with universal human rights. Their struggle highlights the extent of their determination, capacity to mobilize the masses, which eventually bore fruit and brought the reform of the Mudawana.

Although Moroccan women are vital to the family structure on which society is based, the 1957 family law gave them few rights. Based on Islamic law (*Shariâ*), the old Mudawana used to leave women in a vulnerable position within the family. Husbands could unilaterally divorce their wives and threw them out of their homes, while it was very difficult for women to get out of abusive relationships, as their right to divorce was highly restricted. Women could not marry without the legal consent of a guardian or tutor, and wives were forced by law to obey their husbands; while men could marry multiple women without their wives' approval.

The first Mudawana was established by an all-male committee of religious scholars, and thus was strongly based on Islamic law. It was a patriarchal code, with the man being described as the head of the family, and the woman as a dependent minor under the male responsibility; women were treated more like men's property than independent individuals. A woman, no matter how old, was under the guardianship of her father until she got married, and then she fell under her husband's authority.

A wife could be repudiated or divorced by the husband without any justification, and without providing any compensation for herself and her children. It was enough for the husband to disavow her. She could ask for divorce only under special restricted circumstances, like being abandoned without any financial support for a long period of time by the husband or only if she pays him a material compensation.

Children were not protected. The mother lost custody over her children if she re-married or if she behaved 'indecently' by taking a lover, for example. A child-born from relationships outside marriage was recognized neither by the State nor by society; he could neither have a family name nor a seat in school. He was basically an outcast, a burden to society (Ennaji 2012).

Since the early 1960s, secular women's NGOs have been fighting for reforming this family code to guarantee equal rights (Pittman and Naciri 2010).[1] Two major women's rights NGOs, known as the "Association Démocratique des Femmes" (ADFM), and the "Union de l'Action Feminine" (UAF), and their allies campaigned to reform these excessive laws and ensure equal rights for women under the family code, thus giving momentum to the Mudawana reform movement.

Secular feminists have argued that the *Qur'an* (holy book of Muslims), the *Sunna* (Muslim culture and lifestyle), and the *Hadith* (sayings of the Prophet Mohamed) had been subject to a masculine and conservative interpretation and propose a re-interpretation of the Qur'an in light of modern times (*Ijtihad*).

One of the most significant strategies and forms of activism at the time was the petition of 'one million signatures'. This campaign, which was national and massive in favor of the Mudawana reform, was initiated by UAF in 1992, using its newspaper called "8 Mars". The campaign was a vast victory and gained huge public support. Subsequently, the late King Hassan II ordered that a reformed code be drafted in consultation with some women's groups. The reform, which was enacted in 1993, included a few changes beneficial to women. For example, women were now allowed to designate the guardian or tutor who would give approval for their marriage; fathers were no longer allowed to compel their daughters into marriage, and polygamy became slightly restricted and subject to the agreement of the first wife (Ennaji and Sadiqi 2012)

Though the UAF, ADFM, and other secular women's groups were disappointed by the limited nature of the reforms, they considered them a victory, because they broke a taboo: once the Mudawana was amended, it could no longer be seen as an irreversible text, thus lifting the mask of sacredness around it, as we mentioned earlier. Women's NGOs continued to lobby the government by raising awareness about women's rights, gender-based discrimination, and domestic violence. They continued to strategize and campaign for broader legislative changes and altered their communication capacities to integrate a human rights agenda and democratization arguments together with the necessity to re-interpret Islamic laws (Pittman and Naciri 2010).

King Mohamed VI, who accessed the throne in 1999, showed hints of being less repressive than his father and expressed his will to reform the family law. Advocacy campaigns intensified under the socialist-led government, and after a heated debate with Islamist groups, a new Mudawana was passed in 2004. Unlike the previous reform, it advanced women's rights and eliminated many discriminatory provisions. The minimum age for women to marry was raised from 15 to 18, the same as for men; women no longer needed to obtain permission from a guardian before marrying; men were forbidden from unilaterally divorcing their wives; women were given the right to file for divorce; and restrictions were imposed on polygamy such as the approval of both the first wife and the second would-be wife and only with the approval of a judge.

The secular feminist movement did not stop once it had achieved its original goals. Since the promulgation of these reforms, women's progressive groups in Morocco have been lobbying to change some discriminatory laws that survived the reforms. They have also been organizing demonstrations and providing education to the public, aiming to ensure that the reforms are understood and are incorporated into daily life.

The Mudawana reform was opposed by *Salafists* (religious fanatics), the *Ulama* (religious scholars), and many Islamic educators, who claimed that the new family code was against the Islamic values traditionally predominant in the country. Islamist groups campaigned robustly to hold back the impact of secular liberal women's NGOs.

Latifa Jbabdi, AUF founder states: "My goal now is to spread the word to some of the most remote areas [...] I want the people of Morocco to know that our new law is not only a victory for women, but also for the family, society, and generations to come."[2]

Secular feminists endeavored to engage Islamists in debates by integrating religious arguments in their discourse. As a case in point, though personally committed to secularism, Jbabdi, who was elected Member of Parliament, studied the Qur'an and the Hadith in order to include religious evidence into her communication, given that religiosity was high among most Moroccans. Armed with patience and knowledge about the principles of Islam, she could engage with Islamist groups who claimed that the reforms contradicted Islam, effectively arguing that several religious texts supported gender equality.

Activists adopted a global approach arguing for reform as predicted by *ijtihad* (re-interpretation of the Qur'an), and based on the current path the nation was taking towards more democratic structures that aligned with principles of human rights, justice, and equality. They put forward arguments in favor of the Mudawana reform using religious, institutional, cultural and legal discourses (Ennaji and Sadiqi 2012; Pittman and Naciri 2010).

Nevertheless, during the period of 1999–2000, an Islamist counterattack intensified, and secular activists and their allies were increasingly charged with being anti-Islam and sold to the West. Secular women's NGOs faced a strong countermovement that diverged from their progressive aims. Traditionalists and Islamist political factions began to deploy religion to "sturdily refute the secular women's struggle for gender equity" (SchrÖter 2014).[3]

Fanatic religious scholars claimed that any Mudawana reform would oppose Islam. Instead, they insisted that there should be more respect for Islam and its customs. Likewise, political Islam proponents characterized the reforms advocated by secular NGOs as part of a Western conspiracy with the purpose to demolish Muslim values and family structure.

Due to allegations from the Islamist opposition that secular women activists were 'loose', progressive women's NGOs intensified their campaign, which led to the reform (Pittman and Naciri 2010).

Thus, over the past three decades, the family law has been one of the most controversial issues and driving forces in Morocco. The new reforms aim at strengthening certain basic rights to favor women and children while fighting abuse and discrimination. They make both spouses responsible for the family and reorganize the norms regulating marriage and divorce, while seriously protecting children. Hence the new code, which grants more rights to children, women, and men, will positively impact family democratization. The feminist, democratic civil society has succeeded in reducing the holy aspects of the family law, and it is the secular women's movement that has largely opened doors for civil society and for democratic culture (Sadiqi and Ennaji 2006).

As a result, women's legal rights in Morocco have noticeably been enhanced since 2004. These improvements are often ascribed to the joint venture endeavors of the state and a strong push of the secular women's NGOs, which are among the strongest and most effective throughout the Islamic world (Ennaji 2012).

The Islamic women's movement

Women's Islamic movement is deeply rooted in Moroccan society, as it is centuries old, and marked by the great contributions of Muslim women leaders and religious scholars.[4] This is the case of Fatima al-Fihriya (8th century), who built Al-Qarawiyyīn Islamic University in Fès. Zaynab al-Nafzāwiya (12th century), who built many Islamic schools for women in Morocco, helped her husband Sultan Yūsuf ibn Tāshafīn to rule the country. Saida Tiṭīliya (12th century), a great woman saint, studied and spread the Qur'an, hadith (the Prophet's sayings), and other Islamic teachings. Lalla Mḥilla (12th century) devoted her life to research on Islamic knowledge.[5] Khnata bint Bakār (17th century) was a Sufi woman and a great politician who helped her husband Sulman Mulay Isma'īl pacify Morocco and make peace with Western powers of the time. Such historical women leaders and their construction of sainthood within the context of Sufism are relevant to contemporary discourses on gender and feminism in Morocco (see Ouguir 2013).

Today, Moroccan feminists are both impressed and impacted by these historical female figureheads' knowledge and strong personalities that challenge patriarchy. They regard them as role models and as sources of inspiration, whose footsteps they are determined to follow. They are, thus, eager to continue the struggle and undertake social and political activities, within the framework of their religion and their own cultural heritage and life conditions. Most of them use Moroccan history and female saints as primary sources to enrich their debate on feminist activism. For instance, Basima al-Haqqaoui, a founding member of the moderate Islamist Party of Justice and Development (PJD), considers women saints who achieved religious scholarship and political leadership "a reference" that stems from Islamic and Moroccan cultural heritage. She acknowledges the importance of understanding the historical background of women's activism.

According to her, feminists today should know these sources in order to carry on the struggle for women's rights and empowerment.

The contemporary Islamist movement is often referred to as a conservative and patriarchal reactionary force. It regularly clashes with the secular liberal women's activism. The secular women's organizations are perceived by large parts of Islamists as representing a foreign 'feminist' approach which threatens local culture, values, and religion, as mentioned above.

Nadia Yassine, who is one of the icons of Islamic feminism, has held since the 1980s a high position of leadership in the association of *Al Adl Wal Ihssan* (Justice and Charity). Her struggle for women's equal rights is within the framework of the Islamic reference. Together with her colleagues, they have developed an approach that combines Islam and feminism to fight gender-based discrimination. They have started a woman's collective *Ijtihad* (reinterpretation) project to review the Hadith and Qur'anic scriptures following the sayings of the Prophet (*Sira Nabawiya*) and of his companions (men and women), taking into account the historical and social context of the texts. The goal of this project is to reveal the positive status of women in Islam and to discard any discriminatory interpretation.

The Islamic women's movement, which was particularly dynamic before the Arab Spring, has lately started to lose its appeal given that the Islamist-led current government has not advanced women's rights or other major reforms. Despite their reduced popularity after Islamists took power, Islamic women's rights activists still enjoy a broad local popularity for they appeal to the religious sections of the population. Their movement also challenges existing conservative and traditional groups in new ways and in so doing partakes in the national endeavors to improve the lot of women in society.

Yet, how different is Islamic women's activism from secular women's activism? What are the issues it addresses, and what are the solutions it proposes? Do Islamic activists and secular ones converge or diverge? Is Islamic women's activism basically a new strategy to religiously sanction female submission or does it significantly challenge prevailing gender roles and offer new visions for gender equity? (cf. Julie Pruzan-Jørgensen 2010).

While the Islamic movement is heterogeneous and encompasses a wide range of organizations and individuals, it comprises two trends. The first trend is related to the Movement of Reform and Unity (MUR) or *Harakat al-Islâh wa-at-Tawhid* and the second trend is represented by the Party of Justice and Development (PJD) called *Hizb al-Adala wa-al-Tanmia*. The latter is ideologically related to the Justice and Charity Association (*Jama'at al-Adl wal-Ihsan*).

In Morocco, the Islamic movement includes groups which recognize monarchy as legitimate and operate within the political system, like the PJD, and others which oppose the regime and operate outside of it, such as the Justice and Charity association. These two currents do not share the same political strategies. While Justice and Charity is an opposition movement which struggles for the transformation of Morocco from below into an Islamic state, the PJD seeks to make a change within the system and is officially accepted as it endorses the State's political authority. Both groups advocate gender equality and social justice within an Islamic framework and allow women opportunities for political participation and leadership in the Islamic tradition.

Nadia Yassine illustrates the central role that women play within Islamic groups. Until very recently, she was not only the spokesperson of the group before Western media, but also the director of the women's organization. She worked hard to perk up the dynamic place of women in society based on Islamic teachings. In a number of her talks and writings, Nadia Yassine characterizes Islam as an energizing force which guarantees equality for women, and advocates the importance of re-interpreting Islamic texts and engaging women in the struggle for social change.

The most popular Islamic organization in Morocco is the MUR and its related political party, the PJD. Since the late 1990s, the latter has been integrated into the formal political system in exchange for its recognition of the monarchy as the legitimate political authority running the country, including the status of the king as 'Commander of the Faithful' (*Amir Almuminin*). Both the MUR and its ally the PJD are moderate Islamists and are considered as pro-monarchy; however, they are very conservative in their mindset and hold conservative socio-cultural views, like opposing the consumption of alcohol, prostitution, and homosexuality. Their traditionalism is reflected in the way they dress: men wear beards, and women are veiled and wear Moroccan long-sleeve dresses (*djellabas*) of ordinary design.

Their physical appearance in a way reflects their conservatism and traditional views about society in general and women in particular. Their basic principle concerning women's rights and emancipation is that Islam has in fact given women all their rights. Additionally, they claim that, in order to support women and empower them, one should neither 'abandon Islam' nor adopt Western views of struggle for more rights. For them, the essential task is to be aware of these rights and implement them in everyday life. In their understanding, it is of paramount importance to adopt new interpretations of religious scripture and practices within the Islamic paradigm, and in order to guarantee this they join forces with religious scholars.

In addition, Islamic activists claim that there is a complementarity between men and women and between rights and obligations. Women have the right to be provided for by their fathers or husbands, but they are also obliged to obey them and to take care of their families and children. Moderate Islamic activists claim that complementarity involves only the private sphere and even there domestic tasks should be shared by husbands and wives (Ouguir 2013). Moreover, many of them argue that they center on the 'real' issues of Moroccan women while accusing secular women's rights activists of addressing 'fake' problems. For instance, during the struggle for the Mudawana reform, feminists belonging to the Organization for the Renewal of Women's Awareness, ORWA (*Munaddamat Tajdid al-Wa'i al-Nisa'i*), rejected liberal demands for the eradication of polygamy by alluding to its uncommon practice in Moroccan society (see Yafout, this volume).[6]

One of the major clashes occurred on March 12, 2000, when the liberal feminists and other democratic groups organized a rally in the city of Rabat to demand broader women's rights. But, on the same day, the Islamic movement organized a march in Casablanca, where the women, all veiled, marched in separate lines from men. They dismissed the secular demands because they believed them to be contrary to Islamic law. The Rabat rally was successful, yet it was eclipsed by the Casablanca demonstrations, which attracted a greater number of activists.

While this incident served as a major indication of the force of Islamist groups in the country, King Mohammed VI, who had promised in a nationally televized speech that he would work to improve women's human rights, interfered to change the Mudawana. He responded by a royal decree that CEDAW be implemented. Furthermore, the King set up a royal commission (which included two women experts) to revise the family code, and created a Ministry in Charge of the Condition of Women, Protection of the Family, Childhood and the Disabled in order to enhance equal rights (see Eddaouda, this volume).

These decisions were taken one year after the terrorist attacks on Casablanca in 2003 by "religious" terrorists. The attacks caused outrage among the Moroccan people, making religious extremism unacceptable and helping secular activists to take this opportunity to advance their demands. Subsequently, King Mohammed VI decided to reform the Mudawana in October 2003. It was validated by the Parliament in 2004, thus hugely enhancing women's legal rights in the country (cf. Sadiqi, this volume).

Islamic activists today disagree with claims by liberal secular forces to revise the Mudawana again in order to change the inheritance laws by stressing that this is a false problem, because many women, especially in rural areas do not even receive their share of inheritance already guaranteed by the Islamic law. In fact, they prefer to focus, not on the situation of women, but on the problems of the family and society as a whole. They argue that it is more urgent to address issues of corruption, unemployment, and poverty that are the real causes of women's suffering. They adopt an approach based on reconciliation, rather than addressing solely the rights of the individual woman, because for them preservation of the marriage structure and the family unity is of paramount importance. The most powerful Islamic women's organization is the ORWA, which was created in1992 by members of the MUR.[7] The ORWA, presided by the current Minister of Women, Family, and Solidarity, Bassima al-Haqqaoui, became popular during the hot debate on the Moroccan family code by its strong hostility towards a large list of women's rights proposed by the progressive socialist government of that period. As already mentioned, they opposed these demands because they believed them to be in incongruity with Shari'a and with Moroccan cultural patterns. Nevertheless, they were obliged to accept the reform proposed finally by the king. This reform, which substantially improved the status of women, was finally approved by moderate Islamist currents because they claimed it to be different from the initial proposal of the socialists, as it was partially based on Islamic principles.

Moderate Islamic women activists struggled for the reforms together with the secular feminists and partook in the one million-signature campaign that preceded the reform of the Mudawana. However, they reproached the secular feminists the fact that their approach was too liberal (see Sadiqi, this volume).

Post-Arab Spring

Morocco was not immune to the uprisings witnessed in the Arab world following the outbreak of the Tunisian revolution in December 2010. The mass demonstrations were led by February 20 Movement in 2011 in various Moroccan cities. During these protests, they brandished slogans that varied between constitutional, political, social and economic reforms.

The debates that followed the Feb. 20 demonstrations, and the dramatic changes in other North African countries like Libya and Egypt, had pushed the priority of reform to the forefront and contributed to multiplying demands for change, accelerating the intensity of the protests. In an attempt to protect the country from the haphazard of the "Arab Spring," King Mohammed VI delivered a speech on March 9, 2011, in which he presented an agenda for reform, including the adoption of a new constitution.[8]

The latter voted in July 2011 recognizes gender equality and equal political representation for women in article 19. The state guarantees women's increased political participation, as full citizens, and as people's representatives in parliament. For the first time in the contemporary history of Morocco, a veiled political woman, Bassima al-Haqqaoui, was appointed as Minister of Solidarity, Women, Family, and Social Development in 2012. This political shift is symbolic of the latest prospects opened up for women by the Arab uprisings; the regime would clearly have barred a veiled woman from accessing parliament or government had it not been for the Arab Spring effect and pressure from the public.

In the reshuffled government of 2013, one more veiled political woman, Soumiya Benkhaldoun, became "Ministre Déléguée" for

Higher Education, and three liberal unveiled women took the reins of the Ministries of Foreign Affairs, Mines and Environment, respectively; but they were all "Ministres Déléguées", which is equivalent to Deputy Ministers. By contrast, the government prior to the Arab Spring included a total of seven women ministers from 2007 to 2011. This regression in the number of women in the cabinet has caused unease amongst secular-liberal activists who view it as a regression in women's political representation.

In an interview with "iKnow Politics" organization, Jamila El Mossalli, member of parliament from the ruling PJD, asserted: "This is my third term in parliament. I entered parliament in 2002 and was the youngest parliamentarian. I am particularly interested in community and women's affairs. From this perspective I can say there has been substantial progress in Morocco on both the legislative and political fronts.[9] For her, the Arab Spring has positively impacted Moroccan women, as it has brought a new constitution and more reforms enhancing their political participation.

Iman El-Yaacoubi, a member of the same party, added that "for years our party has had the most female representation in parliament which shows the explicit trust the party has in women, but choosing the ministers has to take into account the ministries the party won and not their gender."[10]

The PJD has one of the highest rates of female members of parliament among all Moroccan parties, as six out of the party's current 46 parliamentarians are women. Nonetheless, this high percentage does not inevitably mean that women have an important impact within the party itself. Only two women are members of the party's general secretariat and only six female parliamentarians have been elected on regular terms, as all the others have been elected through the 'national list' or quota system, which was introduced by the government to guarantee female political representation of 10% in parliament.

Bassima al-Haqqaoui, Minister of Family and Solidarity and head of the PJD women's organization, demands a stronger public presence of women, more rights for female workers and peasants, as well as more family support. But the PJD has been silent on the difficult implementation of reforms made in the 2011 constitution. Today, activists fear a conservative approach to equal rights could slow – or reverse – progress (Ennaji 2013).

Secular feminists particularly fear that, with the Islamists leading the government, the already difficult application of reforms will come to a halt. Despite obstacles, progress has been achieved in implementing the new family law since the last decade. New family courts have been established, and the judicial personnel has been re-trained to meet the high demands of the new code. But many judges have refused to apply the new laws, and many Moroccan women lack the education or the means to defend their legal rights.

Moroccan feminists have equally called for changes to criminal laws, including article 475 of the penal code that allowed a rapist to escape punishment if he married his victim. This law has recently been supplanted by a new one which stipulates that "a rapist goes to jail and cannot marry his victim."[11]

The abortion law must also be reformed. Up to now, pregnancies can be legally terminated if and only if the mother's life is at risk. Doctors who carry out abortions, including in the case of rape, can be sentenced to years in prison.

The situation of unwed mothers and their children is no better. According to a survey by the *Insaf* aid organization, half a million of these children were born between 2003 and 2009. Because extra-marital sex is forbidden in Morocco, these children are regarded as "illegitimate." The organization "Solidarité Féminine", which provides a contact point for single mothers and their children in Casablanca area, stated that the situation is unfair to children (Martina Sabra 2012).[12] Aicha Chenna, Founding President of this organization, pointed out to me that many of these children born outside marriage were not allowed to access school nor have full rights as citizens.

It is unclear whether reforms to family policies will be undertaken in the near future, not just because the current government is led by Islamists but because, for secular activists, it is vital that Morocco adopts a secular political system where religion is separate from the State. This would be totally new, since even in the West religion is never totally separated from the State, instead they adopt a kind of moderate secularism, with the State accommodating religion in the public sphere but without privileging one religion above the other. See Modood (2009) among others.[13]

Thus, despite female participation in the Arab Spring protests, it is feared that women's rights are being left on the political margin by the Islamist threat. Across Morocco secular women activists are concerned about the intentions of Islamists and fear that the Islamist-led government will implement reactionary policies discriminating against women. Only when repressive governments are replaced by democracies can we consider the popular uprisings in the Middle East and North Africa to be meaningfully progressive. Since women make up half of the region's population, any democratic developments must improve the social and legal status of women in the Arab world. However, since Morocco has strong civil institutions, there is much hope that democracy can take hold in this country.

How do secular and Islamic feminists converge?

Both secular and Islamic feminists struggle in different ways using dissimilar strategies to better the situation of women. They are, however confronted with hurdles like a strong patriarchy, machismo, and autocracy. These obstacles demand the unity of Moroccan feminisms in order to achieve women's emancipation and empowerment in the region. Both movements use different approaches of analysis within which they fight against gender-based discrimination (Eddouada, this volume and Jhososn-odim 1992). Although all these feminists seek to determine and eradicate oppression against women, they hold different views depending on their political agendas, cultural and educational background, and have different ideologies and societal projects in mind. Given the particular and the complex issues that feminism as a framework of analysis addresses, it is hard to presume that the pathway to gender equality can be planned and put into effect in a context like Morocco, a majority-Muslim society, without taking into account the cultural dimension, the political context, and the aspirations of the people. Within this context that is not receptive to a feminist perspective, addressing issues of women's oppression and the need for their liberation and emancipation is a challenge for all feminists.

For the time being, there is a conflict between two basically contradictory views on gender equality. The first one is anchored in a secular mode of thought and takes the "West" as a model, and the second defends Islamic reference as a framework and political tool to achieve women's rights. Secular feminism is in a way confined by the requisites of the Western model and is, thus, socially and politi-cally alienated from Moroccan society, whereas Islamic feminism, although able to adequately address the social ills of women in par-ticular and of the society in general, it does not exploit its fame to attain women's empowerment. Instead, its approach and discourse are based on a restricted rigid interpretation of Islam (Eddouada, this volume).

Thus, one can state that, on the one hand, secular and Islamic feminists converge because they all fight against patriarchy and autocracy, and struggle to promote reforms leading to women's rights and their participation in public life. On the other hand, the two currents diverge because they use different referents, dissimilar strategies and discourses, and entertain contradictory ideologies and societal projects. While Secular feminists are all for equal rights and full emancipation, following the Western model of universal human rights, Islamic feminists prone women's rights within the confines of Islam; they do not support full gender equality; rather they argue for constrained polygamy, for the implementation of *Shariâ* law as far as social issues like inheritance and unwed mothers are concerned. Regarding polygamy, Nadia Yassine and her sisters see it as "an exceptional solution for exceptional cases." (see Yafout, this volume).They also support minors' marriage and complementarity between man and woman (see discussion above).

Conclusion

The feminist movement in Morocco plays a major role in defending women's rights and in sensitizing women, families, and social actors as to the importance of integrating women in sustainable development.

Secular feminism adopts Western feminist views while main-taining national and cultural identity. Its proponents think that, although feminism can be easily refuted in the name of religious and ideological conservatism, it cannot be simply refuted in the name of cultural authenticity.

The Islamist groups, which have been flourishing throughout the Middle East since the mid-1980's, have ignited debate over the role of women in contemporary society. Their social agendas propagate

Islamic practices, although there has always been lack of consensus on the content of those practices.

Islamic feminists preach the improvement of women's lives within the precepts of Islam and emphasize the Islamic character of their feminist activities, which, according to them, is the only guarantee to women's liberation. They also think that the State regulates the public life, but religion regulates family life, as Islam has been used to shore up family-based patriarchal controls and prerogatives.

By contrast, many radical secular feminists adhere to the view that Islam is incompatible with feminism. For them, women's liberation requires a thorough de-Islamization of all aspects of life. In fact, a number of radical secular scholars attribute the problems of contemporary Arab women to Islam (Sadiqi 2014; Tibi 2009).

While not rejecting the text, reconciliatory secular feminists adhere to the view that Islam as culture is compatible with feminism. They, in a way, compromise the views of both the moderate Islamists and the radicals. The Moroccan writers Fatema Mernissi and Asma Lamrabet are good cases in point.[14] "In her new introduction to the 2011 edition of her Ph.D. dissertation, "Beyond the Veil", Mernissi argues that women's powerful presence in over 500 Arab satellite TV channels, including as news presenters, commanding show anchors, film and clip stars, supports her theory that Islam as a religion celebrates female power (see Yafout, this volume).

For some Egyptian secular feminists like Nawal Saadawi (1997: 246), Islam is not the only culturally legitimate framework of reference. She argues that present-day feminists from the Arab-Islamic world need to re-read their history, in order to understand their culture.

A natural follow-up of feminist journalistic and academic writings is the relatively expanding development of feminist activism through women's NGOs. These associations attest to the dynamism of feminist movements in the region. Most associations, which struggle for secular feminism and civil rights, are mainly led by upper and middle class women (Ennaji 2010).

These middle class feminists play a major role in the democratization process and they fill in a gap, as they are part of the elite which is struggling to keep a balance between secular and Islamist groups, and to enhance women's legal rights and political participation

(Moghadam 2012). Thanks to their resilience and battle, Moroccan women have successfully contributed to the reform of the family code, the penal code, and the constitution, as well as consolidated women's participation in political power.

Further measures in favor of protecting women's rights are badly needed to guarantee their empowerment and contribution to society's democratization. Laws must be enacted to fight all forms of violence against women, particularly polygamy, unjust inheritance laws, and child marriage. The new constitution must be implemented to guarantee gender equality and to foster women's participation in political power and decision-making.

Notes

1 Pittman, A & R, Naciri 'Winning Women's Rights: Cultural Adaptations and Islamic Family LawIn J Gaventa & R McGee (eds) 2010. Citizen Action and National Policy Reform: Making Change Happen. London: Zed.

2 For details see this URL: https://tavaana.org/en/content/moudawana-peaceful-revolution-moroccan-women (accessed on Dec. 29th, 2014).

3 For comparison's sake see similar situations of women's movements and countermovements in the Middle East, as tackled by Claudia Derichs (2014).

4 It is important to make a distinction between Islam and Islamism. Islam refers to Muslim faith. "Muslim" is the term used to describe a person who follows this religion. "Muslim" or "Islamic" can also be used as an adjective to refer to objects, actions and communities. "Islam exists as an ideal in the hearts of devout Muslims" (Sayeed 2014). Islamism generally stands for an ideology that is illiberal to its core—for instance, its refusal to recognize gender equality. There are many currents of Islamism, some of which use violence and are radical; others are peaceful and centralist. Cf. Sarah Sayeed's interesting article: http://www.huffingtonpost.com/sarah-sayeed-phd/searching-for-common-grou_b_5376617.html (accessed on Jan, 11, 2014)

5 See Ouguir's chapter (this volume).

6 They say that only 700 men are polygamous in the whole country.

7 In addition to the ORWA, numerous local women's associations are part of the Islamist women's network referred to as Az-Zahra, which is formally dependent on the MUR. Most of these associations focus on women and problems facing youth and society in general.

8 For more on this, read this article: http://www.al-monitor.com/pulse/politics/2014/02/failure-gradual-reforms-morocco-february-20-movement.html#ixzz3OA2YHfwJ (accessed on Jan.7th, 2015).

9 See the entire interview on this link: http://iknowpolitics.org/en/knowledge-library/interview/jamila-el-mossalli (accessed on 20 Apr. 2014).

10 Personal interview

11 See this link : http://www.theguardian.com/global-development/poverty-matters/2014/feb/07/ngo-change-morocco-rape-law (accessed on Dec. 19, 2014).

12 I refer the reader to this article: http://en.qantara.de/content/womens-rights-in-morocco-activists-see-little-hope-for-gender-policy-reforms (accessed on Dec. 20, 2014).

13 For more on this, read this: http://www.tariqmodood.com/uploads/1/2/3/9/
12392325/moderate_secularism_and_multiculturalism.pdf (accessed on May 29, 2014).
14 See Mernissi's *Beyond the Veil* (1975)

Bibliography

Collins, Patricia Hill. 2008. *Black Feminist Thought: Knowledge, Consciousness, and the Politics of Empowerment.* New York: Routledge.

Crenshaw Kimberle, Neil Gotanda, Gary Peller, and Kendall Thomas, eds. 1996. *Critical Race Theory: The Key Writings That Formed the Movement.* New York: The New Press.

Daoud, Zakia. 1993. *Féminisme et politique Au Maghreb.* París, Eddif.

Derichs, Claudia. (Ed.). 2014. *Women's Movements and Countermovements.* Newcastle upon Tyne : Cambridge Scholars Publishing.

Di Marco, Graciela & Tabbush, Constaza. (Eds.) 2012. *Feminisms, Democratization, and Radical Democracy.* San Martin: UNSAM Edita.

Eddouada, Souad. This volume. "Women and The politics of Reform in Morocco."

El Saadawi, *Nawal. 1997. The Nawal El Saadawi Reader.* London: Zedbooks.

Ennaji, Moha. 2013. "Arab Women's Unfinished Revolution". *The Project Syndicate* of Feb. 23, 2013. http://www.project-syndicate.org/commentary/women-in-politics-after-the-arab-spring-by-moha-ennaji (accessed on 21 Nov. 2014).

Ennaji, Moha. 2008. "Steps to the Integration of Moroccan Women in Development", *The British Journal of Middle Eastern Studies*, Volume 35, N° 3, December 2008, pgs. 339–348.

Ennaji, Moha 2004a. "Civil Society, Gender and Social Cohesion", *Société Civile, Genre et Développement.* Fès, Fès-Saiss, pp. 81–89.

Ennaji, Moha. 2004b. "Le Nouveau Code de la Famille, une Réforme de Fond", *Le Matin*, November 28, 2004, http://www.lematin.ma/ (accessed on 21 Nov. 2014).

Ennaji, Moha. 2012. "The New Muslim Personal Status Law in Morocco: Context, Proponents, Adversaries, and Arguments." In di Marco, Graciela & Tabbush, Constaza (Eds.), *Feminisms, Democratization, and Radical Democracy.* San Martin: UNSAM Edita, pp.193–208.

Ennaji, Moha and Sadiqi, Fatima. 2012. "Women's Activism and the New Family Code Reforms in Morocco". In *The IUP Journal of History and Culture*, Vol. VI, No. 1,:1–19.

Ennaji, Moha., Sadiqi, Fatima. 2008. *Migration and Gender in Morocco.* Trenton, Red Sea.

Inhorn, Marcia. 2015. Multiculturalism in Muslim America? The Case of Health Disparities and Discrimination in "Arab Detroit," Michigan".

In Ennaji, Moha (Ed.). *New Horizons of Muslim Diasporas in Europe and North America.* New York: Palgrave-Macmillan.

Johnson-Odim, Cheryl and Strobel, Margaret. 1992. *Expanding the Boundaries of Women's History: Essays on Women in the Third World.* Indiana: Indiana University Press.

Mernissi, Fatema. 1989. *Doing Daily Battle.* New Jersey, Rutgers University,

Moghadam, Valentine. 2012. Democracy and Women's Rights: Reflections on the Middle East and North Africa. In Di Marco, Graciela & Tabbush, Constaza (Eds.), pp.33–50.

Mullings, Leith. 1996. *On Our Own Terms: Race, Class, and Gender in the Lives of African-American Women.* New York: Routledge.

Ouguir, Aziza. This volume. "The Empowering Legacy of Women Saints: Venerators and Islamist Feminists."

Ouguir, Aziza. 2013. *Female Religious Agents In Morocco: Old Practices and New Perspectives*. Ph.D. Dissertation. University of Amsterdam.

Pittman, Alexandra and Naciri, Rabea. 2010. "Winning Women's Rights in Morocco: Cultural Adaptations and Islamic Family Law". In J Gaventa & R McGee (Eds.) *Citizen Action and National Policy Reform: Making Change Happen*. London: Zed, pp. 174–185.

Pruzan-Jørgensen, Julie. 2010. New female voices within the Islamist movement in Morocco. *IPRIS Maghreb Review* 6: 15–18.

Rhiwi, Leila. 2000. "Mouvement des Femmes Au Maroc", en *Rapport Du Social*, Rabat, OKAD, pp. 21–28.

Sadiqi, Fatima. 2014. *Feminist Discourses in Morocco*. New York: Palgrave-Macmillan.

Sadiqi, Fatima. , 2003. *Women, Gender and Language in Morocco*. Leiden and Boston, Brill Academic.

Sadiqi, Fatima and Ennaji, Moha. 2006. "The Feminization of Public Space: Women's Activism, the Family Law, and Social Change in Morocco", in *Journal of Middle East Women's Studies* (JMEWS), Volume 2, N° 2, Indiana, Summer 2006, pp. 86–114.

Sayeed, Sarah. 2014. " Searching for Common Ground: Are Muslim Terrorists Islamic or Islamist? "*The Huffington Post*, May 29, 2014. URL:http://www.huffingtonpost.com/sarah-sayeed-phd/searching-for-common-grou_b_5376617.html (accessed on Jan, 11, 2014).

Shröter, Susanne. 2014. "Progressive and Conservative Women's Movements in Indonesia". In Derichs, Claudia (Ed.). *Women's Movements and Countermovements*. Newcastle upon Tyne : Cambridge Scholars Publishing, pp.79–106.

Tibi, Bassam. 2009. *Islam's Predicament with Modernity: Politics, Religious Reform and* Cultural Change.London: Taylor & Francis.

Tuquoi, Jean Pierre. 2003. "Mohammed VI et les Marocaines", *Le Monde*, París, Oct. 18, 2003. http://www.lemonde.fr/

Yafout,.This volume. "Islamic feminism in Morocco: Concepts and perspectives."Association Démocratique des Femmes du Maroc 2013. "Le Processus d'Examen et d'Evaluation des Progrès Réalisés dans la Mise en Œuvre du Programme d'Action de Beijing en Afrique (Beijing +10) », Electronic document: www.wildaf-ao.org (accessed on Jan. 3, 2013).

Other Materials consulted

Jeune Afrique l'Intelligent, 21 October 2003

Le Monde, 18 October 2003

Le Matin, 28 November 2004

Al-Ittihad Al-Ishtiraki, 4 January 2004

King Hassan II Speech of 20 August 1992

King Mohammed VI Speech of 30 July 1999

Chapter 3

AN ASSESSMENT OF TODAY'S MOROCCAN FEMINIST MOVEMENTS (1946–2014)[1]

Fatima Sadiqi

Introduction

What would be qualified as "Moroccan feminist movements"[2] started as secular[3] social trends and developed into diverse, polyvocal and complex voices, hence the use of "feminist movements" instead of "feminist movement. "The secular feminist movement started in 1946 and is still alive and vibrant. During the 1990s or slightly before, the Islamic feminist movement appeared on the Moroccan public scene and is still going on. Although they may converge for political reasons, the philosophical and ideological concepts on which secular and Islamic feminist movements are based are inherently divergent: Being based on an Islamist ideology where religion is foregrounded, Islamic feminism cannot converge with secular feminism, based on a (leftist) progressive ideology where religion is backgrounded.

With the advent of the twenty-first century and especially in the aftermath of the so-called Arab Spring, the secular/Islamic paradigm is becoming too narrow a space that it fails to encompass the other growing and poorly understood feminist voices where concepts like "diversity," "online synergy," "Berber," and "rural" are increasingly gaining momentum across the boundaries of space, gender, and class.Although still in the making, these new developments are real. In order to give as clear a view of the various feminist voices in today's Morocco as possible, this chapter focuses on contextualizing the main feminist movements, secular and Islamic, comparing them, assessing their achievements and failures, and gauging the new feminist trends that seem to transcend them.

The Secular Feminist Movement[4]

Born in the 1940s as "al-wathiqa" (document) drafted in 1946 by the first Moroccan NGO (Akhawat Al-Safa – Sisters of Purity, itself part of the Parti Démocratique de l'Indépendence – PDI: Democratic Party of Independence), the first female feminist voices came from a group of elite urban educated women with close male relatives in the then nationalist movement decided to voice their demands both as women and as nationalists. In so doing they focused on promoting girls' education and providing charity to the families of the martyrs. These goals were dictated by the imperatives of the then colonized Morocco: the struggle for independence, strong nationalism, the promotion of Standard Arabic (in the face of colonial French),[5] the respect of Islamic tradition (in the face of French "modernity"), and the promotion of urban ideology (maintenance of a class system). In spite of the strength of these contextual imperatives, Akhawat Al-Safa succeeded in making women's personal and communal aspirations heard in the public sphere. In their public speeches, they focused on three main things in addition to education and charity: the abolition of polygamy, dignity at home, and dignity outside home.[6] Ever since, the movement has been focusing on legal rights as it developed into an increasingly complex social movement where activists, academics and politicians have been joining efforts. The fact that these pioneer women did not highlight religion positions them as "secular."

The "Akhawat Al-Safaa" spirit and message continued after the independence of Morocco and have been developing to the day in congruence with the ups and downs of the Moroccan society and state. The postcolonial neopatriarchy (a mixture of modernity, state feminism, and patriarchy), globalization, and Islamization have been impacting the movement. This impact increased with the advent of the new millennium, state Islamism, sophisticated technology, and the recent uprisings in the region.

Chronologically, the secular feminist movement witnessed three major waves: the first wave (1946-end of 1970s), the second wave

(1980s and 1990s), and the third wave (2000s – present). Although they share secularism as a common hard core, the three waves differ in their overall historical and socio-political backgrounds. However, together, they constitute a continuum that regenerates itself from within and that has been having a profound impact on Morocco's politics, gender policies, and international image. This was made partially possible by the fact that the secular feminist thought was grounded in the universal human rights and avoided religion without dismissing it. For example, patriarchy and not Islam has constantly been defined as the source of oppression. Without positing shari'a (Islamic law) as the main source of legislation, secular feminists have been keen to include civil law and human rights conventions (as adopted by the United Nations) as supplementary frames of reference. Like in any social movement, secular feminists' attitudes towards Islam range from extreme to moderate. Hence radical secularists privilege rationality, consider religious texts as inherently anti-women, and highlight modernity as the sole path to guaranteeing women's rights. As for the moderate trend, it focuses more on international human rights conventions than Islam as a basic reference, and when addressing religious issues, it highlights more *maqasid al-shari'a* (goals of shari'a law) than *shari'a* itself, and encourages the re-reading of the religious text in the light of social changes in society. Moderate secular feminists fluctuate between seeing Islam as valid for all times and places, and using Islamic principles to justify a modernist approach.

The first wave was constituted of the first generation of women who benefited from education and, more importantly, who communicated their thoughts in the public sphere of authority. Most of these feminists belonged to the urban upper and upper middle classes, and were aware of the fact that although they belonged to well-off families they did not have the same opportunities and choices that their male counterparts enjoyed.

The larger socio-political context that characterized this wave was marked by a combination of state-building and postcolonialism, which reinforced the "modernity/tradition" co-habitation in the lives of these women. The Moroccan state wanted to be "modern" and follow the way Western states developed and postcolonialism forced a critique of the state. Within their families and communities, these women felt privileged in comparison to the women of lower classes and rural areas but at the same time they knew that they lacked status when compared to the male members of their own class. For example, after independence, many women had their husbands positioned in various functions of power such as higher military ranks, ministers, higher functionaries, etc. with the prospects of marrying younger women; they also felt crippled by an oppressive and humiliating legislation whereby, for example, a woman needed her husband's written permission if she wanted to have a passport. Indeed the first family law (promulgated during the November 1957–January 1958) obliged women to obey their husbands, who could repudiate[7] them at will and without justification. These women were aware that, on the one hand, French colonization deeply disrupted Moroccan traditional modes of living, and on the other hand, the French "modernity" liberated them from strict Islamic dogmas. Much as they felt the heavy burden of tradition, they also understood that women were heavily instrumentalized in accommodating the competing sets of paradigms that the two modes and lifestyles brought about. For example, during the struggle for independence (1912–1956) both the nationalists and the colonizers capitalized on women in implementing their opposing agendas: the former saw in women the gatekeepers of tradition and, hence, restricted their roles to keeping the family cohesion and bringing up "appropriate" future citizens; and the latter saw in a female elite a guarantee for the dissemination of Western norms, values and lifestyle. Women's status and appearance served both agendas in different ways: whereas the women's *djellaba and litham*[8] was adopted as a sign of nationalism and authenticity, Western attire was adopted as a measure of spreading modernity. In spite of the central position of women in both the nationalist and the colonialist agendas, neither of these agendas was genuinely interested in the education, let alone promotion, of women for their own well being. The pioneer secular feminists were caught between the two powerful poles of tradition and modernity and endeavoured to make the best of both. They saw in tradition a comforting anchor of identity and in modernity a path to emancipation, salaried work and self-esteem. Although the use of Arabic was maintained, the general tendency leaned more towards the use of French because it facilitated the expression of taboo topics and allowed a space of free expression for many feminists. French also allowed these women to inscribe themselves in an interesting nascent Moroccan Francophone litera-ture that, though couched in French, transmitted, among other things, women's concerns, as well as local imagery, folk culture, and values. To publicly voice these concerns, women of the first wave produced journalistic articles on the need for girls' education, the need to balance tradition and modernity, the need for legal reforms, and the need for women's access to politics. In addition to journal-ism, scholarship, political engagement, and activism were used by the first wave. An example of such women is Malika Al-Fassi, a journalist who wrote the first recorded journalistic piece by a Moroccan woman in 1935.[9] Al-Fassi started writing under the pseudo-name of *al-fatat* (the girl). She was followed by other women like Zahra Chraibi and Fatima Kabbaj. Other women were politicians such as Khnata Bennouna, who belonged to a leftist political party. These and other women challenged patriarchy without displacing or dismantling it.

The nature and discourse of the first wave started to change as dramatic global events erupted by the end of the 1970s and the beginning of the 1980s: the success of the Iranian revolution in 1979, the downfall of the Soviet Union in 1989, and the gradual emergence of the United States of America as the sole super-power in the following decades. Political Islam was brought about by the first event, a weakening of the leftist ideology by the second event, and globalization by the third one. Of these three events it was political Islam that brought about the Second Wave of Moroccan feminists as a reaction to it. The main characteristic of this wave was located in the female "newcomers" to the movement: younger educated urban women from lower social classes, many of whom with a rural background. This made the then feminist community more heterogeneous classwize and more discursively polyvocal. The strategies used by the second wave were twofold: a combination of politics and activism, and a combination of scholarships and journalism.

In matters of politics and activism, the Second Wave feminists quickly realized that their issues and demands had never constituted a priority for the state throughout Morocco's national history, nor in the ideologies of the country's formal post-independence political parties (Daoud 1993, Naciri 2008). As a result, young university women entered the Opposition leftist parties en masse. The political climate of the time was conducive to militantism within leftist parties and organizations as a way to express anger with an authoritarian regime[10] and a class-based oppressive social system that excluded a growing mass of poor and illiterate population. The feminists of the time were torn between their feminist commitments and their political allegiances. The male-dominated and hierarchical structure of the leftist parties, as well as their focus on broader national issues, pushed feminists to organize themselves in independent feminine associations (NGOs) without discarding their leftist orientation. The first such association was L'Association Démocratique des Femmes Marocaines– ADFM (Democratic Association of Moroccan Women) which developed from the communist Parti du Progrès et du Socialisme (Progress and Socialism Party – PPS) in 1985. In 1987, L'Union de l'Action Féminine – UAF (Union of Feminine Action) developed from L'Organization de l'Action Démocratique et Populaire OADP (Organization of Democratic and Popular Action). The creation of these two NGOs not only marked the birth of women's activism in the public sphere of power, but also the subsequent feminization of this sphere as hundreds of feminist associations of various sizes followed suit. This, in turn, played a significant role in the feminization and democratization of the public sphere. When the Socialist Union for Popular Forces took power in 1998, the Second Wave feminists considerably gained in visibility and decision-making not only in numbers (more than five women were promoted to the executive body of the party) but also qualitatively in pushing women's issues to the forefront of national politics. Further, in their strategies, the Second Wave feminists both criticized and supported the governments of their time. They criticized them for backgrounding women's issues and supported them in the face of ramping Islamism. The actions of the two pioneering associations expanded from social services to consciousness-raising, which made of them serious mobilizing forces. They also offered psychological, medical, and legal assistance to women victims of violence, as well as literacy classes and legal knowledge to a large number of beneficiaries in urban areas. They also put pressure on the state to reform the family law along CEDAW principles.

In 1992, Action Féminine (Feminine Action) spearheaded the One Million Signatures to reform the family law (Mudawana) which led to the 1993 first reforms of this law. Although disappointing,[11] these reforms stripped the family law from its "sacredness" and, as such, constituted a genuine symbolic breakthrough which enhanced the secular feminist movement's remarkable action to obtain more reforms as the progressive 2004 family law attests to.[12] Female public figures like Latifa Jbabdi, Nouzha Skalli, Amina Lemrini, and Rabea Naciri are associated with these actions.

Secular feminists' actions were strengthened by a coalition between the first socialist government (which came to power in 1998), political parties and women's associations and led to the creation of the "Plan pour l'Intégration des Femmes dans le Développement" (The Plan for Integrating Women in Development), also known as "The Plan" in 1999 (See Eddouada, this volume). The Plan was spearheaded by the then socialist Secretary of State for Social Protection, Family and Children Mohamed Said Saadi. The main demands of the Plan were: the rise of the age of the first marriage of a girl to 18, the prohibition of matrimonial guardianship, the registration of children born outside wedlock under their mother's name, making all types of divorce judicial, abolishing polygamy, and dividing the accumulated wealth between spouses upon divorce. In parallel, secular feminists quickly realized that Islamists targeted women, especially the lower classes, through their call for veiling and their carefully packaged discourses that comforted the patriarchal tendencies among men, especially young unemployed males who were easily led to think that women's work outside the home robbed them of opportunities. Second Wave feminists also realized that by pushing politicized women to demand rights from a religious perspective, Islamists were trying to highjack the discourse, space and fruits of years of efforts by secular feminists.

The main strategies that secular feminists used to react to this state of affairs were a gradual downplay of the 'religious' role of the veil in their writings and practices, more and more usage of Arabic, Qur'an and Hadith (Prophet's sayings and behavior), a call for more flexible readings of the Qur'anic texts, a gradual inclusion of the children's oppression in women's issues, and a reinforcement of Islam as culture and spirituality. These secular feminists also endeavored to draw the attention of the younger, often veiled, generation to the real problem that women faced: absence of legal protection in front of the law. They made an excellent use of the media in depicting the social misery of women and children victims of divorce, thus targeting the very social issues that the Islamists capitalized on. By so doing, the secular feminists maintained their focus on the necessity to reform the family law.

Overall, the secular feminists of the 1980s sought to assert themselves and affirm their own identity and the existence of their own history in spite of the powerful Islamist movement. They did this through journalistic writings, associative work, and anthropological, sociological, and political studies, as well as through narratives and poems. These feminists were conscious that if they rejected Islamic precepts, they would face a double sanction: in Morocco, they would fail to connect with the vast majority of Moroccan women who were poor, illiterate and deeply religious, and outside Morocco, they would be accused of not representing their own authentic culture.

The political and activist endeavors of the Second Wave were reinforced by a combination of scholarship and journalism. Much of this literature aimed at deconstructing Morocco's gendered history and highlighting the marginalized voices, amongst which women's. Women's legal rights, the veil, and public freedom were at the heart of this multilingual literature (Arabic, French, and to a lesser extent English). However, like the First Wave, the Second Wave did not address issues like diversity and the Berber language and culture in spite of the secular nature of the latter. These issues had to wait for the Third Wave.

The Third Wave grew from a rather complex overall socio-political context where four major factors intersect: identity, Islamism, globalization and new technology, and the uprisings in the region. It is a more versatile and complex wave in terms of class, level of education, Islamic dose, language, gender, strategies, and internationalization. More lower class and multilingual youth (male and female) are making their feminist voices heard. The use of Moroccan Arabic and Berber in texting, Facebook, Twitter, and other social media facilitated this, and the images of the revolutions in the region added more fuel.

Of the four factors that shaped this wave, the most spectacular one was an identity politics, which "transformed" Berber from a marginalized to a full-fledged official language in the new 2011 constitution.

In a parallel way and significantly, the new constitution also recognizes equality between the sexes and parity.[13] Indeed the fates of Berber and women have always been parallel. The two were marginalized during the Protectorate and state-building and the two are investing the public sphere of authority almost synchronically.[14] Secular feminist consciousness is increasingly congruent with Berber consciousness as the two share secularism. This is reflected in the reciprocal networking between the two on the ground. Hence, the secular feminist Spring of Dignity Network, a coalition of twenty-two secular feminist associations, originally created in 2008 but redynamized in the aftermath of the uprisings in the region, supports the Berber movement's initiative of One Million Signature to implement the new constitution. Further, cultural rights have been added to secular feminist demands, and Tifinagh (Berber alphabet characters) is now systematically included in the secular feminist slogans.

The Third Wave had also to define its stance with respect to Islamism, which is now part and parcel of the government for the first time in the modern history of Morocco. The Islamist Parti de la Justice et du Développement – PJD (Justice and Development Party) won the 2011 elections and took power. Disillusioned by the failure of mainstream national parties and attracted by the Islamist "corruption-fighting" slogans, many young and less young secular Moroccans gave this Islamist party a "pragmatic," not a religious, vote. However, after a couple of years, the Islamists proved to be just like the other parties, failed to deliver on issues such as employment, and as a result, somehow "demystified" political Islam. This disillusionment with political Islam in Morocco was further enhanced by the failure of the Muslim Brotherhood in Egypt and the pragmatism of Moroccan youth who seem to opt for keeping religion outside politics. Another factor which greatly neutralized the impact of Islamism in Morocco is the fact that democratic transition in this country took place long before the uprisings in the region and activism as well as the policies targeting women's roles and rights were part and parcel of this transition as shown in the previous sections. The recent (and unexpected) victory of the secularist camp over the Islamist one in Tunisia is further blow to political Islam in Morocco.

In addition to Berber identity politics and Islamism, the availability of new technology, as an offshoot of globalization, had a huge impact on the Third Wave. By facilitating communication and democratizing the linguistic landscape through the use of Moroccan Arabic and Berber (mainly written in the Arabic and Latin scripts), or a mixture of both in email, Facebook, Twitter, Youtube, cellular phone texting, blogs, as well as street advertisements, the new social media affected the Third Wave in significant ways. Internet-based tools allowed a quick and relatively unregulated sharing of information which appealed to the youth of this wave.

Finally, the 2011 uprisings in the region affected Morocco by leading to the 20 February Movement. This movement did not demand a regime change as was the case in Tunisia, Egypt and Libya, but it certainly gave renewed vigor to, among other movements, the feminist secular movement. On February 20, 2011, crowds gathered across Morocco asking for more legal, civil, and cultural rights, as well as freedom and dignity. The king responded quickly, and within two weeks important constitutional reforms were announced such as having the Prime Minister from the party that has won the majority of votes, the elevation of Berber to the status of an official language, and the constitutionalization of gender equality and parity. These reforms were approved in a referendum on July 1, 2011, by 98.5 percent of voters.

The main strategies that the Third Wave of use are (virtual) activism and scholarship/journalism. With respect to activism, the core ideas of the Second Wave re-emerged with the Third Wave. For example, the March 2011 creation of the "Spring of Feminist Democracy and Equality," a coalition of a thousand organizations working for human rights and the rights of women, presented a list of demands to the Advisory Committee for the Revision of the Constitution. Among the demands was the state's commitment to combat all forms of discrimination against women, the ensuring of gender equality (a 50 percent quota for women) in all fields, including decision-making. The demands also included the fact that the constitution should recognize the principle of the indivisibility of human rights, so that women could enjoy their civil, political, economic, social, environmental, and cultural rights. They also included the fact that the constitution should enshrine the primacy of international law over national law. Thanks to among other groups, women's pressure, most of these demands were satisfied in the 2011 constitution.

Women's post-2011 legal gains were not, however, matched by similar advances at the social and political levels. For example, in the parliamentary elections of 2011, there were only 67 women MPs elected out of 395. Admittedly, this was a step forward compared to previous elections where there were only 30 women MPs; however, it was expected that at least a third of seats would be allocated to women. More significantly, there was a drastic decline in the number of women Ministers from seven in 2007 to only one in 2011. This was somehow remedied by the inclusion of five more women on the October 10, 2013[15] second version of the Islamist government. This new version reduced the space of the Islamists in decision-making as they now need to share more power with other parties.

The Third Wave also gained more strength in fighting violence against women. Thus, for example, the March 2012 suicide of the sixteen-years-old Amina Filali, who swallowed poison after being forced to marry her rapist, pushed the Equality Now association to issue an Act demanding legal reforms to strengthen punishment for sexual violence and the prevention of child marriage. This association demanded the revision of Article 475 to no longer exempt a "kidnapper" from punishment if his victim, being a minor, marries him. These demands were advanced in defiance of the mutism and inertia of the Islamist Ministry of Solidarity, Women, Family and Social Development. The Equality Now Act led to national debates and heated discussions in the parliament, and finally in February 2014 Article 475 was revised, precluding the exemption of the "kidnapper" from punishment if he marries his victim and raising the sentence in such cases to 30 years of prison: a great victory for secular feminist civil society.

As for virtual activism, it may be illustrated by the role of women in the 20-February Movement, created in the context of the uprisings in the region. This movement was partly started by a young woman, Nidal Hamdache Salam,[16] who initiated a Facebook forum discussion on the political and socio-economic issues in contemporary Morocco. Issues like the separation of the executive, legislative and judiciary, individual freedoms, secret detention centers; corruption of state elites, nepotism, clientelism, regular violations of human rights and personal freedoms, as well as unequal access to education, health care and work were discussed.

Videos calling people to demonstrate in big cities followed suit and the movement materialized in big demonstrations on February 20, 2011. Hamdache coordinated the Youth Commission (of the Moroccan Association for Human Rights) and was instrumental in the mobilization phase. It is reported that more than 50 percent of the protesters in the movement were women.

Even after the March 9, 2011 King's speech where substantial reforms of the constitution were announced, the February-20 Movement continued to demonstrate. Their main demands were that the members of the commission in charge of the reform of the constitution were appointed by the king, and not democratically elected by the Moroccan citizens. Such demands were instrumental in changing the Moroccan political scene in the sense that it allowed taboo topics to be discussed openly. Ups and downs in the intensity of the movement followed and regardless of its fate, there is no denial that it brought people on the street and united them across age, class, and gender.[17]

In sum, the secular feminist movement had to adjust to the new developments and in its attempt to bridge the generational gap seems to have experienced some kind of renewal with the emergence of two new players on the public scene: youth culture and the movement for the recognition of Berber culture and language (Berber being a centuries-old women-related language which became an official language after the recent uprisings).

The Islamic Feminist Movement[18]

Islamic feminism is an intellectual endeavour which denotes awareness of gender power dynamics that privilege men and that are enshrined in family and society as part of Islam. As such, it is mainly concerned with women's rights, gender equality, and social justice from within the Islamic framework (Badran 2005, 2008). Islamic feminism is often geared towards using gender as an analytical tool to produce *Ijtihad*-based reforms that offer new women'-friendly interpretations of the sacred texts. It is, thus, anchored in the discourse of Islam as vehicled by the Qur'an (holy book) and the Hadiths (sayings of the Prophet) as the main references. Islamic feminism triggered a substantial body of literature in non-Muslim majority democratic countries (cooke 2001, Barlas 2002, Mahmoud 2005, Wadud 2006, Mir-Husseini 2006, Moghadam 2009, among many others).

In Morocco, Islamic feminism is a relatively new reality that has emerged in the heat of the 1990s' ideological crisis over the woman issue. The then debates around the reform of the family law opposed the modernists (feminists and democrats in general) and the conservatives (traditionalists and Islamists in general). The scale of the debates was big and involved the entire nation, transcending the parliament to the street, the university, the mosque, and the home. The first peak of this ideological confrontation was the political turmoil and social anarchy that followed the above-mentioned 1992 One Million Signatures campaign to reform the family law. At that time, cushioned by the support of monarchy, the left, and the state, secular feminists were gathering considerable momentum but were also faced with fierce resistance from the Islamists. In the midst of this turmoil, the male Islamist leaders of the time realized that the success of their project depended on their ability to "curb" the female secular feminists by proposing a "new" brand of "female veiled Islamic feminists."[19] The second peak of the confrontation that opposed the modernists and the conservatives was the above-mentioned socialist government's Plan to integrate women in development. The Plan provoked a number of fatwas (religious decrees) condemning feminists as atheists (hence eligible to death) and depicting them as "enemies of Islam" in mosques, as well as in cassettes distributed on the street and in public spaces. In addition, bearded men would stand at roundabouts making gestures to unveiled female drivers that they needed to cover their heads and some women were openly aggressed on the streets for not wearing the veil. The Plan itself was demonized as lacking an Islamic reference and a march was organized on March 12, 2000 to condemn it. In parallel and along the male Islamist leaders' "push" for veiled women's visibility in the public sphere, more Islamist associations were created and the Forum Azzahrae pour la Femmes Marocaine (Azzahrae Forum for the Moroccan woman) was founded in 2002 as a network umbrella that covered these associations. The confrontation between the modernists and the conservatives cooled off after the Casablanca

May 16 terrorist attacks,[20] the state's crackdown on the Islamists, and moderate Islamists' decision to partake in the government.

These events show that Islamic feminism in Morocco was initiated and largely instigated by male Islamist politicians' tactics to counter secular feminists who were gaining considerable momentum.[21] The Islamists saw in this Islamic feminism an arm of their ideology that would both counter the then sweeping trend of the secular feminists and earn them more followers, especially amongst women, most of whom illiterate.[22] Gradually, female Islamic feminists started to appear on the scene first to support the political Islamist project and later to challenge the paternalism within this movement.[23] The majority of Islamic feminists acted more as politicians than feminist theoreticians. This was largely the result of the fact that the Islamists succeeded to a great extent in collectivizing a larger segment of laywomen to endorse the ideological viewpoints of the Islamist movement.

There are two types of Moroccan Islamic feminists: the moderate Party of Justice and Development (PJD) feminists and the more extremist Justice and Benevolence (JP) Association feminists, both of whom in line with their political and associative respective ideologies. For both types of feminists, the biological difference between men and women leads to different social statuses and different rights, hence equity, and not equality, should be targeted. In other words, for these feminists, gender justice is perceived in terms of equity (difference based on biological difference), not equality (similitude). This perspective maintains and reproduces the complementarity of sexes, and the division of sexual labor. For Islamic feminists, it was not a question of applying equality to Islam but of applying correctly the textual predispositions of equity that Islam came with. The question to explore, thus, was not the extent to which textual predispositions were egalitarian, but to explore how male Muslims never ceased to betray them since the Umayad Caliphate in the seventh century. While secular feminists talked about how insufficient Islam-accorded rights were, Islamic feminists talked only about the non-application and/or violation of these rights. It was not a betrayal of the ideal of equality that was at stake but a rupture with the imperative of equity. That is why neither equality in inheritance, nor equality in the number of spouses (polygyny) nor equality in the choice of a spouse (the right of a Muslim woman to marry a non-Muslim) were debated from an Islamic perspective. In a sense, equity was presented as legal and legitimate inequality of rights and seemed to be founded on a rejection of individual autonomy as a woman was first and foremost a wife and a mother (the pillar of the household and the first vector of values). All in all, the project of Islamic feminists in Morocco is still a moral order doubled by the traditional political patriarchy founded on sexual discrimination. They are called feminists in this chapter because they are trying to challenge patriarchy by, for example, calling for complementarity in the private sphere (Yafout 2008).

Both the PJD and the JB count high numbers of female feminist members. These women share a number of characteristics: a strong belief that Islam provides women with rights, an adherence to the veil, work within the ideological tenets of the party/association they are affiliated to, and a belief in complementarity (instead of equality) between men and women and between rights and obligations, a tendency to consider women's problems within the larger context of the family, and not as individual problems. However, there is a difference between the two groups: the JB women are more vocal and outspoken than the PJD ones. A reason for this may be that the former is not recognized by the state, hence the apparent erasure of gender and class in its discourse.[24] All in all, while these female Islamists refute the idea that women in conservative parties are silent, they also present Islam as the only source of women's rights. The main channels that Moroccan Islamic feminists use to disseminate their thoughts and ideas are: preaching, activism, and to a certain extent scholarship.

The topics of preaching revolve mainly around how a believer should live and practice his/her religion. For example, Islamic feminists both advise women on how to practice their faith and by the same token disseminate the sociopolitical perspective that Islam has become misguided due to political interests and misogynistic readings. As for activism, it includes the organization of religious gatherings and study groups to empower women and allow them to transform their roles in their families. The inspiration they get from the lives of the Prophet and his Companions is very positive for most women. As for scholarship, it includes a reading of the Qur'an from a feminist point of view.

In addition to the PJD and JB Islamic feminists, two other types of Islam-based feminism are found in Morocco: "self-based" and "state-based". While the latter is widespread and may include feminists from the PJD party or the JB association, the former is rather restricted to a few women and is independent. Further, the two types are characterized by a non-affiliation to a unifying Islamist movement or association. Both start from the Qur'an and Hadith to support equality between the sexes and underline the egalitarian and universal message of Islam. An example of self-based feminism is Asma Lamrabet, a pathologist and writer. Although wearing a "modern" veil, Lamrabet does not see the veil as mandatory. According to her[25] by focusing on the veil, theologians reduce women to "bodies" and background the fact that Islam is a religion of equality, knowledge and compassion, values deemed by her as more important than the veil. Furthermore, Lamrabet prones more involvement in female Ijtihad and fatwa-production.

As for state-based Islamic feminism, it appeared in the aftermath of the 2003 terrorist attacks in Casablanca as a state's endeavor to control and monitor the religious field in order to eradicate terrorism, and a way of developing a positive international image of Morocco. To achieve these goals, the state, through the Ministry of Endowment and Religious Affairs, created the Islamic association Munaddamat at-tajdid Al Wa'yAl-Nisaa?i (Organization of the Renewal of Female Consciousness) in 2005 with the benediction of the moderate Islamists and the Ulama (religious leaders). The main mission of this association is the "nesting" of an "Islamized" version of feminism which would channel the shared interests of the state and its allies, and ensure their positioning as "democratic" and "open" vis-à-vis national and international community. The Ministry of Religious Affairs was also in charge of training and supervising the first cohort of female religious preachers/guides (Murshidats) in 2005,[26] a pioneer move in the history of Morocco.[27] The Murshidats program was geared towards reviving Islam's tolerance and moderation, fighting radicalization, and underlining the religious legitimacy of the Moroccan regime. To enter the program, the would-be Murshida needs to be under forty-six years of age, hold a B.A. degree or an equivalent diploma with high grades, and succeed in the entry exam (an interview where she needs to prove that she memorized half of the Qur'an). Ever since 2005, the program has been training fifty women each year and the courses include Islamic affairs, psychology, sociology, computer skills, law and business management, as well as Islamic history and geography, Qur'anic recitation techniques, and the art of preaching and communication.

Upon graduation, the Murshidats are assigned tasks that include guiding women (and men) in their religious practices in mosques, as well as in various public institutions, such as prisons, youth clubs, hospitals, and so on. This move is revolutionary in itself because Moroccans in general, and Moroccan women in particular, often find it difficult to seek religious guidance on intimate things pertaining to their lives from men. When addressing mixed audiences, the preachers share their interpretations of the Qur'an and Hadiths (Prophet Muhammad's sayings), but when addressing all-female audiences, they also give advice on private and sometimes intimate issues, such as how to dress in private and public spaces, how to interact with men in those spaces, how to deal with sexual problems, and so on.

The state also encourages women to participate in the religious lectures that are delivered during Ramadan (al-Durus al-Hassaniyya) in the presence of the king, in the local scientific councils (Majalis al 'ilmiyya), and in the Rabitat– councils – where twenty out of seventy Ulema are women). Furthermore, *'alimat* (women religious leaders) have been integrated into the regional delegations of the Ministry of Religious Affairs and Habous, where they direct family units. All in all, just as it appropriated some secular feminism the state, in its endeavor to keep a balance and control ideologies, appropriated some Islamic feminism.[28] State-instigated Islamic feminism may also be viewed as a response to increasing demands from religiously-based women's activists in recent years.[29]

Given their nature, both the self-based and state-based Islamic feminist initiatives are welcomed by the secular feminists for three main reasons: they draw on the Sufi (rather than legal orthodox) Islamic heritage,[30] they adopt the principle of equality, and they introduce change in gender relations within a powerful public space: religion.

A Comparison of the Secular and Islamic Trends[31]

The secular and Islamic feminist movements in Morocco are products of specific contexts where historical, social, political, and international factors intersect. Hence while the secular movement is to a large extent a product of the leftist ideology where the political use of religion is backgrounded, the Islamic movement is the product of an Islamist ideology where the political use of religion is foregrounded. The intrinsic ideological opposition between these two movements makes them intrinsically divergent although they may converge for political reason such as lobbying for a feminist cause. In other words, although Islam is in a sense part of both trends, it is not instrumentalized in the same way, hence the core difference that gave rise to other divergences, namely on issues of reference, goals, perspective on tradition, religious identity, equality vs complementarity of rights, the gender issue, and knowledge-production.

With respect to reference, secular feminists privilege *maqasid sharia* (goals of shari'a), international conventions of human rights, and universal values. As for Islamic feminists, they privilege the sacred texts: the Qur'an and Sunna (Prophet'. The bone of contention between the two is that while Islamic feminists resist Western values and acknowledge Islam as the sole source of inspiration for any reform, secular feminists highlight universal values and prone a more human rights interpretation of the sacred texts.[32] The issue of universality is linked to attitude to the West. Many Islamic feminists refute the "universality" of women's secular rights and see these as representations of a particular (not universal) Western point of view – which contradicts and challenges Islam.

So far as goals are concerned, while the secular movement targets women's rights, the Islamic movement uses preaching, charity, and global activism with the purpose of advancing the Islamist movement, not women's rights. For example, the way the secularists and Islamists address women victims of violence on the ground is particularly revealing. Whereas secular feminists use "listening centers" to increase women's awareness of their rights as citizens, Islamic feminists use "family consulting centers" to enforce the values of the Islamist project: solidarity, justification of polygamy, and so on.[33] The Najma Center, set up by the seculartist network Anaruz[34] (National Network of Centers for Women Victims of Violence in Morocco),[35] initiated by the secularist Democratic Association of Moroccan Women (ADFM), encourages abused women to speak about their traumatic experiences. The center also created a free telephone hotline which provides legal help and counseling to women victims of violence.[36] The Islamic counterpart of Listening centers, are the Family Consulting centers, created by the Mountada Azzahrae li Al-maraa Al-Maghrebiya (Forum Azzahrae for Moroccan Woman)[37] which covers sixty associations that focus more on family as an institution than on women as individuals. The main services that these consulting centers offer for free are family reconciliation, psychological and legal instruction promoting family values as the only guarantee for a stable society, and encouragement of youth to seek marriage as a shield against child abuse and sexual harassment. These endeavors are further supported by fieldwork, lecturing, seminars, training programs on family solidarity, and so on. These family centers also reach out to courts and schools to disseminate their ideas. In their strategies, these centers often invoke the Qur'an and divine laws as tools to curb human instincts. The secular and Islamic centers have, thus, divergent agendas. While the former emphasizes legal action in accordance with the core aims of the secular feminist movement which targets patriarchal legal Islam, the latter stresses family and social solidarity in accordance with the political Islamist ideology which tolerates (and often thrives on) such patriarchy.

The third issue on which the secular and Islamic feminist discourses diverge is tradition. While seen as versatile, dynamic and fluid by secular feminists, at least by the Third Wave, Islamic feminists generally associate tradition with "old" practices that counter "true" Islamic teachings. However, while Islamic feminists tend to combat traditional practices and reject them as acts that diminish women in and outside the family, they stress women's traditional roles as wives and mothers and support a heavy system of prescriptions on how women should behave in and outside home with an emphasis on non-mixity and the segregation of the sexes in public spheres. Furthermore, while secular feminists are more vocal in advocating "progressive" change in women's behavior and practices, Islamic feminists focus more on "protecting" the "threatened" family values.

With respect to religious identity, Islamic feminists highlight cultural identity as an unambiguous Islamic identity, whereas secular feminists generally consider this notion almost obsolete. For the latter, religious identity is part of women's multiple identities and highlighting religious identity is reductive and crippling as its complicates the treatment of gender inequality, injustice, and patri-archy. This is also often seen as highlighting the male establishment as supreme authority. The focus on religious identity by Islamic feminists makes the discussion of women's issues outside religion almost impossible. This is generally seen by secular feminists as a way of reducing a woman's multiple identities to her religion.

As for the issue of equality/complementarity, the Islamic trend capitalizes on men and women having complementary roles in the family in the sense that a woman may choose specific roles in the family next to her fundamental roles of wife and mother, and a man may choose other roles in addition to his fundamental role as the breadwinner and head of the family. In other words, for Islamic feminists, women's rights are as equal to but not similar to men's. Rather than seeing men and women as equal and similar, they are seen as complementary and having different roles and obligations. Islamic feminists' views on complementarity are often challenged by the various types of non-married women such as the widows, divorcees, "spinsters", and single mothers. Further, Islamic feminists' stance on equality is ambiguous and misleading: hence, while some of them label secular women's rights activists "un-Islamic," others underline the "just" and "equal" nature of Islam. This renders the Islamic femi-nists' standards and measures of equality rather shaky.[38]

As for the use of gender as an analytical tool, it is more problematic for Islamic than secular feminists. The former are not sympathetic to the use of "gender" as a tool because it disregards differences and complementarity between men and women. Indeed, CEDAW (Committee for the Elimination of Discrimination Against Women) has become the main "arena" of controversy between the two feminist movements in what concerns the utility of the gender category. For Islamic feminists, CEDAW is associated with "Western individualistic approaches" that seek to make gender relations completely equal, in contradiction with the Islamic view that considers the family, and not the individual, as the primary entity to be protected and where com-plementarity rather than complete equality is crucial. Islamic feminists generally oppose the gender approach on these grounds and often refer to it as "international interference in Moroccan internal affairs."

Finally, knowledge-production is a domain where divergence between the secular and Islamic feminist movements is attested.

Unlike the former, Islamic feminists lack scholarly rigor and border on political Islam propaganda. For example, Nadia Yassine's ambivalent attitude on the family law (Mudawana) reforms as reported in the press is polemical and self-contradictory: in 1999 she was staunchly opposed to any legal reforms and in 2004 she stated that the laws needed to be more aggressive.

In sum, there are deep and substantial divergences between secular and Islamic feminist trends. While Islam is a reality in Moroccan society and culture, and while politicians may have reached a certain comprise, the secular and Islamic movements cannot converge. The two are poles that cannot meet discursively; otherwise they would have to constitute one discourse. However, the two movement may feel the need to collaborate and work together in the face of patriarchy and male dominance such as was attested in various speeches of both camps.

Conclusion

The two main Moroccan feminist movements (secular and Islamic) have come a long way, especially the secular one. However, although these movements are at the forefront of the Arab-Muslim feminist movements, they still fall short of their aims as large portion of Moroccan women, especially in rural areas, are marginalized in both the secular and Islamic feminist discourses and the feminist praxis (Sadiqi 2014). The two movements do not allow enough space for the polyvocal spaces that have been created in the aftermath of the Arab Spring. The new emerging voices are young, cyber-sensitive, and diverse in matters of gender, class and identity. This emerging youth seems to have hope in a secular state where both religious and non-religious feminisms may flourish and where other voices such as Berber women have a genuine space.

Notes

1 In this chapter I address the fight and struggle of educated urban women within a broad social movement that interacts with the other two social movements in the country: the Islamist and the Berber movements. This does not mean that uneducated, mainly semi-urban and rural women are passive and do not have a history of "vocality"; on the contrary, these women have always expressed their agency through other means, such as oral poetry, community service, art, etc. (see Sadiqi et al 2009 and Chapter 5 of Sadiqi 2014).

2 "Feminist movements" is understood here as voices that empower women in the public spheres of authority, as opposed to the private spheres of power (authority being understood as power sanctioned by society. For more details, see Sadiqi 2014, Chapter 3)

3 "Secular" is understood here as "not foregrounding religion" and "Islamic" a "foregrounding religion. "

4 The notion of secularism in Morocco necessarily includes a dose of religion as the king is the highest political and religious authority. As such, while not foregrounding religion, the secular feminist movement seeks to improve, not replace, shari'a law.

5 "Standard" Arabic is written Arabic and is different from "dialectical" or darija (spoken) Arabic.

6 "Al-Wathiqa" (the Document) is published and commented on in *Women Writing Africa. The Northern Region* (edited by Fatima Sadiqi, Amira Noaira, Azza El Khouly and Moha Ennaji and published by The Feminist Press in 2009). It is the first written text by women in modern Morocco.

7 Repudiation means that a man can divorce his wife by uttering stating so verbally. This "right" is accorded to men only.

8 A *djellaba* (a long garment that covers the whole body with a hood that may be used to cover the head as well) is the Moroccan national attire. It was first used by men then by both sexes. As for the *litham*, it is a piece of cloth that women put on their nose and mouth.

9 See Sadiqi et al (2009).

10 King Hassan II's regime was particularly oppressive in the 1970s and beginning of 1980s pursuant to the failure of the two military coups that marked the beginning of the 1970s.

11 The main substantial changes in the 1993 reforms were: a father would no longer compel his daughter to marry, a mother was ensured legal guardianship of her child, a woman must consent to marry by signing a registry witnessed by officials appointed by the Minister of Justice.

12 See Sadiqi (2008, 2014) for more details on these actions.

13 Article 19 of the 2011 constitution states:

> L'homme et la femme jouissent, à égalité, des droits et libertés, à caractère civil, politique, économique, social, culturel, et environnemental, énoncés dans le présent titre et dans les autres dispositions de la Constitution, ainsi que dans les conventions dûment ratifiées par le Royaume. L'Etat marocain œuvre à la réalisation de la parité entre les hommes et les femmes. Il est créé, à cet effet, une Autorité pour la parité et la lutte contre toute forme de discrimination

> The man and the woman enjoy, in equality, the rights and freedoms of civil, political, economic, social, cultural and environmental character, announced in this Title and in the other provisions of the Constitution, as well as in the international conventions and pacts duly ratified by Morocco and in respect of the provisions of the Constitution, of the constants [*constantes*] and of the laws of the Kingdom. The State works for the realization of parity between men and women. An Authority for parity and the struggle against all forms of discrimination is created to this effect.

> (Author's translation).

> Pursuant to this article, a new body called "Authority for Equality and the Fight Against All Forms of Discrimination" was created to ensure that women's

rights are safeguarded. As an offshoot of this "Authority," the Forum on High Parity and Equality was created to ensure the implementation process of Article 19. Also a new section called Libertés et Droits Fondamentaux (Liberties and Fundamental Rights) includes Articles 32 and 34 with statements concerning the rights of women, children and the disabled: Article 21 prohibits sexism, Article 59 safeguards women's rights and liberties during states of emergency and, most importantly, Article 175 states that these rights cannot be retracted in future constitutional revisions.

14 For example, the Royal Institute for Amazigh (Berber) Culture (IRCAM) was created in 2001 and the new progressive family law was first announced in 2003.

15 October 10 is the Moroccan National Day. Although the coincidence is welcomed by most Moroccan women MPs, four of the five new ministers were appointed only as Deputy Ministers and not full Ministers, which implies that women are still not judged able to lead ministries. An MP qualified these new deputy Ministers as the "harem" of the government.

16 See https://www.mamfakinch.com/printemps-marocain-le-role-des-femmes-par-osire-glacier/.

17 It is important to note that the struggle of the third wave was robustly supported by associations that the second wave started.

18 Although the expression "Islamist politics" makes sense, "Islamist feminism" does not because it is self-contradictory. In other terms, while a feminist discourse may be Islamic, Islamist discourse cannot be feminist.

19 Two such female feminists were Bassima Hakkaoui (current Minister of Solidarity, Woman, Family and Social Development in the current Islamist government) and Khadija Messala, a member of the Islamist group in the parliament.

20 On May 16, 2003, Moroccan extremist Islamists killed forty-four people in a terrorist attack. Most of the victims were Moroccan, but some foreigners were among the victims.

21 According to Meriem Yafout (2008) Islamic feminism started in the 1970s but the developments were not homogeneous enough to create a genuine movement.

22 The veil was heavily instrumentalized during this period (the 1990s). The international scene, especially the first Gulf War, accelerated the spread of Islamist ideology among the Moroccan population. In addition, large portions of older educated middle class women embraced a form Islamist ideology, veiled and performed pilgrimage to Mecca to make up for the guilt-related feelings of absence from the mosque. This particular phenomenon was enhanced by the rapid spread of "modern preaches" by the young Egyptian accountant Amr Khalid.

23 It is important to note that generally speaking, the veil does not mean the same thing for men and women in Morocco: whereas most veiled women see their veiling as a token of emancipation from male control, most Muslim men see in it a sign of obedience.

24 Such a phenomenon has been attested in Morocco's struggle for independence during which liberation from the French occupiers primed over anything else, including gender (Abouzeid 1989). However the death of Sheikh Yassine in December of 2012 created a gender issue within the association as his daughter, Nadia Yassine, also the mouthpiece of women's issues in the association, has been distanced from politics.

25 See http://www.panoramaroc.ma/fr/le-hijab-nest-ni-une-priorite-ni-un-pilier-de-lislam-dr-asma-lamrabet/.

26 See Ennaji 2011.

27 This move was facilitated by the status of king as *Amir al-Muminin* (Commander of the Faithful).

28 See Pruzan-Jørgensen, 2010 for more details on this issue.
29 See Eddouada & Pepicelli, 2010 for more details on this.
30 The then and current Minister of Islamic Affairs is a member of the influential Boutchichiyya Brotherhood.
31 In this section I focus on mainstream Islamic feminism and do not include the state or individual Islamic perspectives.
32 This contention is also rooted in the ambiguity that surrounds the way shari'a and fiqh are used. While shari'a is more inclusive and refers to regulations and rules that emanate from the sacred Qur'an and Hadith, fiqh refers to a set of non-sacred regulations and rules that are produced by Muslim scholars. As such, fiqh is open to Ijtihad. It is for this reason that most secularists refer to the goals of shari'a that allow changes in fiqh according to the changing conditions of women in real life.
33 Secularist listening centers were created in the aftermath of the Vienna 1993 international convention and their main aim is to fight violence against women through legal action.
34 See http://www.anaruz.org/portail/.
35 Anaruz was created in 2004.
36 Women victims of violence can either file a complaint with the court or, if they can afford it, hire a lawyer to handle the case.
37 See http://www.blanee.com/etablissements/forum-azzahrae-de-la-femme-marocaine-rabat.
38 Knowledge production in Western countries where Islam is not state law and where individual freedom is guaranteed, does prone an equality-based Islamic feminism; however this type of equality does not constitute part of the Moroccan Islamic feminism.

Bibliography

Abouzeid, Leila.1989.*Year of the Elephant: A Moroccan Woman's Journey toward Independence*. Austin: University of Texas at Austin.

Badran, Margot. 2005. "Between Secular and Islamic Feminism/s. Reflections on the Middle East ;tand Beyond." *Journal of Middle East Women's Studies*(JMEWS), 1:1, 6–28.

Badran, Margot. 2008. *Feminism in Islam: Secular and Religious Convergences*. Oxford: Oneworld.

Barlas, Asma. 2002. *Believing Women In Islam: Unreading Patriarchal Interpretations of the Qur'an*. Austin: University of Texas Press.

Cooke, Miriam. 2001. *Women Claim Islam: Creating Islamic Feminism through Literature*. New York: Routledge.

Daoud, Zakia.1993. *Feminisme et politique au Maghreb: Soixante ans de Lutte*. Casablanca: Editions Eddif.

Eddouada, Souad. & Pepicelli, Renata. 2010. "Morocco : Towards an Islamic Feminism of the State". *International Critique*46: 87–100.

Ennaji, Moha. 2011. "Women's NGOs and Social Change in Morocco." In Sadiqi, Fatima. & Ennaji, Moha (Eds.), pp. 79–88. London: Routledge.

Mahmood, Saba. 2005. *The Politics of Piety. The Islamic Revival and the Feminist Subject* Princeton and Oxford: Princeton University Press.

Mir-Hosseini, Ziba. 2006. 'Muslim Women's Quest for Equality: Between Islamic Law and Feminism'. *Critical Inquiry* 32. *Middle East Report Online*, June 16, 2006.

http://www.zibamirhosseini.com/documents/mir-hosseini-article-quest-for-equality-2006.pdf (accessed on May 29, 2014).

Moghadam, Valentine. 2009. *Globalization and Social Movements: Islamism, Feminism and the Global Justice Movement.* Lanham: Rowman & Littlefield.

Naciri, Rabia. 2008. "The Fight for Reform has Given Much Power to Women's Organizations". In *Proceedings of 11th International Forum on Women's Rights and Development,* edited by Caroline Sin, , 21– 26. Publication of Association for Women's Rights in Development (AWID): Cape Town.

Pruzan-Jørgensen, John. 2010. "New Female Voices Within the Islamist Movement in Morocco." *IPRIS Maghreb Review.* Vol. October/November: 15–18.

Sadiqi, Fatima. 2014. *Moroccan Feminist Discourses.* New York: Palgrave Macmillan.

Sadiqi, Fatima and Ennaji, Moha. (Eds.) 2010. *Women in the Middle East and North Africa: Agents of Change.* London: Routledge.

Sadiqi, Fatima., Nowaira, Amira. El Khouly, Azza. & Ennaji, Moha. 2009. *Women Writing Africa. The Northern Region.* New York: The Feminist Press.

Wadud, Amina. *2006. Inside the Gender Jihad: Reform in Islam.* Oxford: OneWorld Publishers.

Yafout, Meryem. 2008. "Women within Islamist Movements: A Modernization Factor?". Draft Document. EDE Genre en Méditerranée. Rabat – 21/24 April 2008. https://www.academia.edu/426198/YAFOUT_Meriem_Femmes_au_sein_des_mouvements_islamistes_facteur_de_modernisation (accessed on Mar. 21, 2013).

Chapter 4

MOROCCAN FEMINISM AT THE GRASSROOTS LEVEL

Susan Schaefer Davis and Amina Yabis

Introduction

There exist a wide variety of organizations in Morocco that promote feminism, with well-educated and articulate leaders and clear agendas. However, a large majority of middle and working class Moroccan women are not involved in these organizations. Most of those involved are beneficiaries of literacy or small scale economic programs, rather than working to support feminism on a broader scale.

How do middle and working class Moroccan women view and negotiate the larger project of feminism? This article attempts to answer that question by interviewing an "average" Moroccan woman who grew up in a working class family in the Fes medina and is now married to a school teacher and living in a middle class neighborhood of a small town. In fact she is not average at all in some ways, having founded a women's cooperative and a local association, and been nominated for Morocco's prestigious Khamisa Award as a woman leader. Her upbringing, education, and current work place her among other women at a grassroots level rather than feminist activists – although she works to benefit women. This in-depth interview explores how this in some ways ordinary woman became involved in her work with women, and how she sees feminism in Morocco.

Introduction

As an anthropologist who began working with Moroccan women nearly 50 years ago as a Peace Corps Volunteer, two things have remained very important to me: the often underappreciated strength of Moroccan women, and the value of including the realities of their lives at the grassroots level. I hope this article will address both. It is an interview with Amina Yabis, an extraordinary woman from a typical background. I do not claim that Amina illustrates Moroccan grassroots feminism in general; as everywhere, the country and its population are too varied. But she presents a clear example of what can happen for at least some women at the grassroots level.

My goal here is not to define or trace the development of feminism in the Middle East or Morocco. Badran (2009) has done the former covering more than 100 years, and Daoud (1993) has done so for Morocco, Tunisia and Algeria. Evrard's recent book (2014) provides a fine-grained analysis of the current women's rights movement in Morocco. Many support the view that Moroccan feminism is mainly promoted by upper class women (Daoud 1993), with Sadiqi noting that recent Moroccan feminism "...has largely been associated with educated, enlightened, and self-aware upper class women (2003:215)." Yet she argues that feminisms need to be contextualized and thus, because of the wide variety of women in Morocco, we need to include information from feminists of other social levels (2003:215). Some recent works remedy this, with Evrard (2014) describing NGOs run by youth, including rural high school students, and Bordat, Davis and Kouzzi (2011) presenting examples of grassroots level NGOs including local development associations, economic cooperatives, and even hairdressers trained to educate clients about their rights. Amina's story is a valuable contribution to the literature on non-elite feminists.

Amina is a petite, lively woman in her early fifties; her eyes sparkle with intelligence or humor or both when she speaks. I first met her in the early 1990s through a Peace Corps Volunteer who was helping her market her products which consisted of jewelry made from the buttons on the traditional *jellaba* or robe that men and women wear. She had worked with two Volunteers before; all were specialized in small business development. The first one helped her with the paperwork to make official both a cooperative and an association that she founded. While she had some help getting started, it is obvious below that she expanded upon it greatly and it now benefits hundreds of local women. This supports my view of Moroccan women: give them an inch of help, and they'll go a mile. Yet many women have had such assistance, and Amina is outstanding in the distance she has gone and the number of women she has affected.

She describes her early background in the interview. Currently, she lives in a middle class home in Sefrou, with the downstairs devoted to the cooperative where she teaches young women weaving on both upright and floor looms (the latter traditionally used by males), and classes in using vegetable dyes, an almost-extinct skill in Morocco. The button makers usually work at home. In 2013 she was chosen to be an officer in a new women's center the King Mohammed VI Foundation built in Sefrou, so she now spends much of her time there. She uses the computer and emails in both French and '*3aransiya*', which is Moroccan dialect written in Roman letters. She has been to the juried International Folk Art Market in Santa Fe several times, selling the button jewelry made by her cooperative, providing a great economic benefit for the members. She was also chosen there for a museum exhibit as one of ten women worldwide whose co-ops had greatly benefitted women (International Folk Art Market n.d.) and recently has been asked as one of ten artisans worldwide to collaborate with the Folk Art Market in their efforts to benefit artisans.

She has four sons, three of whom are married and living elsewhere, and one still at home. Her husband Si Mohammed teaches in a rural primary school to which he carpools with other teachers; the family doesn't own a car.

Notes on the interview

In what follows, I have transcribed and translated our conversation from Moroccan Arabic. The below is not totally complete: I have not included my encouraging comments, and I have omitted some repetitive phrases. While the latter may be of interest to linguists, I am more concerned with the ideas conveyed. I have included all the relevant information. Rather than summarizing, I think it is important for the reader to have Amina's own words.

There are several works that note, and illustrate, the importance of letting Muslim and Moroccan women speak for themselves. One of the first was *Middle Eastern Muslim Women Speak* (eds Fernea & Bezirgan 1977). Baker (1998) interviewed women from Morocco's Resistance movement, and Gray (2008) interviewed and compared Moroccan and French-Moroccan women. Sadiqi notes that oral histories are useful to add class and gender perspectives to the dominant writing (2003:15), and Fernea notes that Abouzeid's autobiography does just that for the time around Moroccan Independence (1998:i)[1]. In her introduction to *Doing Daily Battle*, Mernissi echoes my feelings exactly in saying she is proud of those interviews, which "..give me a feeling of fidelity to the reality of women's experience (1988:18)." Sadiqi does cite one danger of educated women presenting the voices of other women: it risks presenting these women as passive, which reinforces the way they are seen in the standard discourse (2003:15). The reader will see below that there is no danger of seeing Amina as passive.

A significant point for this interview is that I wanted to ask Amina about her view of feminism: what is it, how does it work in her life and her town. But . . . I couldn't. There is no word in Moroccan Arabic for 'feminism'. So instead my question was framed as about *huquq l mra* or women's rights. One might argue that this led her replies to focus more on the concrete than the abstract, but in fact her life is focused that way, and tells us a lot about how feminism looks at the grassroots level.

Interview

I begin by explaining that I've been asked to contribute to a book by Professors Sadiqi and Ennaji from Fes, and tell her that I'll use both of our names, so will let her read and edit it before it's submitted. (She did so by having it translated into French on Google.) I tell her that they want me to

> S: write something about women's rights in Morocco [*hokuk lmra fel Maghrib*] . . . that is, something like the different kinds of women's rights in Morocco. My idea is to talk to you about your ideas on that. To start, tell me a little about yourself, like where were you born, where you studied, things like that.
>
> A: My name is Amina Yabis. I was born in Fes, in the *medina* [old city].

S: Where in the *medina*?

A: I was born in Rcif...in the old city. I was from a poor family. I started school when I was 7 and I studied for about 5 years. I left school and started working. I learned to do some embroidery in Fes. I learned to embroider fancy slippers, and kept working to help my family out a little.

S: Excuse me, you left school – about how old were you?

A: About 13 – I did one year of junior high and dropped out.

S: And from there you started to learn embroidery and help the family?

A: I started to learn embroidery, I learned sewing ... I did that artisan handwork.

S: And where did you learn? At a traditional women's center, or from an individual woman, or ...

A: I just learned from women at home. We had neighbors who were experts and teachers, and my mother enrolled me to learn with them.

S: You said you helped your family with the money when you worked – about how old were you when you started helping them?

A: From when I was 13. When I left school, I started to work and help out, so my brothers and sisters could stay in school.

S: They stayed in school?

A: Yes. I have three brothers and two sisters. All of them were in school.

S: And you? Why didn't you stay in school?

A I left because I was a little older than them and I had to help out a bit.

S: Are you the oldest in the family, of those children?

A: I have one sister older than me, but that idea .... that the boy needs to go to school, to finish his studies, that if we educate a girl we just waste money because she'll get married, go off to a man, to someone else. My parents had those ideas, and they didn't let me finish my education. [laughs]

S: What a pity – I was going to say that you're the intelligent one.

A: [laughs] Well, it wasn't destined for me to finish school, and they took me out.

S: I was going to say that in my opinion, it was really good that you left. At this point, who in your family has done something like you have? I don't know the others, but you – God bless [your good work].

A: So, I kept working, and staying at home I helped my mother with housework like cooking, and when I finished that I'd have time to embroider and sew. And I got married – I got married to my husband from Sefrou.

S: About how old were you when you got married?

A: Eighteen.

S: Was it your family who decided who you'd marry, or how did you know who you wanted to marry?

A: No, I met my husband, it was me who wanted to marry him. My family didn't want it at first. They said no, you're still too young, that boy – his family is difficult or ... Basically, the family was against it. But I said to th   em "I'll   marry him, or I won't get married. Only him – or I'll die."

S: [both laugh] Was it true, or did you just want to scare them?

A: I wanted to scare them so I could get married and leave, be relieved of having to work. That is, I'll get married, I won't work, my husband will work, and me, I'll rest. But again I just found a lot of problems – it's inevitable. I got married, then I had children, and then I had to help them out a lot because my husband's work wasn't enough, it wasn't enough to ...

S: What was his work?

A: A teacher.

S: Was he always a teacher?

A: No, at first he worked as a secretary, when I married him. He kept on with his studies until he got his high school degree, and when he got his degree he became a teacher.

S: How old are you now?

A: I was born in 1962. So I'm almost 51.

S: OK. Now, your family – how many children do you have?

A: Now I have 4 children, all boys.

S: Are they all in Morocco, or where are they?

A: No, the oldest is in Belgium, married to a Filipino woman. And the second is married in Morocco, he works here in the phosphate industry. The third one is in America, living in New York.

S: And the fourth is still at home with you?

A: The fourth is in the university, in Fes.

S: I also wanted to ask you, when you hear *hoquq lmra* (women's rights) – what do you think when you hear those words? What's their meaning in your opinion?

A: My view is that she gets her freedom, and if she marries she doesn't for example just stay in her house, sitting at home, and if she wants to go out she has to tell her husband she's going out, if she wants to go and see her family . . . .That is, she has to be somewhat free: if she wants to go to school she can, if she wants to travel, she can travel. She would have her freedom. Here, the woman . . . we still have a little . . . Her parents doubt her [proper behavior], and when she gets married, her husband controls her. She always needs to ask someone for permission to do something in her life.

S: And you, when you got married, is that what you wanted? Or did you want it before you got married?

A: Yes, that's what I wanted. I used to say "Ah, Father won't let me, Mother is always telling me this and that. Me, when I get married – you know, it will be the opposite." But when I got married, THEN I saw that my husband told me what to do, his mother and father and siblings . . . MORE than when I was at home.

S: Did you live with them at first?

A: I lived with them at first, until I had two children.

S: About how many years was that?

A: Some five years.

S: Well – that was a really lot, yes?

A: [laughs] Well, they tell you "You're still young, you can't go to live alone, [when] your husband goes to work, you shouldn't stay alone in the house, it's necessary that someone has to live with you." So, you'll stay with your husband's family until you have children who are a little older . . . THEN you can move [out] with your husband, so that when he goes out your children will be with you, they'll watch you.

S: And who told you that?

A: This is what we have in our customs and our culture. It's that when a girl first gets married, she doesn't move [out of the extended family] with her husband. If it's far, if he works far away, he doesn't take her with him. She stays with his family until she has children, then they leave.

S: And why is it they wait until there are children?

A: So those children stay with their mother, they keep her company, they keep an eye on her, they...

S: [interrupts and laughs] I thought that too, they keep an eye on her.

A: They say like if the man went far away and the wife was alone at home, maybe someone would come and say 'that one isn't married' because she has no children, he'd say she's not married. He might . . . . . . That's the kind of thing they say.

S: You said you had ideas about women's rights before you got married...

A: Ah, not...no. No, I didn't have them until I got married. When I got married, it was my husband who was in an association of women's rights.

S: He was in the association, or you?

A: My husband was in that association.

S: Yes? Do you know the name of that group?

A: The association of rights of...ah...people...human rights. [*hokuk linsan*]. The Human Rights Association. He was in that human rights association, and he was on the women's committee. And when he married me, it was him who started to show me, he told me "We work on women's rights, we defend women's rights, but not one woman comes, there isn't any woman with us to work. The men just talk about women's rights. Each leaves his wife at home. It's not possible...it's necessary if we talk about women's rights, she needs to be there too, she needs to talk about her rights." Well, from time to time I used to go with him to that association, and if there was some training course or something, I went with him. I started to learn a little, I was listening and watching.

S: And you were the first woman who went to that association?

A: Yes, I was the first one who went to a meeting. And my husband told them "I talk about women, and I brought my wife – and you, where are your wives?"

S: Did they come?

A: No, after that we weren't in Fes any more. He went to work in the Sahara, and I went to the Sahara with him.

S: So, I was going to ask you, do you know about what year you went with him to those meetings in Fes?

A: Yes, in 1983.

S: So I wanted to ask you, in your life, did you do something that you think helped women's rights?

A: Me, the first thing I did in my life to help women, it's when I came to live in Sefrou: I was a candidate in the elections.

S: Elections for what?

A: For city council. I entered the elections, and I was the first woman to stand for election in Sefrou. I didn't do that to win, and get a job – no. I did it to show that a woman has the right to be in elections. She too can defend people's rights, also can speak for people, and she too has the right to stand for election, not just to vote. That's the first thing I did in Sefrou.

S: And what year was that?

A: 1994.

S: And did you win or not?

A: No, I didn't win, but nearly all the women voted for me.

S: Good – they sort of got it.

A: They voted for me . . . they voted for me without their husbands knowing. Because their husbands told them don't vote for a woman, vote for a man. [laughs] I didn't win. But when I didn't win, that's why I began that co-operative making buttons.

S: Oh? There was no button co-op before?

A: No, it didn't exist, and women didn't used to go out of their homes to sell buttons. It used to be that men came, they came and brought them work in their homes, and they'd do it, and men would come back and take it, and men sell it. The woman worked, but wasn't known at all. Me, when I set up the association and co-op, I started working. It was me who went to the women's homes, I told them you need to go out yourselves to work, and sell your work, "the man" is making a big profit off you. That's it. The women joined, they began to join the association with me.

S: And what's the difference [in price] between the [about 200] buttons of a *qaftan* or *jellaba*? How much did the man take from them? How much does he pay them, and . . .

A: More than half. If she worked for 5 dirhams [about $0.65 US], he used to sell them for 10 dh.

S: So he gets as much as she does.

A: He gets the same as her – or even more than her. But he doesn't work. And she's the one ruining her eyes...she spins the thread, she spends the whole day working. And him, he comes, he drives his car up to the door, he gives her the work to do and takes the buttons. He gives her the raw material, the 'silk' [rayon], and takes the buttons. He goes and sells them for double, or more. Like in Fes he sells them for double, if he goes to Casablanca he'd sell them for triple. The further it is, the more the price goes up. I told the women, some of us will go to Casablanca too, we'll go to Rabat, we'll go and take them ourselves. We imposed that on the men. That was in the first co-op, the first association of women in Sefrou – it was mine.

S: Was it an official co-op, did you register with the government and all?

A: With the government, and the government helped me a lot. They gave me a place to have meetings with the women so I could explain to them. I used to have meetings at the youth center with women so I could explain to them what an asso-ciation is, what a co-operative is. The first time a lot of unmarried women joined. They weren't married, or their husband was dead, something like that. They didn't have husbands. But it was just later that married women started to come. Because at first, their husbands wouldn't let them.

S: Do you know why their husbands wouldn't let them?

A: They used to tell them "No, don't go out, don't travel, don't go, that one [eg Amina]...just lies, she wants to profit herself, she's not a good woman". As you know, here they say that women who go out are not good women. But when they saw me in Sefrou, and the men watched me and they knew I was good and didn't do anything bad, and I went right to work, not to any bad place, they finally started to trust me and to send their wives. They told them "If you're going with Amina, go; if you're not going with Amina, don't go."

S: There has to be trust...

A: They started to go out with me, we'd go to Casablanca, two or three women. Or we'd split up, two would go to Casablanca, two to Marrakesh. And we'd take the work, we'd take it our-selves, and we'd be the ones to profit. We didn't have men sell for us at all anymore.

S: And did the women, for example you said they'd sell for 100 *reals* [5 dirhams]. When they were working with you, did they get more than that?

A: When we all started to work in the cooperative, whatever we earned we'd use to buy our raw materials, and whatever was left we'd divide among us. There wasn't any 100 *reals*; we divided all of the profit between us.

A: At first, we began with 10 women. And we got our capital from micro credit; that's where we got our money. We kept working, and when we had a profit, we'd pay the micro credit. We were in debt for a year, until we paid it off. When we paid it off, we started to keep the money. And women started making 10 dh for a set of buttons.

S: That's double?

A: She started earning almost double – and more. And when she got it, she'd go out, she'd walk around, she'd go to Casablanca, she'd go ... The Handicraft Ministry would invite us to be in exhibitions, we began to meet with government officials, we began to see ... to learn, to go get trainings. The point is, we went out, we saw life, we saw ... And she began, the woman who just used to stay home, and spends all day working in the kitchen, then works on buttons till she goes blind ... she too began to go out, to see the world, to walk around. Two of us went to France, me and another woman. Another time I went with another one to Spain, and another time ... that is, those women never imagined they'd go abroad. We began to go out, thanks be to God, and there were lots of women who wanted to be in a co-op. Now thank God, there are now some 20 co-ops in Sefrou.

S: Really? Good. And you said the year you began the co-op was?

A: In 2000

S: And another time, did you say something about there were some well off women who used to work with you before?

A: No. There weren't any who were well off. Just needy ones, or ones with no husband, their husband was dead, ...

S: Not the ones who make buttons. But like they wanted to run you or something, from Fes or somewhere.

A: There were some; some associations wanted to run us. Some well-off woman would come, a professor with her car. And she'd say [falsetto voice] "You're poor, would you like us to help you, I'll sell for you, I'll do this and that . . . " We worked with one woman at first, but we found that she exploited us, just like the men.

S: Was that after you'd begun a co-op?

A: Before I formed the co-op. When we had an association, she came. She said "I live in Casablanca, we've formed a new association, and you, you don't know . . . We'll teach you, and we'll take your buttons and sell them for you." We gave her our buttons, and we found she did sales shows in France, and that she sold them for a very high price, much higher than that man. And she'd give us just a little bit. It's a big association in Casablanca.

S: Is there something else you did, like . . . . That you think would help women? That one was very important.

A: This work of making buttons, it didn't used to be on the list of professions that we have in Morocco. Only tailoring was recognized, not button making. For the buttons on the *jellaba*, they said a man made the buttons, he tailored it and he made the buttons. I'M the one who showed people that it's women who make the buttons. That skill became part of the [official] list of professions. It wasn't well known before.

S: And you said you began with ten women and girls.

A: Yes, I began with 10 women.

S: And now how many do you have?

A: Now I have 40, but I don't want to let in a lot. People are always coming over, wanting to join with me in the co-op, but I can't do it because it's very hard to have a lot of people who don't get along. They cause problems. So, what I do, I take a woman if she wants to work with us in the co-op, until she works with us a year so I know her character, whether she's easy to get along with, not a nervous type, that she won't cause problems. You know how women are, they get talking,' this one said, this one did . . . ' and they start fighting. We get some experience with the woman, and she has like an internship. We get to know her well, then she can join the co-op with us.

S: Are the association and co-op not the same?

A: No, those in the association, they work in the association in order to help people.

S: So that's something else, not a co-op.

A: Right.

S: And a co-op is to make buttons.

A: Yes. The co-op is so the woman can sell, like a company. So she can profit, can earn money.

S: And in an association, what do . . .

A: It helps people. It works in order to help. Like now in the association, women come to the association and say "We want you to help us. We want you to sell these buttons for us." So the association sells the buttons for them, and doesn't take a benefit or profit. And a co-op, no. In a co-op, the women sell and profit themselves.

S: Ah, OK. And are there more people in the association than in the co-op [that Amina works with], or not?

A: There are some seven officers in the association, and over 300 members. [Each pays 20 dh a year, used for good works.] They don't make buttons, they just help people. They sell for them, they give them trainings, if there's a woman who has a daughter . . . [she hesitates, maybe means 'in trouble'?] , they help her. If there's someone sick with a bad disease [STD] God forbid, they help her with the doctor, with medicine.

S: And what's the name of the association?

A: The Golden Buttons Association

S: Golden Buttons. And the co-op is called?

A: The Cherries Cooperative of Silk Buttons.

S: OK. That's an important thing you did to help women. Is there something else you think of that you did?

A: Well now, I'm always helping women. There is one who wants to go to school, she never went, so I sign her up for literacy classes. There are some 40 women I signed up to learn to read. I've begun working for an association, to manage a women's center. [She was chosen to do so by associations in Sefrou.]

S: Tell me about the association. What's its name?

A: Mohamed the 5th [grandfather of current king].

S: And what do you do in it?

A: I'm the treasurer.

S: And what's the name of that association again?

A: The association of administration of the women's center.

S: The Women's Center, OK. And for that, did the state give you something?

A: They gave us ... they built us a big center. They gave us a lot of equipment in it. They made different rooms in it, so women could learn to read, learn sewing, learn cooking, learn pastry making. Now I work in that center, I help the women here in Sefrou.

S: Is it something like a traditional women's center [*nadi niswi*, government run and teaching home economics skills] or something else..?

A: It's something different from that kind of women's center. It's bigger than those women's centers. Come visit me and I'll take you to see it.

S: And do you also teach people in the area or something? I heard that you go to some Peace Corps sites and show people how to use natural dyes.

A: I do that kind of training in Morocco. I go out, like now I work with PC volunteers who come to Morocco. They go to a place and see the women don't know how to set up a co-op, they don't know how to work, or ... So they call me and I go see the women. All over Morocco, I've gone to see a lot of the women living out in the countryside. I do trainings with them. I talk about how I began, how I worked, in what ways it's possible for them to work ... I do a lot of trainings with them.

S: Who are those groups? You said there are PC Volunteers, but are those women just villagers, or do they have an association or who are they?

A: No, I go see women who want to work, to form a cooperative. There are a lot of cooperatives that I helped get working, more than 20 co-ops that I've helped in Morocco. I began natural dyeing with them too. I learned it, and I teach them how to dye wool using herbs. Whatever I learn, I teach to other women. That's my work with women. I just want women to learn something. And to go out and work.

S: I want to ask you a little about the Khamisa [an award given to outstanding Moroccan women annually]. You didn't do the Khamisa to help women, but [those] people understood that you helped women.

A: I was participating in an exhibition of crafts. The exhibits were the ones the government does, in Casablanca, in

Marrakesh. They saw me, and saw that what I do [button jewelry] is something new and that it sells quickly. When the Khamisa was choosing women that are working well, who help women, I submitted my cv. I told them "I've worked too", I wrote in my cv what I did, all those things I did with women. They chose me – I was one of 5 women who succeeded in Morocco, who got that Khamisa in 2006.

S: Good, good. And it's nice that the government began to show people what women do, that they aren't just sitting around. And it's good that you were among them

A: Those women they had chosen worked in business. But they had BIG companies. Not like me, I'm the one who had a cooperative of poor women, women who had very little

S: And you, were you among them? Were you OK? How was it?

A: It's not only about money. I was . . . I got a lot of [new] ideas, and thank God, I was open-minded. Even if they came and have cars, they have drivers, they have companies with telephones – I see myself as just the same as they are. I was comfortable.

S: And were they nice to you?

A: They were nice, they're my friends and very kind. And they also helped me because I got to know them. One of them contacted me to go to France. The ties with them have helped us a lot. They work in companies and the companies have succeeded . . . that is, they're just like men – or even better than men.

S: Those things you've done, is there among them something you feel helped women more than the other things you did? Or that you like better than other things you've done?

A: What I like, I'll tell you, praise God, is that now I'm satisfied because I can't do nothing – only if I died or something. I really like to work, I like to help women. And I'll continue to help, God willing.

S: Is there something you'd still like to do with women, something you haven't done yet, some new idea?

A: What I haven't done yet . . . It's that there are still a few women here who aren't able to talk about their rights. You'll find a problem like a woman needs some papers from the administration, she comes to my place and says " Come on with me. You Amina, you talk and you raise your voice, when they see you they give the paper to us. When they see you they hurry up." That's the problem we have here, that women still aren't able to go and talk about their rights.

Today a woman came to see me. Her daughter is going to study at the university and her father has no money, so she needs a scholarship. And those who don't have money, they give them a scholarship. She said "Come with me to the governor's office so you can tell them..." I told her "It's one of your rights! You can go and talk about your daughter, and your daughter's in the university, she can talk too." She said "We can't do that, we're afraid, and..." Well, tomorrow I'm going with them to tell them, to speak for them.

S: I was going to ask you, all this work you've done with women in Morocco... there was the co-op, there was the association, you showed people how to do business and things like that. Is there something among them that you'd say helped women more than another thing, or were they all about equal, or..?

A: There are women who worked, and they go to exhibitions. This year there are 2 cooperatives that came to Santa Fe [to the International Folk Art Market] – you saw them. The other year the one from Khenifra came. The women learned a lot, and benefitted a lot. And now, God bless them, there are some who teach others. That's the kind of thing I like a lot – I like that a lot. When I began working, I gave those things, and praise God I see that what I did succeeded. I talk to women, I go and spend 3 or 4 days with them. And when I'm back home, I hear about them "Oh, they started a cooperative, they're selling, they went to an exhibition." The Guigou co-op went to an exhibition in Germany this year – I'm the one who helped them.

S: Well, good. I wanted to ask, are there other people in Morocco who help women? They talk about women's rights – do you hear there are others who do something good about women's rights?

A: They do for them... like if there was a woman whose husband divorced her, or if she had some problem they help her, like they'll get her a lawyer who can defend her. Or if there was someone who has children and she can't find money to send them to school – they send them to school, they help them, they buy them books, they... that is, there are a lot that help women. Even if they're not about women's rights, they help.

S: That's about all I wanted to ask you, but you might have something you want to say that I didn't think to ask you. Is there something you'd like to add?

A: No – if you have a question, I have no problem.

S: No, that's it.

A: If you think of something, call.

Conclusion

So what does Moroccan feminism look like at the grassroots level? Amina's story illustrates this. It shows some of the problems such women face: limited or no education, inability to act without family or husband's approval when young, and suspicion of women moving in the public domain. Yet Amina presents an example of the route an ordinary woman can take, the steps along it, and what she can accomplish for herself and others – if she has determination, support, and intelligence. Her husband's support was important in her first, and continuing, interest in women's rights. That echoes my notion, and that of Evrard (2014) that there are more men involved in women's rights groups in Morocco than in the US. Finally, note that while Amina first went to meetings about women's human rights, her main work was less abstract and based on empowering women economically; from that they obtained more rights, for example to travel independently. Toward the end, she moves again toward advocacy and says she wants women to be more able to speak up for themselves and claim their own rights. Whether you call it feminism or women's rights, Amina is a fine example of Moroccan women's empowerment.

Note

1 The fact that Abouzeid's *Return to Childhood* highlights this period may partially account for the fact that it is required reading in Moroccan *college* or junior high classes.

References

Abouzeid, L. 1998. *Return to Childhood: The Memoir of a Moroccan Woman*, University of Texas, Austin.

Badran, M 2009. *Feminism in Islam: Secular and Religious Convergences*, Oneworld Publications, London.

Baker, A 1998. *Voices of Resistance: Oral Histories of Moroccan Women*, State University of New York Press, Albany.

Bordat, SW, Davis, SS & Kouzzi, S 2011. 'Women as Agents of Grassroots Change: Illustrating Micro-Empowerment in Morocco', *Journal of Middle East Women's Studies*, vol.7, no. 1, pp.90–119.

Daoud, Z 1993. *Féminisme et Politique au Maghreb: Soixante Ans de Lutte*, Editions Eddif, Casablanca.

Evrard, AY 2014. *The Moroccan Women's Rights Movement*, Syracuse University Press, Syracuse.

Fernea, EW & Bezirgan, BQ, (Eds) 1977. *Middle Eastern Muslim Women Speak*, University of Texas Press, Austin.

Gray, DH 2008. *Muslim Women on the Move: Moroccan Women and French Women of Moroccan Origin Speak Out*, Lexington Books, Lanham MD.

International Folk Art Market n.d., *Empowering Women*, available from <http://www.internationalfolkart.org/exhibitions/past/empoweringwomen/africaempower-ingwomen.html>. [Feb. 5, 2015].

Mernissi, F 1989. *Doing Daily Battle: Interviews with Moroccan Women*, trans. MJ Lakeland, Rutgers University Press, New Brunswick, NJ.

Sadiqi, F 2003. *Women, Gender and Language in Morocco*, Brill, Leiden-Boston.

Chapter 5

ISLAMIC FEMINISM IN MOROCCO

Concepts and Perspectives

Merieme Yafout

Introduction

It has been rooted for ages in the collective memory of Muslims' belief system that a woman is physically weak, psychologically fragile, and subjected to man given her nature and that she is an object of pleasure at his disposition. She is perceived as a being to be beaten, to be enclosed, and to be deprived of all her rights including the right to study. In sum, she cannot be equal to man in terms of social, political, legal and economic rights. This perception was especially supported by the legal opinions of some religious scholars who tried to find a basis for this attitude in the *Qur'an* and *Sunnah* (words and actions made or approved by the Prophet).

However, this interpretation of sacred texts has often been contested by other religious men who claim that it is not related to Islam. Indeed, Mohammed Abdou, RachidReda, Al Afghani and some other scholars who belong to the contemporary generation such as Mohammed El Ghazali, Abdelhalim Abouchouqqa, Yusuf Al Qaradhaoui, Rashid Al Ghannouchi, AbdessalamYassine, and others have argued that many social practices, that marginalize woman, and that are endorsed by classic jurisprudence *(fiqh)*, are not Islamic but rather based on traditional customs and rites. For Leila Ahmed (1992), Mohammed Abdou was probably the first to defend the idea that it was Islam, and not the West, as claimed by the Europeans, which first defended the humanity of women and her equality with men. Abdouargued that the degrading practices against women in the Muslim world are not due to Islam but to the misinterpretations that have affected its laws through centuries (Leila Ahmed 1992, p. 139–140).

It is these ideas that have contributed to the expansion of the so-called current "Islamic feminism".These scholars defend the emancipation of women based on an Islamic reference.They believe, in fact, that it is not Islam as a religion that is incompatible with the rights of women, but rather selective and abusive inter-pretations of its laws and texts by classical Islamic jurisprudence. Thus, they don't find a logical or inherent connection between the ideals of Islam and patriarchy. Consequently, their projects are mainly based on the reclaiming of the sacred texts accompanied by a critique of classical jurisprudence. This method is described by some of them as "liberation reading".Moreover, some studies suggest that Islamic feminism emerged in Iran after the revolution (1979) and precisely after the end of the Iran-Iraq War (1980–1988) (Kian 2010, p.45; Mir-Hosseini 2006, p. 640; Latte Abdallah 2010, p. 9). Thus, due to their massive participation in the revolution, Iranian women became aware of their return to a subordinate position and joined a protest movement against inequality based on the reclaiming of sacred texts. By reinterpretation, these women do not intend to change the meaning of the sacred texts in order to be compatible with any hegemonic liberating discourse but to put it in its historical and social context and to identify and adopt the purposes of religion, instead of the literal interpretation of the text. It is, in fact, a return to original Islam: "A revival of the *Sunnah*",to quote the words of few of them. Moreover, the effort of interpreta-tion and re-contextualization (*ijtihad*)[1] was undertaken by Muslims since the age of the Prophet. It forms a stream in the history of Islam that attempts to show that the essence of this religion is the liberation of human beings from all shackles (slavery, despotism, machismo...). However, this effort has often been an exclusively male domain. Certainly, some women have excelled in this field since *Assayida*[2] Aisha, the Prophet's wife, passing through *Assayida* Nafisa, granddaughter of Hussein[3], arriving at the mystical Rabia Al Adaouia and others. Yet, compared to the males, their number remains small.

Therefore, the innovative contribution of Islamic feminism consists of the remarkable women's engagement in a male subject which is *ijtihad*. Moreover, their involvement in this field has its roots in the conditions experienced by women in Muslim societies: in the name of Islam, women are beaten, repudiated, deprived of their rights, and excluded from the public sphere. For this purpose, their effort focuses on the appropriation of religious texts in order to free themselves from misogynistic readings, shackles of tradition, and patriarchy. Not only this, but it would also have the advantage of not forcing women to face the dilemma of choosing between their Muslim identity and faith, on the one hand, and their emancipation, on the other hand.

Furthermore, it is important to emphasize that most of those described as Islamic feminists are not necessarily so. Indeed, the sphere of producers and users of "Islamic feminism" discourse also include those who reject this label or identity. In this sense, many women explain their rejection of this marker by their refusal of the Western model as a unique empowerment model. They perceive feminism as a Western notion, or at least associated with the West. For some of them, this concept is a rejection of the role of women within the family. Others evoke the birth of feminism, in the West, in a context of conflict with religion. Therefore, their goal is to reconcile religion with the promotion of women's rights. In sum, their positions are accounted for by the rise of stereotypical feminism in the Arab world, as it is perceived as an ideology imported from the West. Such a perception is also strongly refuted by Western feminists like Margot Badran, who maintains that feminism in African Muslim countries and Asia is indigenous (Badran 2010, p. 27). Additionally, those who defend this position display a surprising lack of knowledge of the history of feminism in Africa and Asia. They contribute to the perpetuation of negative stereotypes and align de facto with the judgments made by those Westerners who, in their ignorant arrogance, claim that Muslims are incapable of producing feminism, and Islam is inherently sexist (Badran 2010, p. 33). Certainly, the concept of "Islamic feminism" is controversial because it is often associated with the West and therefore is an attempt of alienation and domination. This does not necessarily mean that women who reject it do not defend the freedom of women and gender justice. Among those who reject the concept of "Islamic feminism" while adopting emancipation projects for women, we can mention Nadia Yassine and Khadija Moufid, whose projects will be presented later on.

In this context, the questions this chapter poses are simple: what is Islamic feminism in Morocco and who are its figureheads? What are their principles and challenges? In what ways do they appropriate the sacred texts?

Since the late 1980s, Morocco has seen the emergence of a wave of women who stand against the jurisprudence which uses religion to justify sex discrimination and reinforce the patriarchal logic. They consider that it is up to women, in particular, to make an effort to highlight the liberating spirit of Islam because, in their mind, the jurisprudence has been developed from a purely male perspective. Thus, in order to introduce their thinking, I will present, in the following section, the thoughts of some women whom I consider to be the main figures of Islamic feminism in Morocco.

Fatema Mernissi and the Forgotten Queens

The sociologist Fatema Mernissi, in my opinion, is one of the leading figures of Islamic feminism in Morocco though she does not claim that. In fact, she is one of the first to confess that the Prophet has set a very important status for women in public life, yet there was a manipulation of the sacred texts by the political power. At the time of the Prophet, as she mentions, and in the streets of Medina, the debate around equality of sexes was strongly present. Therefore, men were forced to discuss this issue, even accept it since it was the will of God and his Prophet.

Certainly, Mernissi was blamed for questioning, among others, the integrity of some narrators of *Hadith*, for their hostile position against women. This, in her opinion, shows their lack of intellectual credibility and honesty. Therefore, she deconstructs some decisive *Hadiths* about women which were reported by *Al-Bukhari* and are considered authentic. Therefore, these *hadiths* are thought to be untouchable. In her book "Political Harem: The Prophet and Women"[4], in which she began reading the *Hadith* from a historical, sociological, and anthropological point of view, she studied several *Hadiths* including the one that says people who are led by a woman will be ruined (*Ma aflaha qawmoun wallaw oumourahoum imra'a*). To deconstruct this *Hadith*, Fatima Mernissi went back to the origins of the author Abu Bakra.[5]The latter was a notable of the city of Basra, a former slave who and settled in Iraq after being freed by the Prophet. According to Mernissi, twenty-five years after the death of the Prophet, Abu Bakra will recall this *Hadith* during the civil war between the Caliph Ali Ibn Abi Talib and the mother of believers, Aisha (the wife of the Prophet). Mernissi reveals that Abu Bakra would opportunistically use this *Hadith* to justify his refusal to engage with Aisha and to attract at the same time the sympathy of Caliph Ali. Moreover, the studies of *Hadiths* by Mernissi remain a subject of controversy.

Many researchers, in fact, agree that Mernissi selected *Hadiths* before their appropriation (Göle 1993, p. 118; Ezzat 2007, 2002, p. 255). Besides, she questions the cultural heritage that clogs the completion of gender equality by wondering whether in order to achieve this equality it was necessary to "mutilate the Arab-Islamic past," or rather, "sort out the past to reclaim it". According to the Turkish sociologist Nilufer Gole, Mernissi ended up by opting for the latter (Göle 1993, p. 118).

Furthermore, the *Hadith* which states that "people who are led by a woman will be ruined" (*Maaflaha qawmoun wallaw oumourahoum imra'a*) is often released in different contexts by different male personalities (*Ulema*, preachers, politicians...) to justify their rejection of women's access to political decision-making. They argue, in fact, that the government and the leadership of the state were always men's privilege and an all-male monopoly. In contrast, Mernissi argues that, unlike the sense often attributed to this *Hadith*, Muslim history is full of examples of women who ruled directly or indirectly Islamic states. She devotes her book "Forgotten Queens"[6] to present stories of many women, who were heads of Islamic states, but who are erased from official history and are thus "historically murdered". Mernissi confirms that none of these women ever received the title of Caliph. But Caliph is an extremely valuable title which is reserved for a tiny minority, since it has a religious and messianic dimension. The majority of Muslim heads of state have never had this title unlike the one of *sultan/ malik*(king) which is still taken by heads of Muslim states.

In this sense, Mernissi adopts the distinction made by Ibn Khaldun[7]who defines the *Cilafate* as the opposite of *mulk*. As for the *Cilafate,* it is an authority that obeys divine law, *the Shari'a*. Here, the *Shari'a* applies to the leader himself and makes governing by his own passions illegitimate. The *Mulk* is responsible for managing solely the mundane interests of the governed people, while the Cilafate, given his spiritual nature, will also deal with the afterlife. In this way and based on the sociology of history approach, Mernissi presents Sultana Radia,Shajarat al-Durr, Zineb Nefzaouia, Turkan Khatun, Taj al-A'laam and other female heads of government. Each had her way to run public affairs, to practice justice and manage taxes. Many had personally led battles, inflicted defeats, and concluded armistice. Some remained long on the throne; others barely had time to settle. Besides, the concealment of women heads of government is only one example of the silence about the political and social participation of women throughout the Islamic history.

Nadia Yassine and the Female *Ijtihad* Project

In fact, despite her rejection of the concept "Islamic feminism", Nadia Yassine represents one of the prominent figures of this stream. Indeed, she has led since the early 1980's a struggle within the movement *Al Adl WalIhssan* (Justice and Spirituality)[8] for women's emancipation and for the formation of elite of women who are very conscious of their rights and trust the liberating potential of Islamic repository. With her "sisters",[9] they have developed an approach that attempts to combine a religious and "feminist" consciousness. In this way, their approach is faced by two deeply rooted ideologies: machismo and autocracy deemed to be two sides of the same coin. Certainly, for Nadia Yassine and her "sisters", the deterioration of the status of women in Muslim history is linked to the emergence of autocracy. They thus adopt the concept of "historic break" which distinguishes two main periods of Muslim history:

-   The age of the Prophet and the four orthodox Caliphs, which according to them, was distinguished by the liberation of women and all the oppressed of many shackles that they were imposed during the pre-Islamic period.

- The *mulk 'ad*era (hereditary monarchy) started with the Umayyad dynasty and was marked by the fall of a number of liberating principles established by Islam such as justice and *shura* (consultation). In fact, the so-called "historic break" has had an impact on the condition of women whose status switched from vital liberation to alienation. Indeed, despotism that marked this period has led to the closing of the doors of *ijtihad* and the return to a number of pre-Islamic traditions and patriarchal customs that act negatively on the status of women.

According to Nadia Yassine and her "sisters", the closing of *ijtihad* produced an imitator law (*taqlid*) which is totally retrograding and misogynist. It is for this reason that these women started a female collective *Ijtihad* project to review the *Hadiths* and *Qur'anic* verses in the light of the life of the Prophet (*Sira*) and that of his Companions (men and women), taking into account the circumstances of revelation (*asbab annouzoul*), the historical and social context of the Text, the spirit of progressive change (*attadaruj*) undertaken by the *Qur'anic* message. The objective of this work is to question any restrictive interpretation associating Islam with the subordination of women and to discard any discriminatory theory. Thus, these women face the challenge of acquiring the academic tools of *ijtihad* and hold monthly meetings of reflection in order to restore confidence to women and enhance their self-esteem by showing them the model of empowerment of women Companions of the Prophet (*sahabiyats*).These women, thanks to the place they occupied in the original Islam, contributed to the construction of a Muslim society through their commitment alongside men to support the Prophet and build a new society.

Additionally, they analyze, among others, some controversial concepts that the traditional interpretation is detrimental to women's empowerment while attempting to develop a new understanding. In fact, they perform the task of deconstructing definitions and concepts of classical interpretations to build new designs supported by scripture and historical facts. Thus, regarding polygamy, for example, without going as far as claiming the ban, Nadia Yassine and her colleagues see it as "an exceptional solution for exceptional cases."This means that the rule is monogamy and thus polygamy should only be an exceptional practice, very limited practice for limited cases. Therefore, they do not fail to emphasize the negative consequences of the misuse of this practice on family and society: neglected women, poorly educated children and dysfunctional families. In passing, Nadia Yassine emphasizes that this practice is hardly welcome in the movement of *Al Adl Wallhssan*. This is why all its leaders are monogamous, and the polygamous ones are frowned upon by the various members and especially women members. The research of these women in this regard relates that the pre-Islamic era was very much in favor of polygamy: the number of women to marry was unlimited and extramarital affairs were common. After the advent of Islam and of its method of progressive change, polygamy became regulated and restricted. From these historical facts, Nadia Yassine and her colleagues have developed two observations that allow them to consider polygamy as "exceptional solution for exceptional cases":

-The first thing is that the *Qur'anic* verses and *Hadiths* that seem to legitimize the practice of polygamy establish rigorous conditions so that the scope of this practice is relatively narrowed, given the abuse of Arab antiquity. The *Qur'an* states: "But if you fear that you will not do justice, then only one (one wife)" (Qur'an, 4/3). Then, we read elsewhere: "You will not be fair to your wives, even if you want to be so" (Qur'an IV / 129). To this verse, two *Hadiths* are joined in which God threatens a curse to a polygamous man who is not equitable and fair to his wives. Hence, Nadia Yassine and her "sisters" conclude that polygamy leads to injustice and causes pain to women. Moreover, the Prophet refused that Imam Ali, the husband of his daughter Fatima Zahra, takes a second wife. To express his refusal, the Prophet ascended the pulpit and uttered (talking to Ali): "Fatima is part of me and all that hurt her is painful to me." While discerning the meaning of this event, these women pay attention to the fact that the Prophet ascends the pulpit to respond to the request of Imam Ali. This proves, they argue, that he does not react to the sole case of his own daughter, but he sees polygamy as an injury to any woman.

-The second observation relates to the circumstances of the revelation of the verses that legitimize polygamy. This is, in fact, the exceptional context of *Uhud* battle in which many Muslims were killed leaving behind a considerable number of destitute widows and orphans. In this case, polygamy was a temporary solution within the framework of social solidarity especially in the absence of social institutions to support certain groups such as widows and orphans.

Finally, we should bear in mind that with regard to polygamy deconstruction, the work begun by these women does not claim its prohibition, but it focuses especially on the fact of restricting and rebuilding it as a practice that must be limited to exceptional cases. Furthermore, it is important to note that the dynamics of these women was certainly encouraged by the thinking of Abdessalam Yassine, the founder of the movement (and Nadia's father), who clearly defends women in his theory. According to him, the so-called historical rupture had a negative impact on the status of women by moving them from being active agents, participating in the society development to an "insignificant and oppressed creature, as we see today in our societies hit by illiteracy and heavy macho and unjust traditions"(Yassine 1998, p. 191). Therefore, he welcomes and supports the prompt need to save Muslim women from the "abyss of injustice and negligence"(Yassine 1998, p. 191).

However, the intellectual work of these women has aroused strong internal male resistance that hindered its progress in its practical application. Perhaps even that this resistance was the origin of the rumors around the resignation of Nadia Yassine and of a certain number of leading female figures in the movement.

Khadija Mufid and the notion of *azzawjiya* (duality)

Concerning Khadija Moufid, who is also, I believe, one of the iconic figures of this sort of feminism despite the fact that she rejects this concept. She has been deemed as one of the founders of Unification and Reform Movement (MUR),[10] which was created in 1996. During her presence in this movement, Khadija Moufid generated many struggles for a considerable female presence and participation as regards decision-making in the movement. However, her struggle eventually ended up in her resignation from the Justice and Development Party (PJD)[11] in August 2007, followed by conflicts concerning the mode of selection of the national list of candidates.[12] Indeed, the classification of women of the party follows an election process at an internal scale, followed by a measurement accreditation by the General Secretariat of the party. According to Moufid, the general Secretariat refused to put her on the top of the list because, as she thinks: "a woman with a strong personality and expertise to exercise power is a threat to the power of men" (Yafout 2012, p. 355).

Today, she organizes meetings for women's awareness in the headquarters of the association *AlHidn*, which she presides. She denounces the traditional approach to women's issues, which she describes as Oriental and conservative, because it is based on a restrictive thinking of certain oriental Ulemas. These latter developed a certain conception of women paralyzing half of the society in a way that affects not only women, but also the social process. Therefore, she calls for an intellectual revival that would trigger social and political reform where women's role can be central. In this sense, she develops an approach called *"Azzawjia"* (duality), which considers the origin of the universe. Thus, the universe was created, she argues, from couples. Therefore, all the imbalances through the history of humanity were due to the dominance of one party over another: dominating males confiscate women's rights, or the female dominates and betrays the rights of society because femininity is linked to the whole society, not to just a single entity (Yafout 2012, p. 315).

Thus, based on this approach, Moufid defends the centrality of the family, as she is also the president of the Center for Family Studies and Research within Values and Laws. In fact, she thinks that we should not address the problems of women apart from those of the family. These should be treated with an approach that takes into account the three elements of family: woman, child and family. She criticizes the individualistic and partial approach that favors the interests of the individual, as a subject of law, regardless of his or her impact on the group's interest and, in our context, emphasizes the interest of the woman as an individual at the expense of the interests of the family. She adopts, however, a holistic approach emphasizing the group's interest instead of the interest of the individual. Thus, while ensuring that the priority of the family and the emancipation of women are not two contradictory objectives, the woman can be an effective actor in the public space without betraying her familial responsibilities.

Moreover, she considers that it is necessary to take care of the centrality of the family, to strengthen cohesion and streamline its role so that it can be an effective and influential base in the maintenance of social structure. This, she argues, requires paying attention to two significant pillars for the stability of the family and motherhood: balancing women's responsibilities in the home and public sphere. Achieving this equilibrium is deemed by Moufid as one of the universal problems of the modern woman. She denounces, in this sense, the lack of a family policy likely to allow women the reconciliation between family responsibilities and professional activities.

Furthermore, Moufid develops a concept of polygamy different from that of Islamist feminists mentioned above. Indeed, she believes that before being a man right, polygamy is a right of the second woman because it allows her to become a mother especially that women marry less and their rate becomes higher than that of men. In addition, she evokes the feeling of love: for in a situation where a woman falls in love with a man already married, polygamy is the only solution, since any form of relationship outside marriage is illegitimate in Islam. In this sense, Moufid claims that illegitimate relationships are harmful to women because they enable men to enjoy them without giving them, in return, a guarantee of stable and lasting married life, and, also, without assuming any responsibility towards them. On the contrary, polygamy prevents the first woman's marriage to be broken in cases of infertility or incurable disease because by this measure, the husband will marry a second wife without divorcing the first one. In this case, polygamy is an "adequate solution" that prevents the destruction of family. Finally, Moufid advances another argument that makes polygamy a necessity. She argues that it is a solution for the active woman that needs to reduce the presence of man in her life.

Lamrabet and feminine Islam

AsmaLamrabe tis one of the figures of this movement who assumes the name of "Islamic feminist". For her, feminism is a universal heritage and all women have the right to appropriate and adapt it to their specific cultural contexts. However, she stated that the feminism she adopts differs ideologically from that advocated by a frenzied westernization of femininity. It is, however, similar to it in terms of rights claims. In sum, she believes that Islamic feminists are obliged to use the vocabulary already in vogue which is globally understood.

She also adopts the methodology based on the reference to the lives of women Companions of the Prophet in order to legitimize the freedom of Muslim women and their access to public space. Thus, she bases her study on the life stories of women Companions and especially those of the wives of the Prophet and presents them as liberation models. The importance of such an endeavor is also to confront the practical experience of women Companions of the Prophet to the rules of *fiqh* (jurisprudence) examined as a human production influenced by the cultural context in which it was produced and by people who had generated it. Moreover, in her book, "Aisha, or Feminine Islam", she presents the Prophet's wife from a different point of view given by classical jurisprudence. Thus, she emphasizes her outstanding qualities as a religious scholar and politician, for in addition to having regulated much of the *Sunnah*, Aisha served for forty years according as a *Mufti* (the one who issues legal advice). In this regard, Lamrabet notes that *"Mufti"* exists only in Arabic masculine form. Yet Aisha, the Prophet's wife, was among the first to have personified it.

On the other hand, Lamrabet has lead "feminist" thoughts about the *Qur'an*. Thus, in her book: "The *Qur'an* and Women", she deals with the thorny issue of inheritance by trying to show that inheritance is quite complex and cannot be reduced to a single rule, which mentions that man inherits twice a woman's share. The verse that present this rule should be put in its historical and social context; the man was required to meet all the economic needs of the family, in the sense that the amount inherited by the wife was a net amount added to here property while the sum inherited by man was a gross amount to be deducted from the maintenance of the family expenses. She concludes that the laws of Islam must advocate for the preservation of this spirit in a context where the woman shares the same economic responsibilities and sometimes assumes a double function.

Currently, Lamrabet runs a center for study and research on women in Islam in which doctoral students in Islamic studies examine the sacred texts and undertake a re-reading from a female perspective. The aim is to deconstruct discriminatory interpretations against women. It is important, however, to point out that this center is affiliated to the *Rabita* (the league) of Morocco's *Ulema*, an official institution whose aim is to train clerics but in a strict framework of respect for basic elements (*thawabit*) of the religious policy in Morocco such as the supremacy of the Maliki school or the supremacy of the Commandry of the Faithful.[13] This environment certainly limits the degree of freedom and autonomy necessary for these women to make an effort of reflection on religious texts and go beyond the framework of traditional schools and official Islam adopted in Morocco. This requires not only being free to draw from the scope of different jurisprudential schools but also free to adopt different methods and analytical approaches. In this regard, I will cite two examples reflecting this limitation:

— Some women members of Rabita show that they are unable to get rid of this intellectual grip and produce scientific knowledge by themselves. They carry out their thoughts on the issue of women in the narrow context of a patriarchal model based on the recognition of intellectual and functional superiority of men over women.[14]

— The Arabic translation of the Lamrabet's book "The *Qur'an* and women" and which was undertaken as the first project in the context of that study center was interrupted because of the reflections of the author on the status of women in Islam which were considered "bold".

Conclusion

In sum, we can see that Islamic feminists may agree on the same opinions; they complement and sometimes contradict each other. We have already seen the reflexionof Nadia Yassin and her "sisters" concerning polygamy that calls for a limitation of this practice, to make it an exceptional solution, as it has negative consequences on the familial and social level. This reflexion comes as a complete contradiction of Khadija Moufid's reasoning, which focuses on the second wife and her right to marriage, and considers therefore polygamy as a right of this wife. But the common point between these figures of Islamic feminism is their belief that women's liberation is possible through the sacred texts. This does not necessarily contradict the approaches based on international standards, which can be complementary in many ways. Moreover, interpretations developed by these women intellectuals are not only limited to religious texts but permeate contemporary science and universal human experience including that of Western feminists. They look at all these experiences as "undeniably important lessons" adopted in the *Hadith* that calls the believer to learn all wisdom: "Wisdom is the lost wealth of the believer which he takes where he finds it". Thus, their thoughts involve multiple approaches and disciplines: sociology, history, anthropology, and psychology...

In addition, The *Qur'an* and *Hadith* are perceived by women as bearing universal messages. Indeed, there are many verses in the *Qur'an* that address people in general without specifying Muslims "ya ayouha nnas" (you people!). Others are called believers "ya ayouha ladhina Amanou" (O you believers!) referring to anyone who believes in God, and not just Muslims.

Furthermore, the work of these women scholars is not limited to individual intellectual reflections, but it is also transmitted through meetings, associations, student groups, researchers, etc. The female pioneers cited above are only the figureheads of a movement to which other women adhere as they are fully convinced of the ideas and works cited above. However, they are exposed to a double stigma: a) the stereotypical Westernist conception of the Muslim woman as being veiled, submissive and oppressed; this image is still in vogue in postcolonial contemporary representations; b) macho mentalities at the internal scale which accuse feminists of serving a Western project aiming to distort Islam.

Finally, we can think of the mobilization of this trend of women in the framework of post-Islamism the sense that it helps to show the complex relation Islam/ modernity and to participate in the reforming efforts of a group of modern Muslim intellectuals. In addition, the female intellectual figures, mentioned in this chapter, appropriate the religious knowledge and often adopt a critical stance in relation to Islamic thought, classical jurisprudence and traditionalist *Ulemas*. They contribute, in fact, to the evolution of religious discourse from being exclusive to being inclusive and liberating.

Notes

1 L'*ijtihad* is an islamic concept that requires an innovative effort : rereading the sacred texts of Islam while especially making a liberating spirit prevail in the reinterpretation over the literal meaning of the text.
2 A honorific title usually given to the wives of the Prophet, his daughters and his granddaughters. It means "Great Lady". The wives of the Prophet are also called "Mothers of the Believers".

3 Hussein is the grandson of the Prophet
4 Mernissi, Fatima1987,*Le Harem Politique : Le Prophète et les femmes*, Albin Michel, Paris.
5 Not to confuse with Abou Bakr, the first Caliph of Islam.
6 Mernissi, Fatima 1990, *Sultanes oubliées : Femmes chefs d'État en Islam*, Albin Michel, Paris.
7 Arab historian, philosopher, diplomat, and political leader of the XIVth century.
8 Islamist movement created at the beginning of the 80s by Abdessalam Yassine, and is considered since the 90s as the biggest opposition force facing the Moroccan regime.
9 This term is used to describe the women who share the same thinking and projects as Nadia Yassine.
10 MUR is a union between several Islamist associations created during the 1980s whose Renewal and Reform movement (MRR) was founded by Abdelilah Benkirane in 1981.
11 Islamist party founded in 1996 and currently leading the government. MUR is considered the religious wing of the PJD and its ideological matrix.
12 The National List is a measure that was adopted in 2002 to allow women a representation of 10% in the parliament through a national list dedicated to women. Since the elections of 2011, the National List that once had 30 women is now reserved to women and youth, who are therefore counted as 60 women and 30 young men. Hence, the women's representation in parliament raised from 30 to 60 women.
13 The Commandry of the Faithful is a principle according to which the rule of the Moroccan king is based on Divine Right. Hence, the Moroccans are attached to it by a pact of allegiance. As a consequence, all the instructions issued by the Commander of the Faithful concerning religious or national affairs are a part of the unchangeable values (*thawabit*) that should be respected by all Ulema and preachers.
14 See, as example, Farida Zomorroud, *Conférences sur quelques points en rapport avec l'interprétation du Coran*, Rabat, ministère des Waqf et des Affaires islamiques, 2005, p. 80. A conference presented to the King in the framework of the religious lessons of Ramadan.

Bibliography

Ahmed, Leila. 1992. *Women and Gender in Islam, historical roots of modern debate*,The American University in CairoPress.
Badran, Margot. 2010. 'Où en est le féminisme islamique ?',*Critique internationale*, n°46 janvier-mars, pp. 25–44.
Ezzat, R. Heba. 2007. 'Women and the interpretation of islamic sources', Available from: http://www.sistersinislam.org.my/index.php?option=com_content&task=view&id=581&Itemid=298.[04 Sep 2007].
Ezzat, R. Heba. 2002. 'Rethinking Secularism...Rethinking Feminism',Available from: http://www.islamonline.net/English/contemporary/2002/07/Article01.shtml.
Göle, Nilufer. 1993. *Musulmanes et Modernes : voile et civilisation en Turquie*, La découverte, Paris.
Kian-T,Azadeh.2010.'Leféminismeislamiqueen Iran:nouvelleformed'assujettissement ou émergence de sujets agissants ?',*Critique internationale*, 2010/1, n° 46. Presses de Sciences po, pp.45–66.
Lamrabet, Asma. 2003. ,*Aïsha épouse du Prophète ou L'Islam au féminin, Attawhid*.
Lamrabet, Asma. 2007. *Le Coran et les femmes : une lecture de libération, Attawhid*.

Latte Abdallah, Stéphanie. 2010. 'Le féminisme islamique, vingt ans après : économie d'un débat et nouveaux chantiers de recherche', *Critique internationale*, N°46, janvier-mars, pp. 9–23.

Mernissi, Fatima. 1987. *Le Harem Politique : Le Prophète et les femmes*, Albin Michel, Paris.

Mernissi, Fatima.1990. *Sultanes oubliées : Femmes chefs d'État en Islam*,Albin Michel, Paris.

Mir-Hosseini,Ziba. 2006. 'Muslim Women's Quest for Equality: Between Islamic Law and Feminism', *Critical Inquiry 32*, The University of Chicago.

Moufid, Khadija. 2005. 'Le code de la famille : quelles nouveautés?' (en arabe), In *Du code du statut personnel au code de la famille : quelles nouveautés ?: Les travaux de la journée d'étude organisée par l'association Al Hidn*, Ed Annajah Al Jadida, Casablanca.

Yafout, Merieme. 2012. *Statut des femmes au sein des mouvements islamistes marocains : entre exégèse au féminin et participation politique. Cas des femmes appartenant à Al AdlWallhssane et au MUR/PJD*, Thèse de doctorat, Université HassanII- Ain Chock, Faculté des Sciences Juridiques, Économiques et Sociales Casablanca.

Yassine, Abdessalam. 1998. *Islamiser la modernité*, Al Ofok, Casablanca.

Yassine, Nadia. 2003. *Toutes voiles dehors*. Le Fennec, Casablanca.

Chapter 6

ISLAMIC FEMINISM IN MOROCCO

The Discourse and the Experience of Asma Lamrabet

Sara Borrillo

Introduction: Updating categories like "Feminism" and "Islam"

Women's movements in the MENA (Middle East and North Africa) region have struggled in different ways, throughout the twentieth century and today, and thanks to the historical experience of the 2011 uprisings, they continue to struggle in the social movements, in the public sphere of media (Salvatore, 2011), and in academia. The Moroccan women's movement is characterized by a long historical continuity and by an extremely rich heterogeneity in which it is possible to observe transformative convergences and divergences among its components (Sadiqi, 2008; Salime, 2011). In this chapter, I intend to identify some of the most relevant aspects of the discourse and individual trajectory of Asma Lamrabet as an "Islamic feminist", to contextualize her experience in the Moroccan women's movement and to highlight the elements of continuity and innovation of her approach.

In the Moroccan women's movement, it is possible to distinguish components depending on the field in which women orient their different strategies, their ideological identity, as well as the forms in which they express protest or the practical outputs of their action. In a broad sense, regarding the perspective of analysis based on the dichotomy "knowledge-action", we can identify an "intellectual" feminism, active in the production of discourses that support social and political agencies, and a "militant" feminism, operating more in the political arena to reclaim women's rights *vis à vis* the patriarchal power (Bourquia, 1996). This does not mean that intellectuals and militants have necessarily separate fields of action; on the contrary, in some cases they collaborated and still collaborate in different research-action projects.

Regarding ideological identity, we can observe that feminism and international conventions for human rights (Universal Declaration for Human Rights, 1948 and CEDAW, 1979), on the one hand, and Islam, on the other, represent the two main systems of values around which women's movement perspectives and strategies are articulated in Morocco. In some dichotomical analyses, these two references are presented as oppositional, as associated with two « projects of society » presented as corresponding respectively to a secular or to a religious framework (Daoud, 1993; Gandolfi, 2011). Feminism, secularism and individual liberties are considered as aspects of a Western, materialist, antireligious perspective, while visions of the world inspired by Islam are considered as conservative, opposed to gender equality and broadly hostile to modernity. But this dichotomy can't reflect the complex reality because, firstly, from an analytical perspective, nor the "feminism" nor "Islam" can be conceived as homogenous categories *in sé.* In fact, there are so many different forms in which these two categories are expressed, contested, negotiated or redefined (Gole, 1996; Mahmood, 2005). Secondly, this dichotomy does not speak about the plurality of agencies depending on different ways in which to interpret and embody feminism and Islam (Shaikh, 2011) in individual and collective trajectories, *vis-à-vis* historical, social and political changes (Abu-Lughod, 1998; Ahmed, 1992).

It is possible to identify three main components of the Moroccan women's movement. And this, thanks to the methodological approach that considers "feminism" and "Islam" in a postcolonial perspective, as reference categories of agencies that emerged in women's individual and collective discourses used to self-represent themselves (Sorbera, 2013). On the basis of women's public action and their forms of self-representation we can distinguish secular feminists, women activists in political Islam or Islamist movements and parties, and "Islamic feminists" (Salih, 2008). The Moroccan Uprising animated by the 20

February Movement seems to have changed this classification, encouraging changes between historical forces or within their internal components. The 20 February Movement's struggled for "dignity, freedom and social justice", as the well-known slogan of protest movements in the Middle East and North Africa in 2011 says (*karama, hurriyya, adala ijtimaiyya*). In particular, its demands were referred to the end of the corruption in the national bureaucracy of Makhzen, the democratization of the political system and the amelioration of socio-economic condition of the people. The massive protests in the beginning of 2011 have lad the central power to the reform of the Constitution, announced in the King's discourse of 9 March 2011: the referendum for the confirmation of the text, produced by a Commission appointed by the King, received the boycott of the 20 February Movement. Indeed the new Moroccan Constitution finally was approved also thanks to the support of traditional feminist organizations, because of the provision of the gender equality at art.19. Due to this fact, the relations between feminist associations and the progressive forces of the movement, which were united before, deteriorated. Consequently, we can observe two interesting evolutions in feminist strategies and discourses. Firstly, the end of the monopoly of secular feminist associations of the struggle for women's rights in the progressive block of the civil society: today some informal groups and new associations, of activists, journalists, artists struggle for gender equality in a more autonomous and innovative way. Secondly, it is possible to observe a post-ideological way to demand women's rights in the new historical phase after 2011: the secular/Islamic divide seems to be more nuanced to the advantage of a "new feminism" (Salime, 2012) composed by new and changing alliances for women's rights over the classical boundaries between secular feminists, Islamist activists, Islamic feminists (Borrillo, 2012).

In any case, it seems useful to consider the following classification for a general distinction on the articulation of discourses and strategies about women rights in Morocco.

1   Secular feminists claim women's rights as human rights affirmed in international conventions. They demand the respect of gender equality in a State based on the Rule of Law in which Islam is considered as an aspect of the individual private sphere and not

as one of the primary sources of central power, citizens' identity and social normativity (Dupret,Buskéns, 2011).

2   Women activists in political Islam or Islamist movements and parties consider Islam as the primary source of their individual identity, as well as the main system of laws and values for the collective ideal order (Yafout, 2012).

3   Finally, there are the adherents to the Islamic feminism perspective, supporting full compatibility between the international discourse on human rights and Islam, conceived as a moral and spiritual system of values promoting social justice, solidarity and non-discrimination against women (Badran, 2009; Cooke, 2001; Mir-Husseini, 1999; Ali, 2012).

In this chapter, I will concentrate on the discourse and experience of Asma Lamrabet, as one of the most representative figures in contemporary Islamic feminism, influencing the debate on women's rights in Morocco and in Muslim-majority countries.

Islamic feminism: a critical discourse in Islam, a gender based theology of liberation

In women's emancipatory strategies and discourses that have emerged in the debates about the progress of Muslim-majority societies, an increasingly centrality is occupied by those who demand a reform of Islamic jurisprudence and normativity toward gender equality. From this perspective, feminism and Islam are not ontologically opposed, as some academics assert (Moghissi, 2005). Inspired by a reformist vision of Islamic ethics, this perspective aims to demonstrate the full compatibility between the message of Revelation (*Risāla*) and gender equality, from a spiritual point of view and at a social, political, juridical, and economic level (Hassan, 1999; Yamani, 1996).

The French sociologist Stephanie Abdallah Latte considers that there are three main groups of Islamic feminists:

1   Critical Muslim theologians, some of them self-defined as "feminists".
2   Secular feminist militants, with a cultural and sociological Muslim background.
3   Women of the political Islam or Islamist movements, who are active for the amelioration of women's situation (Abdallah Latte, 2010).

For me it is correct to consider "Islamic feminists" as the exponents of the first group who are struggling for women's emancipation within Islam and through the re-appropriation of the process of interpretation of Islamic sources.

Margot Badran defines Islamic feminism as a "feminist discourse and a practice articulated inside the paradigm of Islam" (Badran, 2002). Asma Barlas talks about "a gender equality and social justice discourse derived from the understanding of the Qur'anic message, which tries to realize rights and justice for all humans in the totality of their existence and in the public-private continuum" (Barlas, 2011). According to Mai Yamani, this discourse is promoted by thinkers with different backgrounds with the common objective of promoting women's empowerment, in the name of a feminism which is Islamic in its form and in its contents" (Yamani, 1996, p.1). In accordance with Moghadam it is "a reform movement based on the Qur'an and promoted by Muslim women who challenge the patriarchal interpretation of Islam, offering alternative readings, based on their linguistic and theological knowledge, in order to ameliorate women's conditions" (Moghadam, 2008). These "Muslim scholar activists" (Webb, 2000) think that the responsibility for women's subordination in laws and social behavior in Muslim-majority societies does not reside in Islam but in its misogynist interpretations that have distorted its egalitarian bias. Thanks to the empirical assumption of "textual and sexual discrimination" against women (Barlas, 2011), well explained by Amina Wadud with the expression "*tafsīr* is hu(man) made" (Wadud, 2000), the ethical horizon of Islamic feminism consists in affirming the Islamic conformity of the principles of social justice and gender equality. The methodological assumption consists in distinguishing *Shariâ*, the ethical dimension of Islam, and *fiqh*, its technical dimension of the jurisprudence: the discrimination against women has been legitimized in Islam because of the confusion between these two concepts (Mir-Husseini, 2006). Amina Wadud suggests that when we speak about Islam it is opportune to specify to what we are referring: what Islamic sources are affirming, Islamic cultural traditions, what Muslims do, or the law established by governments ruling in Muslim-majority countries (Wadud, 2000).

Raja Rhouni defines Islamic feminism as an Islamic gender-based critique, which shares with Islamic reformism the aim to reform

Muslim-majority societies from an exegesis of Islamic sources (Qur'an and Sunna) inspired by an interdisciplinary method that concerns the critical reasoning (*al-'aql*) of the interpreter and the historicized contextualization of the religious message (Rhouni, 2010). This intellectual globalized movement of the religious herme-neutic for gender equality represents a "multiple critique" (Cooke, 2001) emerging through the consciousness of some Muslim women that they are the object of two fundamentalisms to reject: one is the Western cultural hegemony, the other is the patriarchal interpreta-tions of Islamic sources[1]. Islamic feminism appears therefore, as a counter-discourse which is useful for struggling against cultural power, both Western and patriarchal. It is also, according with Asma Lamrabet and Salman Sayyd, a post- and de-colonial emancipatory project, developed in opposition to hegemonic structures inside power relations at a social and at an epistemologically religious level: it can therefore be defined as a "theology of liberation"[2].

Islamic feminism is also conceived as the result of a hybridization process of many identity dimensions, linked to class, gender, ethnicity, Islam and feminism, in a renewed form of citizenship that Amina Wadud calls "intimate citizenship", that combines militancy, public responsibility and subjectivity[3]. In this sense, it is possible to consider Islamic feminism as a political project, because it expresses the capacity of Muslim women to bargain with patriarchy and to find a creative compromise between Islam and self-determination (Kandiyoti, 1988; Moghadam, 2002).

Islamic feminism is a "globalized intellectual discourse" (Salih, 2007) through which Muslim women, whether self-represented as feminist or not, want to achieve gender equality and it becomes a "reform movement" when local organizations and "transnational feminist networks (TFNs)" (Moghadam, 2005) use its argument in a multidisciplinary perspective for militant action. Thanks to the internet and ICT (Information and communications technologies) we can today observe many groups and organizations such as *Musawah, Sisters in Islam, WLUML – Women living under Muslim law, Karamah – Muslim women lawyers for human rights* and WASILA – *Women's association and society for Islamic learning and awareness*.

The use of the two terms "discourse" and "movement" in these definitions, helps to observe the changing nature of the phenomenon of Islamic feminism, which is currently in a phase of constant evolution. In this perspective, Islam must not be conceived of as a dogma to be blindly followed, but as a moral, religious, and political guide that inspires different interpretations, life-styles, *performances* and *agencies*, that we cannot conceive of as an absolute definition (Mahmood, 2005).

The discourse and experience of Asma Lamrabet is a geo-localized version of Islamic feminism, which has a remarkable impact on the international level.

Asma Lamrabet: a gender *jihād* discourse and experience

With the expression "gender *jihād*", Amina Wadud refers to women's capacity to bring about a "cognitive subversion" inside Islam (Wadud, 2006), which can offer an alternative to the male monopoly of the religious exegesis of the sacred texts of Islam and of related jurisprudence (Barazangi, 2006).

In this perspective, I define Asma Lamrabet's work as gender *jihād*, for two reasons: she affirms the right for women to be authoritative in the Islamic structures and in the construction of Islamic knowledge, and from the point of view of the contents, her work aims to affirm the egalitarian and emancipatory principles of the Qur'an. Here I analyze these two aspects of her personal experience: the first concerns her process of acquisition of religious authority; the second one more deeply concerns the contents of her exegetical work.

Regarding the first aspect, I would like to pay attention to the self-negotiated authority process of Asma Lamrabet that has led this author to become Director of the Center for Studies and Research on Women questions in Islam (CERFI) of the *Rābiṭa al-Muḥammadiyya al-'ulamā'* in Rabat.

We must note that Asma Lamrabet works as a hematologist, at Ibn Sina hospital in Rabat, her hometown, where she gained her specialization. Since she was young, she has travelled around the world: she has lived in France and Algeria, because of her father's political exile[4]. Then, thanks to her marriage with a diplomat, she lived in various cities in South America and Europe, where she served in some hospitals as volunteer. Back in Morocco in 2003, she rediscovered her original society, and she started to consider the dominant Islamic system of values as "schizophrenic": it is neither suited, in her opinion, "to the demands of the rapid evolution and changes in Moroccan society, nor to the Qur'anic original message of equality between all individuals"[5].

I participated in an event of presentation of her last book, *Femmes et hommes dans le Coran : quelle égalité ?* (Lamrabet, 2012), in the same bookshop of Casablanca (*Karamah*, in Arabic "dignity") in which Fatima Mernissi had also delivered some speeches during the 1980s. There she explained why and how she started her research:

"My personal research has lasted twenty years. I came from a family that I can define as schizophrenic: a nationalist and socialist father, representative of the Moroccan left in the 1970s, progressive in the public sphere, but firm about conservative Islamic religious values in the private sphere. In my adolescence, Islam was not clear for me: my father was talking about freedom and justice at an ideological level, but in his daily life, in social practices, he was a conservative man. After my Ph.D. in Hematology, it was my wish to know *by myself* what the Qur'an said. It was my wish to know *by myself* [she repeats] what Islam means. And I was feeling myself free to be able to conduct my research alone, without any association, group, or movement"[6].

After the first period of her research, where she published her first book, *Musulmane tout simplement*, from 2004 to 2007 Asma Lamrabet was the coordinator of a research group about Muslim women's issues and intercultural dialogue in Rabat, while she continued to publish comments and articles on her personal blog (www.asma-lamrabet.com). Then, in 2008 she was elected President of the International Group for Studies and Reflections on Women in Islam (GIERFI) based in Barcelona, with the aim of debating women's condition in Islam and following from this, on women's condition in societies influenced by monotheism. Since 2011 she has been director of the Centre for Studies and research on women's issues in Islam (CERFI) of the Association of *'Ulamā'* of Morocco, where today she directs the research work of five women and one man.

I find her evolution very interesting, from an intellectual position of someone who reads the Qur'an and questions herself – in her words "by myself" – about the normative power of its *surat* in contemporary society, to the role of director of a research center on women's issues in Islam based in a religious institution. One initial answer of course concerns her personal commitment, determination, and ability to persuade and negotiate with the Moroccan Islamic establishment. A key moment of this process was in 2008, when she promoted the partnership between the Group for International Studies and reflections on women in Islam (GIERFI) and the Association of *'Ulamā'* of Morocco, directed by Ahmed Abbadi, the General Secretary of this League. Then, when she edited the book *Femmes et Coran: une lecture the liberation*, she asked Abbadi to review it, and he promoted the Arabic edition of the text published by the Association of *'Ulamā'*. His proposal was, however, blocked by the Academic Council of the Islamic Association, made up of a group of *'Ulamā'*, who refused to publish this book in Arabic, demonstrating a general perplexity towards Asma's progressive ideas, justifying this rejection by the fact that she does not have a traditional or officially recognized religious authority. Effectively, Asma Lamrabet does not yet have a traditional and officially recognized authority as *'ālima*: she does not have a traditional diploma in Islamic studies; she did not attend the *Dār al-ḥadīṭ al-Ḥassaniyya*, nor the *Dār al-Qur'ān*. This is perhaps the most interesting point of Asma's non-official religious authority. Despite this, in 2011 Abbadi appointed her "director" of CERFI, the Center for studies and research on women's issues in Islam of the Association of *'Ulamā'*. Evidently, therefore, in the same Islamic institution there are different ways of understanding the religious authority of Asma Lamrabet. When, during an interview, I asked the General Secretary of the Association of *'Ulamā'* the reasons for the opposition of the Academic Council of this Association against the publication of Asma's book in Arabic – and in particular I asked whether the reason for this opposition was that Asma did not have the characteristic of a traditional *'ālima* –, Ahmed Abbadi answered that "nobody can say that she is not an *'ālima*"[7].

Even though the Association of *'Ulamā'* does not have the absolute official power to dictate the requirements for the definition of Islamic authority in Morocco, Abbadi's answer represents a significant precedent regarding the identification of Islamic female religious authority (Kramer and Schmitdkte, 2006) by an institution of the Islamic establishment of a country where the role of *'Ulamā'* is very important for the legitimation of the central power. Anyway, for the work of Asma Lamrabet to be more effective, consensus and legitimation on the part of other *'Ulamā'* is important, something that, as yet, Asma does not completely have.

Supporting the Qur'anic concept of equality instead of complementarity

The idea of women's right to have access to Islamic authority in Asma's approach, which leads us to the second part of this paper, is oriented towards the promotion of a re-reading of Sacred texts (Qur'an and Sunna) aiming at gender equality and individual interpretative effort (*ijtihād*) to adapt Islamic sources to reality as an alternative to the interpretations based only on the imitation of tradition (*taqlīd*).

As she said in an interview : "I'm sorry, but closing the door of *ijtihād* is really inadequate, because it makes the adaptation of Islam to reality very difficult. Islam has an evoluative nature and *ijtihād* is a necessary tool for the adaptation of Islam to contemporary reality. *'Ulamā'* rely too much on the predecessors, not the sacred texts, but this *taqlīd* is blind".

Thanks to this general perspective, Asma offers an egalitarian exegesis of the Qur'an and the Sunna. The theological reference of her approach is the concept of *tawhīd*, the oneness and the unicity of God, which puts all the beings created by God on the same level. She explains the Qur'anic legitimation of the concept of gender equality (*musāwā*) instead of the concept of the complementarity (*takāmul*), which is the most popular in Muslim-majority societies.

The idea of complementarity between women and men in Muslim-majority societies is founded on the gender-based division of labor, related to the biological roles of men as responsible for the family and society and for productive work, and of women as mothers, daughters and wives, responsible for the work of reproduction and care. The core problem of complementarity is that it creates a fixed system of gendered obligations and rights, leading to a juridical complementarity between women and men, which keeps women inferior in family and in society. The consequence is the affirmation of a juridical inferiority of women under the male responsibility of the family, of the *umma* and of the State, legitimized by the umbrella concept *al-qiwāma*.

Asma, as an alternative to this classical vision, promotes the argument of gender equality ("*musāwa bayna al-jinsayn*") based on eleven basic concepts that she extrapolates from a direct reading of the Qur'an, as she explains in her most recent book *Femmes et hommes dans le Coran: quelle égalité ?*.

It is important to note that her Qur'anic reading is based on three hermeneutical levels:

a The holistic reading of the Qur'an (*al-qirā'a al-šumūliyya*) enables the restoration of the issue of women's rights within the universal spiritual message of equality for all human beings.

b The teleological reading (*al-qirā'a al-maqāṣidiyya*) which aims to shed light on the purposes of the Qur'an.

c The contextual reading based on the effort of reflection (*ijtihād*), as a fundamental tool, enabling the consistency of the spiritual message within its context and the pertinent challenges of its era.

Thanks to the consideration of the importance of these different readings of the Qur'an, in the opinion of Lamrabet gender equality in the Qur'an is defined in at least the following eleven concepts:

1 In the process of creation of human beings, equality is unquestionable, because there is a clear Qur'anic declaration of equality in the first verse of the 4th Sura, where Allah "created you from a single soul" (where "from a single soul" in Arabic is "*min nafsin waḥidatin*"; Qur'an, 4:1). This idea is not new, as it was explored by others Islamic feminists like Amina Wadud (Wadud, 1999).

2 The responsibility of human beings (*al-khilāfa*) on the earth belongs to both men and women. This concept confirms the interpretations of Amina Wadud and other Islamic feminists.

3 Moral integrity or piety (*al-taqwa*), and not gender, is the only criterion of evaluation of human beings by Allah.

4 The Qu'ran speaks to both women and men; when there are plural male nouns in its text it is because Arabic group nouns, expressed in a plural male form, refer to both women and men.

5 Marriage is based on Qur'anic ethics, so it is a mutual union inspired by love, harmony, and respect between husband and wife: it is not a contract to buy a woman and her reproductive power. The aim of a marriage is welfare and good feeling (*ma'rūf*),

as emerges from verse 187 of the second *sura*: "they are like your clothes, and you are like their clothes" (*"wa hunna libās lakum wa antum libās lahunna"*; Qur'an 2:187).

6 Political and familial responsibility (*wilāya*) is valid for both men and women. In Asma's opinion this concept is inserted in the Moroccan Family Code – the *Mudawwana* reformed in 2004 – where the family is under the responsibility of both husband and wife, and women are not obliged to pay obedience to the husband, as was the case before 2004.

7 The concept of male responsibility (*qiwāma*), traditionally conceived of as male superiority (*darāja*) over women on the basis of the patriarchal interpretation of the Qur'anic verse "Men are guardians over women, because Allah has given the one more (strength) than the other" [*"al-riǧāl qawwāmūn 'alā al-nisā' bimā faḍala Allah ba'dahum 'alā ba'd"*; Qur'an, 4:34], concerns only the validity of male economic responsibility for the family in the social system of the first Islamic period. Due to this concept, woman to inherit half of the inheritance of the male of the same degree of kinship. Today, however, the *qiwāma* of men over women is simply anachronistic, Asma argues, because it is shared by both husband and wife: in fact, also women today work in the public sphere and have great economic responsibility in the maintenance of the family.

8 For this reason also, the concept of inequality in inheritance between women and men is conceived of as anachronistic in Asma's vision. On the basis of this idea, together with the CERFI center and with the economic support of UN Women, Asma is promoting a study about 500 families to analyze the effective redistribution of economic responsibilities between partners.

9 The fact that in classical interpretations the juridical testimony of two women is equivalent to the testimony of one man is not valid in Asma's opinion because it only concerns some financial contracts in the first Islamic period, as the Qur'anic verse 2:282 suggests. Today, there is no reason for this discrimination because of the professional capacity that women also have in this sector.

10 Regarding marital divorce, there is no doubt that women have the right to ask for a divorce, as envisaged by the new *Mudawwana* of 2004.

All these concepts are well explored in her last book, but there is another recent concept that she explains on her blog:

11 Asma also affirms the right of a Muslim woman to marry a non-Muslim man, in opposition to the classical interdiction of marriage between them because of the patriarchal need to conserve the lineage. In her opinion, Islam allows a woman to marry a non-Muslim because there is no Qur'anic evidence for the interdiction of this kind of marriage for women only. Asma affirms that the possibility to freely chose the husband or the wife has to be valid for all, otherwise the interdiction used by the conservatives jurists on the basis of the interpretation of the Qur'anic verse 2:221 ["Do not marry unbelieving women, until they believe"] must also be valid for men because of the fact that the Qur'an speaks equally to men and women[8].

Conclusion

The well-known Moroccan sociologist Fatima Mernissi says that "only when women wake up and stop washing and cooking, and start to understand why norms are not created by themselves, will women surely find the way to change the rules and the entire world" (Mernissi, 1994). According to Mernissi, the Qur'an and Sunna can be used as a "weapon" to adapt the Islamic message to contemporary society (Mernissi, 1991). This idea is shared by Asma Lamrabet, whose activity aims to propose a new interpretation of the sacred texts based on a reformist approach, which aims to show the emancipatory character of Islamic revelation.

The experience of Asma Lamrabet denotes an example of self-negotiated authority in which we can observe a "self-made" trajectory of the "female subject" that controls, chooses and organizes her proper *agency* to build a religious authority.

We must also observe that the incorporation of feminist militants or reformist intellectuals into official Moroccan religious institutions is part of a strategy of Moroccan power defined as "State Feminism" or "Islamic State Feminism" (Alami Mchichi, 2010; Eddouada,Pepicelli, 2010). In this regard, we may observe that Asma Lamrabet is conscious of how her freedom is constantly "negotiated", and even if she does not consider this "bargaining with patriarchy" (Kandiyoti, 1988) as sustainable forever, she surely considers it as necessary today to change the patriarchal system from within.

In a recent interview at her house, Asma Lamrabet defined Islamic feminism as a "third way" alternative to secular feminism and to religious conservatism, which aims to make Islam and gender equality compatible:

"I am Muslim, but I'm a modern woman too. I share Western values about human rights but I think that everybody must respect the proper context of belonging"[9].

All this leads me to conclude that Asma Lamrabet is a fundamental voice in the debate about gender equality and the future of the status of women in Morocco and in all the Islamic world.

Notes

1 Ziba Mir-Husseini, personal interview, Rabat, 3 April 2010.
2 Both authors presented papers to the Summer School *Critical Muslim Studies Thought: De-colonial Struggles, Theology of Liberation and Islamic Revival*, organized by University of Berkeley in Granada, 4–13 June 2012.
3 Amina Wadud, personal interview, London, 11 September 2011.
4 Asma Lamrabet, personal interview, Rabat, 11 July 2012.
5 Asma Lamrabet, personal interview, 2012.
6 Asma Lamrabet, personal interview, 2012.
7 Ahmed, Abbadi, personal interview, Rabat, 4 May 2012.
8 Lamrabet, Asma, "Les 11 concepts clés de l'égalité femme-homme dans le Coran": http://www.asma-lamrabet.com/articles/les-11–concepts-cles-de-l-egalite-femme-hommes-dans-le-coran/
9 Asma Lamrabet, personal interview, Rabat, September 2014.

Bibliography

Abdallah Latte, Stephanie. (Ed.). 2010. *Le féminisme islamique aujourd'hui – Critique Internationale*, n. 46, Paris :Les Presses de Sciences Po.
Abdallah Latte, Stephanie. (Ed.). 2010. *Féminisme islamique*, REMMM – Revue des mondes musulmans et de la Méditerranée, n.128, December Issue.
Abu-Lughod, Lila. 1998. *Remaking women. Feminism and Modernity in the Middle East*. Princeton: Princeton University Press.
Ahmed, Leila. 1992. *Women and Gender in Islam. Historical Roots for a Modern Debate*. New Haven: Yale University Press.
Alami Mchichi, Houria. 2010. *Le féminisme d'Etat au Maroc. Jeux et enjeux politiques*, Paris : L'Harmattan.
Ali, Zahra. 2012. *Féminismes islamiques*, Paris, La Fabrique.
Badran, Margot. 2009. *Feminism in Islam. Secular and Religious Convergences*. Oxford: Oneworld publications.
Badran, Margot. 2002. "Islamic Feminism: What's in a Name?", *Al-Ahram Weekly Online*, 17 – 23 January Issue No.569, http://weekly.ahram.org.eg/2002/569/cu1.htm (accessed on Apr. 21, 2014).

Barazangi, Nimat Hafez. 2006. *Woman's Identity and the Qur'an. A New Reading.* Gainesville: University Press of Florida.

Barlas, Asma. 2011. "On Anti-anti fundationalism of Nasr Abu Zayd's Rethinking of Qur'an", paper presented to the Conference *Islamic new thinking*, Essen, 26–28 June 2011,http://www.asmabarlas.com/TALKS/2011_Abu_Zayd_Memorial. pdf.(accessed on Apr. 27, 2014).

Barlas, Asma. 2006. "Does the Qur'an Support Gender Equality. Or, Do I Have the Right to answer this question?", http://asmabarlas.com/PAPERS/Groningen_ Keynote.pdf. (accessed on June 24, 2014).

Borrillo, Sara. 2012. "Le mouvement du 20 Février et la réforme constitutionnelle au Maroc : un compromis démocratique suffisant?", in Sadiqi, Fatima (Ed.), *Femmes et nouveaux media dans la région méditerranéenne,* 303–324. Image Pub : Fez..

Bourquia, Rahma. 1996. *Femmes et fécondité.* Casablanca, :Afrique Orient

Cooke, Miriam. 2001. *Women Claim Islam. Creating Islamic Feminism Through Literature,* New York – London : Routledge.

Daoud, Zakya. 1993. *Féminisme et politique au Maghreb. Soixante ans de lutte (1930–1992).* Casablanca Eddif.

Dupret, Baudouin, Buskéns, Leon. 2011. "L'invention du droit musulman. Genèse et diffusion du positivisme juridique dans le contexte normatif islamique", in Pouillon, François, Vatin, Jean-Claude (Eds.). *L'Orient créé par l'Orient,* pp. 71–92. Paris : Karthala.

Eddouada, Souad, Pepicelli, Renat. 2010. "Maroc : vers un "féminisme islamique d'Etat", *Critique Internationale,* Sciences Po. Press, Paris, pp.87–102.

Gandolfi, Paola. 2011. "Etnografie e lavori sul campo in Maghreb e in Marocco prima e dopo le "rivoluzioni"", *Archivio antropologico Mediterraneo,* XII-XIII, , n.13, 2:89–104.

Gole, Nilufer. 1996. The Forbidden Modern. Ann Arbor: University of Michigan Press.

Hassan, Riffat. 1999. "Members, one of another: gender equality and justice in Islam", http://www.religiousconsultation.org/hassan.htm. (accessed on Jan. 2014).

Kandiyoti, Deniz, 1988. "Bargaining with Patriarchy", *Gender & Society,* September, 2: 274–290.

Kramer, Gudrun, and Schmitdkte, Sabine. (Eds.), 2006. *Speaking for Islam: Religious Authorities in Muslim Societies,* Leiden-Boston: Brill.

Lamrabet, Asma. 2012. *Femmes et hommes dans le Coran : quelle égalité?,* Lion: Tawhid.

Lamrabet, Asma, 2012. "Islamic Feminism", paper presented to the Summer School *Critical Muslim Studies Thought: De-colonial Struggles, Theology of Liberation and Islamic Revival,* University of Granada, 4–13 June.

Lamrabet, Asma. 2011. *Femmes, Islam, Occident. Chemins vers l'universel.* Casablanca: Les Croisée des chemins.

Lamrabet, Asma. 2009. *Aisha, ou l'Islam au fèminin.* Imperia:Alhikma,

Lamrabet, Asma. 2008. *Musulmane tout simplement.* Paris : Tawhid.

Lamrabet, Asma. 2007. *Le Coran et les femmes. Une lecture de libération.* Lion: Tawhid.

Lamrabet, Asma, 2002. "Les 11 concepts clés de l'égalité femme-homme dans le Coran": http://www.asma-lamrabet.com/articles/les-11-concepts-cles-de-l-egalite-femme-hommes-dans-le-coran/ (accessed on May 21, 2014).

Mahmood, Saba. 2005. *Politics of Piety. The Islamic Revival and the Feminist Subject.* Princeton: , Princeton University Press.

Mahmood, Saba. 2005. "Feminist Theory, Agency, and the Libratory Subject". In Fereshteh, Nouraie-Simone (Ed.). *On Shifting Ground: Muslim Women in the Global Era*, p. 111–153, New York: The Feminist Press.

Mernissi, Fatima. 1994. *Dreams of Trespass: Tales of a Harem Girlhood*. New York: Addison-Wesley.

Mernissi, Fatima, *Women and Islam*. 1991. *An Historical and Theological Enquiry*. London: Basil Blackwell.

Mir-Husseini, Ziba. 2006. "Quest for Equality. Between Islamic Law and Feminism", *Critical inquiry*, 32:.629–645.

Mir-Husseini, Ziba. 1999. *Islam and Gender. The Religious Debate in the Contemporary Iran*, Princeton: Princeton University Press.

Moghadam, Valentine. 2008. "Desengaños y expectativas del feminismo islámico", in AA.VV., *La emergencia del feminismo islámico. Selección de ponencias del primer y segundo Congreso internacional del feminismo islámico*, Oozebap, Barcellona, p. 135–158.

Moghadam, Valentine. 2005. *Globalizing Women: Transnational Feminist Networks*. Baltimore : Johns Hopkins University Press.

Moghadam, Valentine, 2002. "Islamic Feminism and its Discontents: Toward a Resolution of the Debate", *Signs*. Vol.27, 4: 1135–1171.

Moghissi, Haideh. 2005. *Women and Islam. Critical Concepts in Sociology*, Vol. III, London-New York: Routledge.

Rhouni, Rajaa. 2010. *Secular and Islamic Feminist critiques in the Work of Fatima Mernissi*. Leiden: Brill.

Sadiqi, Fatima, 2008. "Facing Challenges and Pioneering Feminist and Gender Studies: Women in Post-colonial and Today's Maghrib", *African and Asian Studies*, n. 7:.447–470.

Salih, Ruba. 2008. *Musulmane rivelate. Donne, Islam, modernità*. Roma: Carocci,

Salih, Ruba, 2007. "Femminismo e Islamismo. Pratiche politiche e processi d'identificazione in epoca post-coloniale", in *Jura Gentium – Rivista di filosofia del diritto internazionale e della politica globale*, http://www.juragentium.org/top-ics/islam/mw/it/salih.htm (accessed on June 7, 2013).

Salime, Zakia. 2012. "A New Feminism? Gender Dynamics in Morocco's February 20th Movement", *Journal of International Women's Studies*, 13(5):101–114.

Salime, Zakya. 2011. *Between Feminism and Islam. Human Rights and Sharia Law in Morocco*. Minneapolis: University of Minnesota Press.

Salvatore, Armando, 2011. *Between Everyday Life and Political Revolution: The Social Web in the Middle East, Oriente Moderno*, XCI-1, Istituto per l'Oriente C. A. Nallino, Roma.

Sayyd, Salman. 2012. "Orientalism and Theology of Liberation", paper presented to the Summer School *Critical Muslim Studies Thought: De-colonial Struggles, Theology of Liberation and Islamic Revival*, University of Granada, 4–13 June.

Shaikh, Sa'diyya. 2011. "Embodied tafsir: South African Muslim Women Confront Gender Violence in Marriage". In Badran, Margot (Ed.). *Gender and Islam in Africa. Rights, Sexuality and Law*, pp. 29–48. Stanford :Stanford University Press.

Sorbera, Lucia. 2013. "Early Reflections of an Historian on Feminism in Egypt in Time of Revolution", *Femminismi nel Mediterraneo, Genesis* – Rivista della Società Italiana delle Storiche, XII, 1:.13–41.

Wadud, Amina. 2006. *Inside the Gender Jihad. Women's Reform in Islam.* Oxford: Oneworld,

Wadud, Amina. 2000 ."Alternative Qur'anic Interpretation and the Status of Muslim Women". In Webb, Gisela (Ed.). *Windows of Faith. Muslim Women Scholar-Activist in North America,* pp.3–21. New York : Syracuse University Press.

Wadud, Amina. 1999. *Qur'an and Woman. Rereading the Sacred Text from a Woman's Perspective.* New York : Oxford University Press,

Webb, Gisela. Ed., 2000. *Windows of Faith. Muslim Women Scholar-Activist in North America.* New York: Syracuse University Press.

Yafout, Miryam, 2012. *Le statut des femmes au sein des mouvements islamistes marocains: entre exégèse au féminin et participation politique. Le cas des femmes appartenantes à Al-'aadl wa al-iḥsān et au MUR/PJD,* PhD Thesis in Sociology, University of Casablanca-Ain Chok.

Yamani, Mai, 1996. *Feminism and Islam. Legal and Literary Perspectives.* Londra: Ithaca Press.

Personal interviews

Ahmed Abbadi, Rabat, 4 May 2012.
Asma Lamrabet, Rabat, 11 July 2012.
Ziba Mir-Husseini, Rabat, 3 April 2010.
Amina Wadud, London, 11 September 2012.

Chapter **7**

DECOLONIZING FEMINISM

A Look At Fatema Mernissi's Work
And Its Legacy[1]

Raja Rhouni

> *It is necessary to avoid generalizing, to avoid projecting on poor women our own preoccupations and problems, and, above all, to do our work as intellectuals. By this I mean: to develop our listening capacity, to be sure that we hear everything, even those things that don't fit into our theories and pretty constructs. (Fatema Mernissi 1988, p. 176)*

> *A ritual is established whereby the writer appeals to religion as the cause of gender inequality just as it is made the source of underdevelopment in much of modernization theory. ...(Marnia Lazreg 1988, p. 87)*

Introduction: Decolonizing feminism

The above statement of Fatema Mernissi urges feminist scholars to be open minded and develop their 'listening capacity' to listen. As a major feminist scholar and activist in Morocco, Mernissi was pioneering in giving the floor to marginalized female voices; illiterate women, peasants, factory workers or maidservants, as early as the 1970s. Her work has been concerned with identifying and critiquing the different structures that oppress women as well as highlighting the strategies of resistance they adopt in their daily struggle for dignity and decent livelihood. However, according to Marnia Lazreg (1988) Mernissi did not listen enough. Lazreg criticizes 'the religious paradigm' in the social sciences' scholarship and feminist writings on the Maghreb region, namely a focus on religion as the major factor explaining *the plight of Muslim women* (Lazreg 1988, p.83–85) Mernissi is criticized as belonging to those scholars who construct women as homogenous non-historical beings, and thereby colonize their voices. Like other postcolonial feminist scholars such as Chandra Mohanty (1984) or Gayatri Spivak (1986; 1988), Lazreg argues that Western feminist writings on Maghrebi women follow up on the colonial discourse, in that they consider Islam as inevitably antifeminist and impervious to change. Religion ought to be abandoned for Maghrebi women to attain the liberation Western women have achieved; preference is given to specific themes like the veil, seclusion, or clitoridectomy. According to Lazreg, however: "Religion cannot be detached from the socio-economic and political context within which it unfolds. And religion cannot be seen as having an existence independent of human activity" (Lazreg 1988, p. 95). Focusing exclusively on religion, moreover impedes any serious apprehension of the living reality of women in the region and therefore hinders change and women's empowerment.

Whereas Lazreg rightly criticizes Mernissi's 1975 study, *Beyond the Veil: Male Female Dynamics in Muslim Society* (1987a),[2] as being overtly secularist in character, Mernissi's stances have changed significantly in the years after. *Beyond the Veil* does entail an unambiguous secularist critique that identifies Islam as the main stumbling block to women's rights, as discussed below. However, Lazreg ignores the way Mernissi's standpoint has shifted since the late 1980s towards a position that has been identified as 'Islamic feminism,' one that sees Islam as possessing the tools of women's empowerment rather than the opposite. Lazreg also fails to highlight the way Mernissi's work even in its secularist phase demonstrates another interesting model of a decolonized feminism, namely an anti-capitalist feminist critique that targets capitalism as an important structure of women's oppression. It is these two important paths towards decolonization that this paper seeks to highlight, using Lazreg's critical insights, which remain valid not only to revisit Mernissi's work, but also to continue imagining an enabling decolonized feminism.

From Lazreg's approach, that we need a decolonized feminism, this paper summarizes the – sometimes thorny – journey that Mernissi's feminist scholarship has undertaken towards decolonization. I will evaluate to what extent Mernissi's work comprises such a decolonized feminism that allows ordinary women's voices to emerge. I will argue that Mernissi's work is a guidepost for feminists today, both in Morocco and around the globe.

Mernissi's Secular Feminism and the Religious Paradigm

On closer look, Mernissi's study *Beyond the Veil*, criticized by Lazreg (1988, 103) appears to be both a critique of colonialist premises and a reproduction of these very assumptions. Mernissi starts her book by an unequivocal criticism of Eurocentrism:

> It is a well-established tradition to discuss the Muslim woman by comparing her, implicitly or explicitly, to the Western woman. This tradition reflects the general pattern prevailing in both East and West when the issue is "who is more civilized than whom." In this book, I am not concerned with contrasting the way women are treated in the Muslim East with the way they are treated in the Christian West. I believe that sexual inequality is the basis of both systems. (7–8)

Mernissi makes it clear that the liberation of women is an indigenous project that has, nonetheless, regressed as an effect of colonial aggression of Arab soil and culture: "Muslims found themselves defending anachronistic institutions (by many Muslims' own standards) such as polygamy, arguing for example that it is better to institutionalize man's polygamous desires than to force him to have secret mistresses" (7). She further argues that, contrary to a widespread belief in the West, Islam does not have an ideology of female inferiority. Women are, on the contrary, believed to be strong beings whose potential power of social disruption is feared; hence the attempt to contain this female power through customs and practices like the sexual segregation of space.

Next to this critique on western approaches, *Beyond the Veil* voices an explicit secularist critique that produces Islam as essentially against gender equality, being based on a fundamental principle of sexual segregation and patriarchal norms. She states from the outset, for example: "In this book, I want to demonstrate that there is a fundamental contradiction between Islam as interpreted in official policy and equality between the sexes." Yet even when she might be viewed as only targeting *"Islam as interpreted in official policy"*, in this case, the Moroccan Personal Status Code or Moudawana, Mernissi makes essentialist statements about Islam (as a divine message). She continues: "Sexual equality violates Islam's premises, actualized in its laws, that heterosexual love is dangerous to Allah's order." (9) Significantly, in this respect, she ends her preface by the following statement: "One wonders if a desegregated society, where formerly secluded women have equal rights not only economically but sexually, would be an authentic Muslim society." (9) The book is a plea for the Moroccan postcolonial state to embrace modernity and universal human rights and abandon Islam as a source of family legislation.

It is important to note that the secular, modernist position displayed in a book written in the beginning of the 1970s was in tune with the times. The book is originally Mernissi's PhD dissertation in sociology written between 1970 and 1973 at Brandeis University, Massachusetts. In the United States at that time, the feminist movement is in its apogee. In an interview, Mernissi mentions that at the time she was at Brandeis, it was home to important figures like Herbert Marcuse, considered the father of the student movement in the US and one of the finest theorists of the New Left, and Angela Davis, a radical African-American activist for human rights and Marcuse's student (Mernissi 1996, p.110) Before Brandeis, Mernissi had studied political sciences at the Sorbonne in Paris and Mohammed V University in Rabat, where, like a number of key figures of Moroccan feminism, she took part in the national student movement UNEM (*Union National des Étudiants Marocains*), the breeding-ground of leftist politics during the tumultuous era of political repression, known as 'the Years of Lead.' At the time, the Moroccan regime, like other authoritarian governments in the region that aligned with the United States, was encouraging political Islam as the antidote to 'the threat of communism.' This political background helps explain the distrust of Mernissi and a number of intellectuals in Morocco towards Islamism and Islam as an 'ideology'. Mernissi's first foreign destination, France, is also the fertile ground of leftist politics, culminating in the tumultuous events of May 68.[3] These biographical elements explain the secularist position and the Marxist feminist approach that characterize Mernissi's critique in the 1970s up until the beginning of the 1980s.

Mernissi's secularist stance towards Islam has easily lent itself to various critiques in addition to Lazreg's, especially since the 1980s. Her position was found guilty of a failure to distinguish between Islam as a divine message (understood here to be fundamentally egalitarian), and its patriarchal human interpretation, Islam and *fiqh* (here the Maliki school, or rather its positive codification), or Islam and the Moudawana. The book was also criticized for its selective, reductionist and ahistorical, literalist approach. Criticism also questioned the solidity of the claim that purports to study "male-female dynamics in a modern society," as the title announces, by referring to medieval interpretation of Islamic sources.[4]

However, one thing that Mernissi's secularist critique avoids doing at this stage of her scholarship is to single out Islam as the only explanatory factor behind women's oppression in Morocco. Her subsequent writings, based on pioneering interviews with lower class women, target state capitalism and its exploitation of female labor. Her efforts to give voice to the marginalized is also a laudable and landmark initiative, that offers lessons today on how to subvert 'the religious paradigm' and address more pressing issues for ordinary women in the region.

Displacing the Paradigm of Religion through an Anti-Capitalist Critique

Mernissi's fieldwork studies written in the 1970s and beginning of 1980s are among the first and most invigorating feminist critiques of capitalism and the weakening of women's power with the integration of the various Third World countries into the capitalist world market; and it is unfortunate that this aspect of her work is not well known or discussed. Her essays "The Degrading Effect of Capitalism on Female Labour in a Third World Economy" (1978–79), "*Le Proletariat féminin au Maroc*" (The Female Proletariat in Morocco, 1980), "Women and the Impact of Capitalist Development" (1982–3), "Zhor's World: A Moroccan Domestic Worker Speaks Out" (1982), or *Doing Daily Battle: Interviews with Moroccan Women* (1988) represent one of the first attempts in Morocco and in the world, at the time, to make visible subaltern women's labor and its non-avowed importance for the economy. The fact that they are largely ignored in the West, at least in comparison to her books on Islam, is in itself revealing of the entrenchment of Orientalism and its paradigms.

It is important to delineate the cultural and intellectual background of this particular aspect of Mernissi's work. The fieldwork studies are conducted after her return to Morocco in 1975, the year she starts teaching at the department of sociology at Mohammed V University. Mernissi has explained her choice to go back to Morocco, in spite of the many opportunities offered to her in the States after her graduation from Brandeis, to be motivated by a desire to be deeply rooted in her society (Mernissi 1996, p 102). In Morocco, she finds a team of sociologists *engagés* like the late Paul Pascon, Abdelkébir Khatibi or Mohammed Guessous, who were animated by the desire to produce a decolonized knowledge of the Moroccan society, focusing their attention on social classes, peasants or urban craftsmen whose history lay outside the scope of Orientalist (especially French) scholarship. It is noteworthy that a member of their team is a woman, Malika Belghiti, who is the first sociologist to have conducted fieldwork on the condition of peasant women in Morocco, with whom Mernissi will work together a few years later.[5] Both this national spirit and the global atmosphere of social change, as described above, led Mernissi to give voice in her work to subaltern women; peasants, factory workers, or maidservants, in short those written out of national and international economic accounts and calculations. The value of Mernissi's work lies in gendering Moroccan sociology which at the time was characterized by a Marxian outlook that, in spite of its merits, tended to focus much of its attention on class as the privileged category of social analysis. Using an approach informed by both Marxism and feminism, her work strived to show that workers or peasants do not constitute a homogenous group and that, besides class, gender lenses are necessary to apprehend Moroccan society and the subalterns' reality.

Mernissi's first article, "The Degrading Effect of Capitalism on Female Labour in a Third World Economy," based on interviews with carpet weavers in 1977 and 1978 in Rabat and Salé, is one of the first attempts in Morocco and in the world at the time, to make visible subaltern women's labor and its non-avowed importance for the economy, and to show "how detrimental are the forces controlling the international capitalist market to the women's interest." (43) Mernissi's study underscores a consolidation of religious and scientific patriarchal discourses in obscuring women's labor. For Mernissi, modern concepts like 'unproductivity' and 'illiteracy,' in which the majority of illiterate women are categorized, have become legitimizing concepts for the exploitation of female labor.

In 1980, she publishes another article with the provocative title "Le Prolétariat féminin au Maroc" (The female proletariat in Morocco) which forces Moroccan sociologists to acknowledge and pay attention to the existence of a female proletariat, whose specificity lies in being subject to a double marginalization, based on class and gender. Mernissi observes women's exclusion from some important industrial sectors, like the sugar industry, their lack of access to professional training and technological knowledge, their absence from permanent job positions created in key industries and their concentration in seasonal jobs. She strongly concludes that women's employment conditions as observed in Morocco necessitate a radical change, which must take into consideration a fundamental element: recognizing women who belong to poor classes as legitimate job applicants within the national job market. This also propels the state, she continues, to provide nurseries and generalized structures of education and professional training (356).

One year later, Mernissi publishes another landmark study "Women and the Impact of Capitalist Development," which as the title suggests, seeks to assess the impact of capitalist development, or rural modernization as imagined by the state, on peasant women's material lives. From interviews with both women and state technicians, juxtaposing their worldviews, rises a "fundamental *contradiction* between the statements of the peasant women on development, and those of the planners, directors and agents of this development, the vast majority of who are men" (69). Women's narratives show that what the state calls 'rural modernization' meant more burdens and a further lowering of their social status. Rural modernization appears to be primarily a technical project designed to ameliorate the technological aspect of agriculture in large production units, which are either owned by the state or private investors, usually city-dwellers. It ignores the needs of small landowners and agricultural workers, especially women. She also argues that the destruction of small agricultural unit, or family farms, due to the expansion of large state-owned or private farms, has not been accompanied by the creation of wage labor for people in rural areas; and even in cases where they are created, she continues, the scarce jobs are mainly designed for men (72). Mernissi concludes: "the prevailing view of development—of its models, its practices, and its values—is essentially a male view," hence her desire to juxtapose it with the female peasant's worldview (69).

In addition to her critique of capitalism and the male, urban and bourgeois biases of state development policies and their negative impact on subaltern working women, another objective of her interviews is to trace women's resistance to the patriarchal system. One of the conclusions she reaches in "The Degrading Effects of Capitalism on Women's Labor" is that young women are "dropping out from [the] traditional value system altogether" (45), inciting them to be patient and submissive. Mernissi states that women start voicing purely economic concerns: illiteracy, unemployment, exploitation, inflation, or uncertainty about jobs and pay. She concludes that this is a major shift in women's self-perception.

But did the feminist imperative to shed light on subaltern women's agency and resistance to traditional norms, foster or, on the contrary, impede Mernissi's 'listening capacity'? Let's have a look at Mernissi's article 'Zhor's World': does Mernissi's approach allow for the subaltern to be heard?

The Feminist, the Subaltern and the Perils of Representation: Can the Subaltern Speak?

Published in 1982, "Zhor's World: A Moroccan Domestic Worker Speaks Out" is another instance that epitomizes Mernissi's project of foregrounding the voice of the female subaltern. The title of the study strongly suggests Mernissi's ambition to redefine the status of the Moroccan maidservant as a legitimate worker. For Mernissi, the interview with Zhor indicates the aspirations and the desire of this category of underprivileged working women for economic independence. These women, she argues, no longer dream only to have a husband who provides for them, but aspire to a regular paid job. It is necessary to emphasize here that Mernissi's objective is to prove that the patriarchal model of the family promoted by the Moudawana is obsolete. She argues that the paradigm of *nafaqa-ta'a* (alimony in exchange for obedience) at the heart of the 1957 Moudawana is untenable, since the male is no longer the sole family provider, as demonstrated by the situation of the maids whom she has interviewed. It is this agenda that makes Mernissi fall prey to the pitfalls of representation and authority. Mernissi prompts Zhor to speak on different subjects seemingly designed to capture her spontaneous worldview, but which unwittingly controvert such spontaneity. First, one can argue that the mere organization of Zhor's narrative under particular headings displays Mernissi's hand at work in framing this narrative. The headings interrupt the free flow of Zhor's voice, which becomes caught within the power relations between the (feminist) *representer* (Mernissi) and the (subaltern) *represented* (Zhor). Mernissi's framing power is clearer in a section under the heading "God, Hope, and Education." Zhor is never left room to express herself freely on the meaning of God, and the place of religion in her life as the first question addressed to her on this topic is overtly leading: "Do you think that God helps the poor?" to which Zhor, not surprisingly, answers with silence, as Mernissi stresses. The question and Mernissi's emphasis on Zhor's incapacity to answer, suggest the strong presence of Marxist ideas, namely the Marxist distrust of religion being the opium of the people that distracts the proletariat from challenging the capitalist system that oppresses them.

Another revealing sub-head, "Status and Clothing: The Veil, Symbol of Poverty," displays the preoccupations of a native feminist author, with a certain agenda, writing for a Western feminist audience. Zhor's transcribed narrative never includes mention of the *veil* per se; she only speaks about the marginalizing aspect of wearing a poor traditional dress, a poor *Djellaba*, as opposed to Western dress (or to fancy Djellabas nowadays), in a highly class-conscious Moroccan society. The 'text' or narrative of the protagonist, Zhor, published in an American feminist journal, *Feminist Issues*, is infiltrated by the discourse of a Western feminist's sympathetic concern for 'the plight of the Muslim woman,' which becomes evident in the use of the word 'veil.' Zhor's voice thus has become a commodity for

western feminist consumption. In "Zhor's World," the feminist representer's consciousness is exalted at the expense of Zhor's own
consciousness; Zhor cannot really speak.

What is more pernicious is the way the reader's attention is devi-
ated from class oppression and the material conditions producing
female pauperization that Zhor's narrative reveals in favor of issues of
veiling and religious oppression. The presence of the Veil as a signifier
in "Zhor's World" is an instance of the colonization of subaltern women's
voices and struggles as well as an example of the way Muslim feminist
writings reproduce the religious paradigm by concentrating on Islam
and veiling, producing an undesired obliteration of socio-economic
issues. This neglect further alienates subaltern women and stresses
their inability to speak through the medium of feminism.

But if Mernissi's secularist feminist critique cannot fully achieve
decolonization, what happens in her later work? Does her adoption of
a feminist position sympathetic to Islam, necessarily guarantee decolonization? To answer this question I will now turn to her *The Veil and
the Male Elite: a Feminist Interpretation of Islam* (1991), which is considered one of the foundational texts of Islamic feminism.

Decolonizing Feminism by Theorizing Islamic Feminism

Originally written in 1987 as *Le Harem Politique: Le Prophète et les
femmes* (Mernissi 1987b), *The Veil and the Male Elite* is a text that
marks a radical shift from Mernissi's earlier secularist position to
what has been described as 'Islamic feminism.' The text comprises a
critique of women's oppressed positions, which advocates women's
rights and equality, on the basis of an egalitarian interpretation of
Islamic faith, rather than arguing against it. The notoriety of Mernissi
in addition to the originality of her endeavor greatly contributed to
the theorization and dissemination of this new feminist paradigm,
tracing an interesting route for a decolonized feminism. However,
this decolonization is undermined by the inadvertent endorsement
of an Orientalist approach.

Although Mernissi has never explained the reasons behind her
change of perspective, an examination of the context of the production of the book allows us to see the change as a result of both an

intellectual development and a response to a changing socio-political reality, rather than an abrupt volte-face. In their efforts to contextualize her transition, Rebecca Barlow and Shahram Akbarzadeh (2006) stress the socio-economic and political context of the 1980s in which Mernissi's text is produced. They note the way the economic crisis of the 1980s in Morocco has led to a widespread distrust of western secularism and modernization in Moroccan society and the rise of Islamism as a popular discourse. Within this context, they argue, "it appeared necessary for Fatima Mernissi to redefine her feminist project in a manner that Muslim women perceived as a more authentic accommodation of modernity to their religion and culture (1486). However, an overview of Mernissi's scholarship shows that this shift is not simply a response to a changing socio-political situation, but a gradual and thoughtful intellectual progression.

A major moment of this transition is her encounter with male progressive scholars of Islam who advocated reform of women's rights using Islamic arguments. Mernissi takes part in a multidisciplinary research group on "Woman, Family and Child," created in 1981, where she encounters Ahmed Khamlichi, a member of the national council of ulama and an advocate of the reform of the Moudawana. In his writings, Khamlichi makes a clear distinction between Sharia and *fiqh*; for him, while the first is divine, the second is human and subject to change, and since the Moudawana is issued from Maliki fiqh, it is not sacred and might be subject to reform using *ijtihad*.[6] Khamlichi's insights have no doubt served to shake Mernissi's secularist take on Islam. It is significant to note that Mernissi mentions his name in the acknowledgement page of *The Veil and the Male Elite*, as her main source.

The discovery of Sufi Islam is another equally important factor of this change. In 1984, she publishes a series of articles in the magazine *Jeune Afrique*, collected in 1986 and published in a book entitled *L'Amour dans les pays musulmans* (Love in Muslim countries). The book marks the turning point in Mernissi's feminist trajectory. Its thesis is in complete opposition to *Beyond the Veil*; Islam is not against love. Mernissi discovers the way Sufi Islam granted women a more egalitarian status, allowing an important female mystic like Rabia Adawiya. In contrast to her earlier works, which rely on the androcentric interpretation of some orthodox male theologians, the present book sheds light on liberal religious scholars, who preached faithfulness in heterosexual relationships, like Andalusian scholar Ibn Hazm (born in 384 Hegira [994 AD]).

In *The Veil and the Male Elite*, Mernissi re-reads the Qur'an and the Prophet's tradition using a contextual approach that highlights the way the egalitarian or feminist aspects of the religion as preached by the Prophet were compromised, distorted or simply forgotten. She fore-grounds the important public roles played by women especially Mohammed's wives, like Aisha or Umm Salama. She also highlights how the new religion granted them spiritual equality with men in addition to property rights, for example. However, the revolutionary social project of the Prophet, she continues, is subject to a strong male resistance that stopped its impetus and brought about a resurgence of Jahiliya misogy-nous norms and values. The book sets to restore the original egalitarian aspect of the religion through a corrective revision of some texts, in the Qur'an and the Hadith, which supposedly supports women's inferior social status in Islam. The *Veil and the Male Elite* offers a very interesting revision of a few misogynous hadiths that are believed to be sound but that Mernissi sees as incongruous with the egalitarian politics of Prophet Mohammed. She also offers an interesting contextual and his-torical reading of a few verses in the Qur'an.

However, in spite of comprising a model of a decolonized femi-nism, *The Veil and the Male Elite* in some respects still reproduces the Orientalist approach to the study of Middle Eastern women's issues. From the onset of the book, Mernissi justifies her investigation of a hadith discouraging women from political leadership, "Those who entrust their affairs will never know prosperity," by its importance in explaining the weak presence of Moroccan women in politics in the late 1970s and 80s. Mernissi's legitimizing strategy is problematic as it makes religion the primary explanatory factor behind women's low political representation. It serves to occlude other factors usually taken into consideration when accounting for women's low partici-pation like the level of education (or here illiteracy), access to information and training in professions leading to positions of power, or the workload for women with families. Overemphasizing religious issues at the expense of development issues reinforces the idea of the entrenchment of the religious paradigm in Mernissi's work.

Conclusion: Mernissi's legacy and decolonization

The above division of Mernissi's feminist scholarship in its two phases, secularist and Islamic, provides important insights to the reflection on an enabling decolonized feminism. In her secular stage, we saw how Mernissi reproduced the Orientalist assumptions of an oppressive Islam, yet her critique of capitalism as an equally powerful structure of violence subverts the religious paradigm. The above analysis also revealed how Mernissi strived to make the subaltern women's voices audible to the State, yet her secularist feminist agenda stifled at times the subaltern's voice, inadvertently resulting in its colonization. Mernissi's Islamic feminist work clearly departs from and undermines the Orientalist discourse on Islam, but contains some remainders of it as well, namely a unilateral focus on religion as *the* factor explaining the underrepresentation of women in politics, while ignoring socio-economic and developmental obstacles.

It is significant to note in this respect that the shift Mernissi takes towards Islamic feminism in the 1980s is accompanied by an intriguing abandonment of her anti-capitalist critique, and it is both regrettable and instructive that this takes place at the moment when anti-capitalist feminist politics is most needed. The 1980s saw the social ravages of neoliberalism as the Structural Adjustment Programs represent which had pernicious impact particularly on women in vulnerable social classes.[7] This kind of retreat interestingly mirrors the situation of American feminism as critically described by American philosopher Nancy Fraser (2013) in an article she published recently in the Guardian with the provocative and suggestive title "How Feminism Became Capitalism's Handmaiden – and How to Reclaim it." Frazer discusses the way the American feminist "movement which started out as a critique of capitalist exploitation ended up contributing key ideas to its latest neoliberal phase." This is the result of feminism's gradual neglect of redistribution, or socio-economic issues, in favor of recognition, identity and cultural issues, which "dovetailed with neoliberalism's interest in diverting political-economic struggles into culturalist channels." This incisive assessment seems not to be restricted to the American, or Western, context alone, but describes the state of feminism in other parts of the world as well.

This critique could be extended to assess feminist activism in Morocco today, as it has tended to be mainly civil and legalistic, focusing on recognition at the expense of redistribution. Eddouada (2003), who studied two important women's organizations, ADFM and UAF, signals this shortcoming in the Moroccan feminist movement in the conclusion of her doctoral dissertation. It is ironic that Moroccan feminism was at its very inception the child of the left (albeit unwanted and rebellious) yet grew up dropping its audacity and utopian energies by losing touch with material issues like inequality and poverty. Salime (2007), has already showed how feminist action, in both its secular and Islamist variants, contributed to making hegemonic the narrative of the War on Terror after the Casablanca bombings in 2003 and the Moroccan state's alignment with the US foreign policy and its decision to promote a moderate Islam through mobilizing feminism. This complicity is the indirect result of women's organizations' appropriation of the major themes of this narrative. Women activists, Salime suggested, emerged as agents of the State. Building on Salime's study, Eddouada and Pepicelli (2012) discuss the way the State appropriated or co-opted the discourse of Islamic feminism to embellish its image on the international scene, producing what she identified as "Islamic State feminism". Therefore, feminists, whether secular, Islamic or Islamist, emerged as the handmaiden of the State and the US foreign policy. To what extent they have become the handmaiden of capitalism or neoliberal economic policies locally is a question that invites further explorations.

To conclude, I would like to state that the critical revision of Fatema Mernissi's work presented here was not intended to debase Mernissi's brilliant work but to continue learning from it, which is the best tribute we can pay to it today. It has rather sought to identify the obstacles impeding feminism's listening capacity and reflect on ways to restore or enhance its critical cutting edge.

Notes

1 Although in many of her publications Mernissi's first name is spelled "Fatima," Mernissi herself spells it as "Fatema;" see her website http://www.mernissi.net/.
2 I am using the revised edition of *Beyond the Veil*, published in 1987.
3 I must say that, to my knowledge, she has never evoked being in Paris during those events. However, the account she has given of her stay in France corresponds to this period.
4 See, Rhouni 2010; Barlas 2005; Zayzafoon 2005; Majid1998.

5 For an account of sociology in Morocco, see Rachik and Bourqia (2011), and Tozy (2013).
6 See for example a text co-written with another Moroccan scholar of Islamic law, Abderrazak Moulay Rchid (Khamlichi and Moulay Rchid1981).
7 See, for instance, Skalli (2001).

References

Barlow, Rebecca, and Shahram Akbarzadeh, 2006. "Women's Rights in the Muslim World: Reform or Reconstruction?" *Third World Quarterly* 27, no. 8: 1481–94.

Barlas, Asma, 2005. "Qur'anic Hermeneutics and Women's Liberation." Paper presented at the International Congress on Islamic Feminism, Barcelona, Spain, October 29. http://www.asmabarlas.com/TALKS/Barcelona.pdf accessed on May 29, 2014

Eddouada, Souad, 2003. *Women, Gender and the State in Morocco: Contradictions, Constraints and Prospects*. A thesis submitted in partial fulfilment of the requirement of Mohammed v University for the degree of Doctorat National. Mohammed V University, Rabat, Morocco.

Eddouada, Souad, and Renata Pepicelli. 2012. *Morocco: Towards an Islamic State Feminism*. Publication. SciencePO, 2012. Web. <http://www.sciencespo.fr/ceri/sites/sciencespo.fr.ceri/files/ci_feminism_iran_se_rp.pdf>.

Fraser, Nancy. 2013. "How feminism became capitalism's handmaiden – and how to reclaim it", the Guardian, Monday 14 October 2013. http://www.theguardian.com/commentisfree/2013/oct/14/feminism-capitalist-handmaiden-neoliberal, (accessed on Sep.1, 2014).

Khamlichi, Ahmed, and Abderrazak Moulay Rachid. 1981. "Moudawanat al-ahwal al-shakhssia ba'da khamsata 'ashara sanatin min suduriha" [The Moudawana: Fifteen years after its issue]. *Al-Majalla al-maghribia li al-qanun wa al-siyassa wa al-iqtissad* [The Moroccan magazine of law, politics, and economics], no. 10 (1981): 128–53.

Lazreg, Marnia. 1988. "Feminism and Difference: The Perils of Writing as a Woman on Women in Algeria." *Feminist Studies* 14, no. 1: 81–107.

Majid, Anouar. 1998. "The Politics of Feminism in Islam." *Signs: Journal of Women in Culture and Society* 23, 2 : 321–61.

Mernissi, Fatima. 1979. "The Degrading Effect of Capitalism on Female Labour in a Third World Economy: The Particular Case of Craftswomen in Morocco," *Peuples Méditerranéens* [Mediterranean peoples] 6: 41–57

Mernissi, Fatima. 1980. "Le Prolétariat féminin au Maroc". *Annuaire de l'Afrique du Nord* [Yearbook of North Africa], 345–356. Paris: Centre National de la Recherche Scientifique (CNRS).

Mernissi, Fatima. 1982 a. "Women and the Impact of Capitalist Development in Morocco." Pt. 1. *Feminist Issues* 2, 2: 69–104.

Mernissi, Fatima. 1982 b. Zhor's World: A Moroccan Domestic Worker Speaks Out." *Feminist Issues* 2, 1: 3–31

Mernissi, Fatima, 1983. "Women and the Impact of Capitalist Development in Morocco." Pt. 2. *Feminist Issues* 3, no. 1: 61–112.

Mernissi, Fatima. 1986. *L'A mour dans les pays musulmans*. Casablanca: Editions Maghrébines.

Mernissi, Fatima. 1987 a. *Beyond the Veil: Male-Female Dynamics in Modern Muslim Society*. 1975. Rev. ed. Bloomington: Indiana University Press.

Mernissi, Fatima. 1987b. *Le Harem politique: le Prophète et les femmes* [The political harem: The Prophet and women]. Paris: Albin Michel.

Mernissi, Fatima. 1988. *Doing Daily Battle: Interviews with Moroccan Women*. Translated by Mary Jo Lakeland. London: The Women's Press.

Mernissi, Fatima. 1991. *The Veil and the Male Elite: A Feminist Interpretation of Women's Rights in Islam*. Translated by Mary Jo Lakeland. New York: Addison-Wesley.

Mernissi, Fatima. 1996. "Fatima Mernissi." Interview by Serge Ménager. *Le Maghreb littéraire* [The literary Maghreb], 2, 4: 87–119.

Mohanty, Chandra Talpade. 1984. "Under Western Eyes: Feminist Scholarship and Colonial Discourses" In *Third World Women and the Politics of Feminism*. " Boundary 2 12 (3) :333–58

Rachik, Hassan, and Rahma Bourqia. 2014. "La sociologie au Maroc ", *SociologieS*, Théories et recherches http://sociologies.revues.org/3719 (accessed on Sep. 30, 2014).

Rhouni, Raja. 2010. *Secular and Islamic Feminist Critiques in the Work of Fatima Mernissi*. Leiden: Brill.

Skalli, Loubna H. 2001. "Women and Poverty in Morocco: The Many Faces of Social Exclusion". *Feminist Review* 69 (1): 73–89

Spivak, Gayatri Chakravorty. 1988. "Three Women's Texts and a Critique of Imperialism." "Race," In *Writing, and Difference*, edited by. Henry Louis Gates, Jr., 262–80. Chicago: University of Chicago Press.

Spivak, Gayatri Chakravorty. 1988. Can the Subaltern Speak?" In *Marxism and the Interpretation of Culture*, edited by Cary Welson and Larry Grossberg, 271–313. Chicago: University of Chicago Press.

Tozy, Mohamed. 2013. "Paul Pascon : un pionnier de la sociologie marocaine", *SociologieS* [Online], Discoveries/rediscoveries, Paul Pascon, Online since 20 février 2013, http://sociologies.revues.org/4322 (accessed on Sep.30, 2014).

Zayzafoon, Lamia Ben Youssef. 2005. *The Production of the Muslim Woman: Negotiating Text, History, and Ideology*. New York: Lexington Books.

Zakia Salime. 2007. The War on Terrorism: Appropriation and Wubversion by Moroccan Women. *Signs*, Vol 33(1): 1–24.

Chapter 8

DECONSTRUCTING FEMALE IDENTITIES WITHIN A POLYPHONY OF FEMINIST VOICES

Soumaya Belhabib

> "It is not our differences that divide us. It is our inability to recognize, accept, and celebrate those differences."
>
> Audre Lorde, *Our Dead Behind Us: Poems*

Introduction

This chapter addresses the female identity issue as a theoretical paradigm where various social, economic, cultural, linguistic and ethnic criteria intervene. Women do not only have multi-layered identities but they are often confronted with various competing socio-cultural models and influences which put them at the heart of the ongoing ideological, philosophical and religious questioning that society goes through. The objective of this chapter is to show that this diversity in women's profiles cannot be represented by one single type of feminist leadership but that it necessarily gives rise to a polyphony of feminist stands with often diverging perceptions of gender equality and justice. I analyze first the way Moroccan women's identity is constructed drawing on intersectionality theory. I argue then that the social cleavage between modernity and tradition enhances patriarchal conservative dogmas while promoting more progressive modern ideals. I show thus how this is translated into two major feminist discourses, the progressive liberal one and the conservative Islamic one. In fact, different types of feminism are emerging due to the diversity in Moroccan society today, the multiple influences of globalization, and the endless virtual possibilities of technology. I conclude with the assumption that even if these 'feminisms' don't always agree, they nevertheless manage through opposing positions to advance women's rights and be in that way truly representative of all identities.

A recent nomination this year has shown that women are gaining visibility and power in the socio-political scene of Morocco. Zineb El Addaoui is the first woman, in the history of Morocco, to be appointed governor (Wali) of the region Gharb-Chrarda-BniHssen, in the province of Kenitra. She was nominated by King Mohamed VI on January 21st, 2014. However, the nomination of a female governor was not received with unanimous support. A colonel of the military auxiliary forces refused to shake hands with El Addaoui, and avoided attending any official activity in which she would be present[1] He declared that for reasons related to his "religious beliefs," he did not want to shake hands with a woman governor.

Such an incident reflects the profound changes in Moroccan gender roles, but it also reveals the way Moroccan men find it difficult to dissociate gender from a function or official status. Within a male dominated context of administrative power, the unusual presence of a woman governor has destabilized a hierarchical order acquainted until then with exclusively male leadership. For this colonel, the sole identity parameter that mattered was her female gender; her status as a 'Governor' was erased by her identity as a woman. His patriarchal mindset, reinforced by the military masculine system to which he belongs, took over his professional status and did not allow him to accept new gender relationships within the public sphere. The usual set order is being shaken as new gender paradigms emerge.

This event reveals a number of social and cultural changes that are taking place at different levels. It is one signal among many that the process of change is already on the move, that modernity, as a transformational dynamic process, is taking hold and that, as it usually happens in these cases, there are those who oppose it and who seek to resist change. Such an overall state can indeed be delineated in various conflicting situations where gender relations are questioned, rearticulated and readjusted. Women appear as the challenging element that comes to disturb a long established order, based on an ancestral patriarchal system in which men's interest prevail.

The public/private sphere issue is being questioned as new gender relationships and regulations emerge within the public sphere, which has been exclusively masculine for so long. Today, women are slowly entering that space, and men must accept this. Long established practices and attitudes are being reinvented, which leads to unexpected reactions of resistance like that of the colonel.

The notion of female leadership is also interrogated here. While female leadership is relatively tolerated and accepted within the private economic sector due to the financial gains it involves, it is still rejected within the more 'official' governmental public sector, which represents the strongly masculinized state power.

These are just some of the implications related to the incident reported above. It is significant to note that competing visions are at stake and that women's attitudes are often under scrutiny. While they are struggling to push for more democracy and equality, Moroccan women and their status are frequently invoked as a barometer for the country's 'progress'. As Morocco is fighting in the midst of a debate between tradition and modernization, between islamization and secularization, between conservatism and liberalism, etc., women appear to be, as they always have been, in the spotlight.

So in order to understand the contradictions that Morocco is facing within its quest for a coherent, unified national identity, it is essential to know who Moroccan women are, what female identity looks like, and what kind of diversity we have. The purpose of this chapter is to consider the way Moroccan women evolve, creating new identity paradigms and see to what extent are these included in the feminist movement demands. With a large spectrum of profiles, feminism in Morocco is inherently pluralist as other needs and priorities emerge. The feminist movement is becoming polyphonic, displaying unique perspectives in its quest to cope with the needs and expectations of all women. The question is: does this multi-faceted feminism serve the main objectives of women, or does it weaken the whole process by creating diverging directions? The cohabitation of different models of feminism raises the issue of whether this diversity contributes to a peaceful coexistence or whether it enhances already existing conflicts.

How is Moroccan Female Identity Constructed?

"Identity is formed in the 'interaction' between self and society" (Stuart Hall, 1996); such an interactive conception of identity and the self[2] is at the basis of the ongoing transformations that the individual is going through and the uniqueness of the experience of each in his/her relationship with society. He/she is impacted by the social and cultural context in which he/she evolves, hence creating a reciprocal sense of stability and unity. People participate in the making of the idea of a nation, represented in the national culture with which they identify. This sense of belonging makes the individual feel secure and has the power to generate a reassuring sense of identity.

However, today the 'subject' is getting 'fragmented', becoming aware that his/her 'I' is far more complex, made up of several layers which lead to a sort of unique composition. There is a "shifting" process which takes the individual from the previously unified and stable identity to a fragmented one, "composed, not of a single, but of several, sometimes contradictory or unresolved, identities" (Hall,1996:598).The feminist theory of intersectionality[3] stems from the premise that people live multiple layered identities which leads them to experience at times both oppression and privilege simultaneously. For example, a female doctor may benefit from respect and privileges within the professional sphere, yet she might experience gender-based oppression and discrimination at home if she is a victim of domestic violence. Indeed, gender intersects with other identities related to a number of factors that include race, skin color, age, ethnicity, language, socio-economic class, religion, language, sexual orientation, geographic location, culture, etc. Each one of these factors intersects with others to create varied identities, thereby multiplying diversity and uniqueness at the same time.

Moroccan women, like all individuals, have multi-layered identities that can make their gender status differ from one woman to another. It is actually significant to see how the intersection of some identity factors can heighten the oppression of women while it can also allow them to be privileged in relation to others or merely reduced to one single identity parameter as has been Zineb El Addaoui when her female gender took over all the other factors that compose her identity.

For any observer of the Moroccan street, it is obvious that new identities profiles are emerging as society is moving ahead creating that social interaction that reciprocally impacts its people. There is not one single model to whom everyone can identify and cultural representations and practices are continuously being reinterpreted. Stuart Hall rightly explains that "the fully unified, completed, secure, and coherent identity is a fantasy. Instead, as the systems of meaning and cultural representation multiply, we are confronted by a bewildering, fleeting multiplicity of possible identities."(Hall, 1996, p.598). Moroccan women are constantly challenged by competing models, from the Western modern influence to the more traditional conservative one. The spectrum in between remains large as it can be a mix of specific identity layers that create endless possibilities. It can be the upper class uneducated pious 'Fassi'[4] woman, or the lower class working young mother from the northern region, or the educated active middle-class Berber woman, or else the elderly poor rural uneducated black widow, etc. Each woman would identify herself in an order of priorities with the criteria she considers most relevant to whom she thinks she is. "As a consequence of their multiple identities, some women are pushed to the extreme margins and experience profound discrimination while others benefit from privileged positions".[5] The intersectional approach reveals that women do not face the same difficulties in the same way and that oppression can be located differently depending on how converging identities overlap. The purpose is indeed to better assess and understand the needs of women as a result of the various facets that compose their identity and devise policies, programs and laws which would be more efficient in meeting their needs. Besides, what is essentially significant for the present analysis is the fact that women's multiple, layered identities mean that their expectations and claims cannot be the same for all. So could Moroccan women even be represented by one feminist leadership, or do they require other leaderships and feminisms?

Subverting Boundaries: Between Tradition and Modernity

With the challenges of globalization on the one hand and the traditional patriarchal ancestral culture on the other, women are often put in embarrassing positions as to which values to adopt. With the era of new technology, the inevitable modernization process of societies, and a large virtual world where previous frontiers are banished, people are exposed to diverse influences like never before. Because of this open framework, in which there is no control anymore, resisting attitudes and reactions develop. The ongoing changes that all communities undergo are to a large extent due to the modernizing process which inevitably invades various social spheres and which meets with resistance from the proponents of tradition and continuity. Modernity, usually inscribed within an unlimited process of change, tends to be defined as a mainly Western concept. Some base it on technological advancement, others on open-mindedness. As opposed to tradition which is defined as something old, rooted in culture and unchanging, modernity is associated with strangeness and outside influence. The usual research tends to associate "tradition with all that is 'native', while modernity implies something imposed from above, usually from the west"(Newcomb, 2006: 290). Hence, modern societies are identified as societies of constant, rapid, and permanent change while the traditional ones locate themselves within a sense of continuity with the past in order to preserve their 'authenticity'. The principal distinction between 'traditional' and 'modern' societies as Anthony Giddens argues is that

> "In traditional societies, the past is honored and symbols are valued because they contain and perpetuate the experience of generations. Tradition is a means of handling time and space...within the continuity of past, present and future, these in turn being structured by recurrent social practices"(Giddens, 1990: 37).

In modern societies, by contrast, it is a reflexive form of life with rapid, extensive, and continuous change, and in which "social practices are constantly examined and reformed in the light of incoming information about those very practices, thus constitutively altering their character" (Giddens, 1990: 38).

However, this does not mean that a clear cut division is to be made between 'modern' and 'traditional' societies. Such a binary opposition of Tradition vs. Modernity can be fallacious when putting them in contentious lights, and creating a value judgment position of one being 'better' than the other while they are rather simply one being different from the other. In fact,

"to sanction a practice because it is traditional will not do; tradition can be justified, but only in the light of knowledge which
is not itself authenticated by tradition. ...even in the most
modernized of modern societies, tradition continues to play a
role"(Giddens, 1990, p.39).

Actually, whenever such an issue is raised in most societies, the
female question is inevitably thrown at the forefront of the debate;
her position in the public sphere; her role within the family, how
she's needed to protect the social institution and preserve social
cohesion; how gender relations are impacted by new roles; and
above all how to preserve her role as 'guardian' of traditions. A number
of issues and long established practices are questioned as soon as
modernity is invoked.

The patriarchal system has been part of Morocco's culture for so
long that it has been acknowledged as the norm, hence providing a
sense of identity and security. Women, in spite of all the progressive
laws and changes that seek to establish equality, still stay subject to
the pressure of a patriarchal system, based on more insidious
implicit social 'laws' (those that are not written), which perpetuate
various inequalities between the sexes. Under the pretext that it is a
woman's role to preserve cultural ancestral values, on which is
based the identity of a whole nation, we legitimize inequality and
discriminatory treatments. Given the 'honorable' role of protecting
ancestral traditions, she finds herself reproducing and maintaining
values of subordination from within an archaic system she is herself
victim of. Besides, if the patriarchal system is the only one that a
society has been exposed to and the one that is continuously being
promoted, it is quite understandable that people may not want to
change it. However, due to the advantages that inevitably come with
modernity, the old system reveals itself to be inappropriate in
today's modern context; it must be challenged and reconsidered in
the light of the new exigencies of today's world, and it must include the
voices of all women.

Modernity does not necessarily bring modernization, nor is
modernity incompatible with tradition as the latter continues to
play an important role in any 'modern' society. And modernization
does not necessarily bring modernity (e.g. the Gulf countries are

modernized but not modern).In fact, the continuity and evolution of cultural values are at the basis of the identity-making process of societies. In any community, it is important to have a stable and agreed-upon point of reference; within Morocco, Islam has always been and still is a kind of secure 'value system'that brings people together and maintains cohesion within society. The feeling of belonging to a group comes from the ability to belong to one specific cultural identity. This is particularly true in the Maghreb for beyond the national and ethnic dimension, the identification to the Muslim community, the notion of 'Umma' (community of believers) can sometimes constitute a more important factor than the national or cultural one. Preserving Islam is not something that people are trying to challenge, they are strongly attached to its values and are simply asking for moving a little bit more towards its Islamic principles of tolerance and respect for all. The position of women in society is often interpreted trough different 'Islamic lenses,' from the most radical discourse to the more moderate one, stigmatizing them and putting them in over-simplified categories of 'modern' vs. 'traditional.' Hence, the Moroccan woman is constantly confronted with different models that exist side by side, competing. On one side, we find the model of the independent, hard-working modern woman, a model promoted by all the institutions of countries in process of democratization and modernization. On the other side, we find the traditional model of the submissive, passive woman, often glorified in her role of mother and wife, an image communicated through conservative and resistant cultural values, often supposedly legitimized by Islamic law.

This is the paradoxical situation of the Moroccan woman: how to preserve her own cultural identity with all the weight of the Arabo-Muslim culture from which it stems, and yet, have access to the advantages that modernity brings, without being accused of mere imitation of the West? She not only has to guarantee the safety of traditional customs and practices[6] but also to avoid being associated with 'imported' hegemonic values of the West. For the sake of preserving authentic family values and stabilizing the cohesion of a whole nation, the role of women within the family has always been a controversial issue. Recent declarations from the actual Islamist head of the government Abdelilah Benkirane in a parliamentary session[7] have not only triggered once again this long-term historical debate but also provoked the anger of the progressive secular feminists and human rights activists. By praising the 'sacred' role of housewives and deploring ancient times during which no woman worked, he is not only refuting the 'Western' model but also taking society backwards in terms of gains in women's rights. Such a discourse is meant to give back to housewives their real value as mothers and as essential 'family pillars', hence reaching a large number of non-working women who get no recognition and esteem for their work at home, neither from their peers, nor from their husbands nor from society at large. Under the pretext of upgrading women's role in the family, a more 'authentic' traditional female model is promoted.

However, it is obvious that social, political, economic and cultural transformations are taking place which are meant to lead societies towards more equity and justice, hence keeping one single model is no longer possible. Women are constantly reminded of their 'natural' role of procreating and child bearing while they also need to adapt themselves and keep up with the new demands that the era of globalization and new technology brings. Rachel Newcomb argues that in order to reconcile the two, the Moroccan government promotes a unitary vision of the "Moroccan woman" as "the guardian of Moroccan cultural values at home and the proponent of modernity outside her house" (Newcomb, 2006, p.305)[8]. By engaging in UN treatises and international conventions in terms of women's rights[9], Morocco is showing its move towards democracy and the establishment of a human rights state within the rest of the world. The local sociocultural values remain, however, prisoner of patriarchal practices and obsolete traditions.

Diverse Feminisms for Diverse Identities

With these opposing cultural frameworks and diverse identity profiles, women necessarily reveal significant differences in the way they define themselves and in their personal view of gender equality. The question is how the Moroccan feminist movement deals with that diversity, which is most liable to develop and extend over socioeconomic and geographical borders. What kind of discourse and ideological framework do feminists use to reach all women? Do they take that diversity into consideration or do they give priority to the realization of their advocacy agenda and its objectives?

When considering the ideological stand of feminism in its large sense, it is commonly referred to as one of the biggest social movements of this century that seeks to eradicate discrimination against women and call for equality between the sexes. Feminist ideology has a long history with different ideological trends and landmark waves (Bryson, 1992) and one of its major traits is that it stems from reality. In every period and in every society, feminism starts by identifying the causes of women's oppression in order to devise and lobby for the appropriate measures to be taken to annihilate these causes. Hence, any feminist perspective, in order to be effective, has to keep closely connected to the needs and the local understanding of what oppression means to the female community it stands for.

So is it reality that shapes feminist demands or is it feminism that changes reality? Though the process is not the same in both ways, it is clear that one necessarily impacts the other. On the one hand, for the feminist claims to be substantial and convincing, they need to be based on ethnographic research and reliable scholarly data, thus clearly located in reality. On the other hand, when a feminist agenda succeeds to further women's rights, this being its major objective, it also succeeds in impacting their lives by granting them more legal rights and challenging locally practiced discriminatory attitudes.

For the sake of keeping in line with the objective of this chapter, the focus will be put here on the first option to show how diverse women identity within a society which is continuously under the influence of new social paradigms is giving rise to a polyphony of feminist voices that cannot be reduced to one single vision. Today, a large literature would mostly refer to a plethora of feminisms (Badran, 2009; Sadiqi and Ennaji, 2005;Salime, 2012) as "feminisms are produced in particular places and are articulated in local terms" (Badran, 2009: 243). Concepts and theories around feminism have been delocalized, reinterpreted and reinvented throughout time and place. Each society adapts them to its socio-cultural and religious values to build up a coherent common ground on which one's identity is constructed.

Interestingly, as has been shown in the previous section, there are two antagonistic trends, the modernist vs. the conservative, that are evolving side by side and that promote a progressive Universalist model as opposed to a conservative Islamic one concerning women's rights in Morocco. Besides, researchers like Asmae Lamrabet[10] and El Madani[11] agree that "there is not one type of feminism in Morocco as there is not one type of Moroccan woman. In other words, the different types of feminisms correspond to the various needs and identities of the population". (Clark, 2013: 14).

When considering the development of the Moroccan feminist movement, two main trends emerge: the secular progressive one with a universal human rights bent which started in the 1980s (Howe, 2005; Sadiqi, 2008), coined as 'liberal' feminism, and the Islamic feminism which developed in the 1990s as a reaction to the former movement and which gained real visibility with the controversial reaction to the National Plan for Integrating Women in Development[12](Sadiqi, 2008; Salime, 2008).

In terms of the development process, the secular feminist movement has a long history of advocacy behind it. The reform of the *Mudawana* (family law) is the result of a long and tedious fight led by the liberal feminists. They had to fight the Islamic trend which was extremely critical of the supposedly Westernization of the movement, perceived as an "aggression towards the Muslim world and an assault on its Islamic identity" (Salime, 2008: 208). Islamism has opposed modernity, making a "confusion between the West and Modernity and takes the West, which may be defined as an incomplete historical manifestation of modernity, for modernity itself" (Sadiqi, 2008: 330).

On the other hand, the progressive 'modernist' feminists were also highly critical of the political affiliation of Islamic feminists regarding their 'feminist' agenda, which is seen to be manipulated to serve the interest of the political party they belong to. Another criticism oriented towards Islamic feminism is that their discourse about gender equality is liable to change whether we are within the private or the public sphere. While they challenge socio-political and economic rights within the public scene, in education, health, workforce, etc., they reconsider gender equality in terms of complementarity when it comes to the private sphere, and specifically within the family. Rajaa Naji[13] clearly makes the difference as she explains:

> When we speak of equality, in Islamic Feminism and simply in Feminism, I think that we make a great error, which is to mix the place of women in society and the place of women in the family. When we speak of complementarity, it's uniquely within the family, not in society. In society we are equals, men and women. (Clark, 2013: 48).

The understanding of gender equality here is considered through the classification of the three roles inherent to the concept of gender[14]. Priority is given to the reproductive role of women, as they take over childbirth, breastfeeding and the nurturing relationship between mother and child. There is a clear division of tasks, which according to this perception of gender roles is 'natural' as men and women have to assume specific roles within the family.

The antagonism between the pro-equality feminists and the pro-complementarity ones as to women's rights within the private sphere is actually linked to the main point of reference to which they relate themselves. The modernists feminist discourse finds its ideological values within the universal human rights framework while the conservative Islamist "discourse and practice is articulated within an Islamic paradigm" (Badran, 2009: 243), seen as a "return to authenticity" and to one's 'real' identity. More radical fundamentalist positions may bring additional nuances for other types of feminisms.

Despite these differences, women can easily relate a personal sense of oppression to a large-scale oppression within society as a whole. What is at stake is their 'womanism' which comes at the intersection of other identity parameters, like social class, education, geographical location, age, etc.. Another common identity criterion to most women is their Muslim identity, whether they adhere to secular or Islamic feminist values. Islam is a state religion in Morocco but it is also largely practiced and is fully integrated in people's beliefs and mode of living. Hence, in order to avoid marginalization and the threat of being labeled 'anti-religious', the secular liberal feminists integrated a religious discourse within the advocacy tools they use in order to reach a large majority of women who are deeply religious together with decision-makers and the population in general. Islamic feminists also included a universal human rights discourse to implement their lobbying for women's rights within Islam to show that Islam is not incompatible with the promotion of democratic values of equity and justice for all. The amendment of the new family law is a good example of the way both social trends were reconciled around progressive modernist laws that found their roots within Islam's precepts. It is equally significant that such an important societal project has been taken over by King Mohamed VI, who has this dual legitimacy both as commander of the faithful and commander in chief[15].

Conclusion

As feminists, of all ideological trends, reveal lucidity and intelligence in finding ways to bridge differences, they also demonstrate that they are attentive to the large variety of women's identities with diverse perspectives and expectations. Such a diversity is becoming more and more visible as new channels of expression, such as ICTs, media, local NGOs, etc., allow more and more women to speak up for themselves. As it has been shown above, the intersectionality in building up an individual's identity highlights the complexity of the process and reinforces the idiosyncratic features of each. It is not surprising then to see different feminist agencies that stand for their own conception of what it means to be a feminist.. The post-Arab spring context, together with the new technologies and social media, has revolutionized ways of protesting, of mobilizing forces and raising awareness. Feminism is in this way not only becoming plural but also getting creative and innovative. Cyberspace today offers a more democratic space where all voices can be heard regardless of their gender, race, age, education, religion, etc. The young generation of women are finding in the virtual world "new ways to engage with politics and feminism" (Salime, 2012: 105) and even advocate new forms of feminisms which would go beyond the 'classic' or 'traditional' one by fighting for human rights and dignity for all, not just for women[16] (Skalli, 2011). The discourse of gender equality is itself evolving and a new generation of women's rights activists, not necessarily affiliated to feminist organizations, is emerging[17]. These often conduct actions, which support the feminist prerogatives of equality and justice, though not necessarily following a feminist movement. Instead, they inscribe their activism within the larger scope of nationhood, citizenship and the quest for democracy.

All these initiatives create friction and disagreement on certain fundamentals, which can be at odds, as it already happened between the two major feminist trends, the secular and the Islamic. However, what is positive about this multiplicity of standpoints or approaches is the fact that it opens up the scope for more public discussions, more visibility and the possibility to reconsider and reinterpret past dogmas and practices. The continuous confrontation of diverging agendas is not easy to handle but at least it has the merit to posit the question as a central one worth consideration by all. As it often happens in most societies, before any decisive change can be made, there are many conversations within the larger community that need to take place, some of which are hard to have and need time. It is actually in the opposition, contradictions and controversy that many big reforms and social causes are pushed for. Feminisms develop thanks to a polyphony of feminist voices, which are definitely different if not contradictory, but which are surely contributing to the reinforcement of a global move towards more democratic rights of respect and dignity which are truly representative of all identities. Change is inevitable though its consequences remain unpredictable. The history of feminisms will tell us...

Notes

1 According to the Moroccan newspaper *Al Massae*, the colonel who had refused to shake hands with Kenitra's Wali (governor) Zineb El Adaoui, has been dismissed from his post as regional commander of the Auxiliary Forces in Kenitra.

2 "G.H. Mead, C.H. Cooley, and the symbolic interactionists are the key figures in sociology who elaborated this 'interactive' conception of identity and the self", as Stuart Hall explains it in "The Question of Cultural Identity", *Modernity An Introduction to Modern Societies*. Eds. Stuart Hal, David Held, Don Hubert, and Kenneth Thompson. Oxford: The Open University, 1996. p.597.

3 I refer here to the concept of intersectionality by Kimberlé Williams Crenshaw. See Williams, Kimberlé Crenshaw. "Mapping the Margins: Intersectionality, Identity Politics, and Violence Against Women of Color". In: Martha Albertson Fineman, RixanneMykitiuk, Eds. The Public Nature of Private Violence. (New York: Routledge, 1994), p. 93–118.

4 Name given to residents of the city of Fes.

5 "Intersectionality: A tool for Gender and Economic Justice", Awid, Women's Rights and Economic change, N°9, August 2004, p. 2.

6 The woman is considered to be the one who is primarily 'responsible' for the children's education in the sense that she needs to teach them 'modern' values of openness and tolerance, but also transmit to them cultural values closely connected to local traditions, customs and rules of sociability. For example, the traditional celebration of religious feasts, celebration of marriages, baptism, the

philosophy of the Moroccan hospitality and the notion of 'souab' or how to be 'polite' according to a conventional 'protocole', which attest of good manners and a kind of savoir-vivre specific to our society.While a woman is expected to provide a 'modern' education so that her children participate in a modern Morocco, she's also expected to educate them culturally in the how to's of Islamic culture or ways of socializing; hence the cycle of modernity vs. traditional culture will continue with her children.

7 On June 17, 2014, Abdellilah Benkirane, leader of the Justice and Development Party (PJD) and actual prime Minister openly deplored, in a parliamentary session, that women have deserted their homes to go out for work and with some nostalgia reminded the audience that mothers who stay homes are like 'chandeliers' that illuminate houses. A sit-in front of the parliament was organized by aCivil Coalition for the application of Article 19 of the 2011 Constitution which comprises several associations of women's rights NGOs and human rights ones. These strongly condemned the Prime Minister's discriminatory declarations that oppose the application of article 19 which stipulates clearly the state's role in establishing equal rights between men and women. Besides, a large reaction of indignation was voiced on social media platforms under the hashtag"#anamachitria" (this is Moroccan dialect to say "I am not a chandelier") to refer to the metaphor and expression used by the head of the government. http://www.marocpress.com/fr/liberation/article-97942.html

8 Rachel Newcomb is referring here to the 2005 Moroccan government. She further explains that "*the Islamist position represented by nationally known figures such as Nadia Yassine and Abdelilah Benkirane,* [who was already] *leader of the religiously oriented Party of Justice and Development, ...is that women's entry into the public sphere and demands for equality threaten the integrity of the Moroccan family and, in fact, the strength of the entire nation.*"(Newcomb, 2006, p.305). It is significant to note that in 2014, nine years later, after the declarations made in the parliament, and as head of the government, his position is still the same.

9 Morocco recognized the Beijing Platform for Action, adopted by the UN World Conference on Women in 1995 and ratified the Convention on the Elimination of All Forms of Discrimination against Women (CEDAW) on August 26th, 1993. It has then withdrawn reservations on article 2&6 (related to the dissolution of marriage and the transmission of nationality from mother to child) in 2008 after the promulgation of the 2004 Family Law.

10 Pathologist in Avicenna Hospital, by profession, Asmae Lamrabet is a leading scholar of Islamic Feminism in Morocco, as author of several books on Islam and women's representation in the Qur'an. She is also Director of Studies and Research Centre on Women's Issues in Islam of Rabita Mohammadia des Ulemas located in Rabat (Since 2011), Former President of GIERFI (International Group of Studies and Reflection on Women and Islam) (2008–2010) and Member of GIERFI Board of Directors. According to an interview transcribed in Emilie Clark, 2013, pp 56–62.

11 Professor of Constitutional Rights, University Mohammad V, Agdal, Rabat, Morocco.According to an interview transcribed in Emilie Clark, 2013, pp 42–47.

12 This plan has been initiated in 1999 by Mohamed Said Saadi, the then Secretary of State for the Family, the Children and the Disabled.

13 Professor of law, specialized in family rights, penal law, and health rights, University Mohamed V, Rabat. She has experience in making comparisons between modern law and Islamic law. She was the first woman to give a talk in front of King Mohamed VI, in 2003, as part of a cycle of religious conferences organized during Ramadan, that are called "Addourouss Al Hassania", and that were exclusively given by male religious scholars until her own participation.

14 Reference can be made here to the three main roles that individuals play in society and which help deconstruct the gender concept: the reproductive role, the economic role or 'productive' one, and the social one. In all these roles, women have inferior positions to that of men. See Isabelle Jacquet, Développement au masculin/féminin: Le genre Outil d'un nouveau concept, Paris: l'Harmattan, 1995, p. 31.

15 In his announcement of the new Family Law during the opening of the autumn parliamentary session, the 10th October, 2003, King Mohamed VI said "as Commander of the Faithful, I can neither prohibit what is legal nor sanction that which is illicit" to clearly underline the religious legitimacy of the Law.["Je ne peux en ma qualité d'*Amir al-mu'minin*, autoriser ce que Dieu a prohibé, ni interdire ce que le très haut a autorisé"].

16 A young woman is explaining in an interview how the way their 'mothers and grandmothers' were militating for women's rights is too 'traditional' and that the youth have a different perspective about feminist activism. She says "I think we will gain more if we all fight for human rights and dignity in our country and not just for women... we need men to help... I don't see how we can do it alone.' Quoted in Loubna H. Skalli (2011):Generational Politics and Renewal of Leadership in the Moroccan Women's Movement, International Feminist Journal of Politics, 13:3, p.340.

17 There are personal actions, like the initiative of a young teenager (Majdouline Al Yazidi, 20 year old) who launched via a Facebook page the "woman choufouch" movement after the slutwalk movement which started in Canada in April 2011. Its purpose is to fight sexual harassment against women and draw attention to the difficulties women face in the Moroccan public space on a daily basis. Another equally innovative activist initiative is the creation in August 2011 of a feminist e-magazine called "Qandisha Magazwine" (by Fedwa Misk, journalist, 32 years) which aims at providing women with a space where they can speak. The name given to the magazine Qandisha[17] is a subversive one as it refers, according to the Moroccan myth, to a beautiful woman considered to be devilish because she upsets men. Hence, the magazine's purpose is clearly to disturb the socially and unquestioned norms, and move away from traditional ways of defining womanhood.

References

Badran, Margot, 2009. *Feminism in Islam*. Oxford: Oneworld Publication.

Bryson, Valerie, 1992. *Feminist Political Theory*. London: Macmillan Press Ltd.

Clark, Emilie K. 2013. *Islamic Feminism: A Theoretical Framework for the Practical Implementationof Women's Rights inMorocco*. Advisor: Jocelyn Lieu. Field Advisor: Said Tbel. Pp.1–68. http://www.academia.edu/6753321/Islamic_Feminism_A_Theoretical_Framework_for_the_Practical_Implementation_of_Womens_Rights_in_Morocco (accessed on Apr. 21, 2014).

Giddens, Anthony. 1990. *The Consequences of Modernity*. Cambridge: Polity Press.

Hall, Stuart, 1996. "The Question of Cultural Identity". In Stuart Hall, David Held, Don Hubert, and Kenneth Thompson (Eds.) *Modernity An Introduction to Modern Societies*, pp.595–623. Oxford: The Open University

Howe, Marvine. 2005. *Morocco: The Islamist Awakening and Other Challenges*. New York: Oxford University Press.

Jacquet, Isabelle. 1995. *Développement au masculin/féminin: Le genre Outil d'un nouveau concept*. Paris: l'Harmattan.

Newcomb, Rachel. 2006. "Gendering the City, Gendering the Nation: Contesting Urban Space in Fes, Morocco". *City and Society*, Vol. 18. Issue 2:288–311

Sadiqi, Fatima., 2008. The Central Role of the Family Law in the Moroccan Feminist Movement. *British Journal of Middle Eastern Studies*, 35(3):325–337.

Sadiqi, Fatima and Ennaji, Moha. (2005)."Feminization of Public Space: Women's Activism, the Family Law, and Social Change in Morocco." *Journal of Middle East Women's Studies(JMEWS)* (edited by Valentine Moghadam and Fatima Sadiqi). Indiana: Indiana University Press. Volume 2, N° 2: 86–114.

Salime, Zakia. 2008. Mobilizing Muslim Women: Multiple Voices, the Sharia, and the State. *Comparative Studies of South Asia, Africa and the Middle East.* Vol. 28, 1.: 200–210. Duke University Press.

Salime, Zakia. 2012. A New Feminism? Gender Dynamics in Morocco's February 20th Movement. *Journal of International Women's Studies*, 13(5), 101–114.Available at: http://vc.bridgew.edu/jiws/vol13/iss5/11 accessed on Jan. 20, 2014.

Skalli, Loubna H. 2011. Generational Politics and Renewal of Leadership in the Moroccan Women's Movement. *International Feminist Journal of Politics,* 13:3, 329–348.

Williams, Kimberlé Crenshaw. 1994). "Mapping the Margins: Intersectionality, Identity Politics, and Violence Against Women of Color". In Martha Albertson Fineman, Rixanne Mykitiuk (Eds.). *The Public Nature of Private Violence*, pp. 93–118 . New York: Routledge,.

Chapter 9

THE WOMEN OF 20-FEBRUARY MOVEMENT IN MOROCCO

A New Feminist Consciousness

Mohammed Yachoulti

In comparison with their action and activism in the last two decade, Moroccan women have managed in 2011 to forge a new political identity in the public arena. Through embracing the February 20th movement claims and strategies of activism and most importantly applying the principle of parity in all aspects of its uprisings that swept the country, the new generation activists of Moroccan women have drawn a new picture of feminist activism in Morocco. In fact, the dissatisfaction with previous forms of feminist activism and its elite nature not to mention the aspire to put the whole society on democracy track are but some of the triggers that pushed the new generation of Moroccan women to seize the Moroccan Arab spring to sweep the public arena with new feminist beliefs and assumptions. Based on the results of my previous research on Moroccan women's organizations as a doctorate student, and through following this new generation on the ground and through media, I believe that it has imposed itself not only as a new and undeniable political partner/actor in the Moroccan political arena but also as a generation that would lead feminist activism in the coming decades. I also believe that this new fact or shift is significant in terms of future action of these actors as well as in terms of democratic political practice.

Introduction

The winds of the so-called Arab Spring have not only triggered political reforms in Morocco but have contributed to the change of
political practice and struggle strategies of vibrant actors in general
and women's movement in particular. Indeed, the new generation of
Moroccan women that invested the public arena in 2011 managed to
forge a new political identity that cut off with the NGO-zation of
feminist activism. In the recent past, Moroccan women worked
within their organizations to defend their cause and achieve gender
equality. However, to obtain reforms, the leading associations within
the women's movement sidestepped the democratically elected institutions and addressed the king in person to achieve gender reforms.
This fact, I believe, had dramatic repercussions not only on the democratic practice in Morocco but on Moroccan women themselves as well.
In this regard, this chapter aims to compare the type of activism performed before 2011 and that of 20-February Movement women and
beyond. The purpose of this comparative approach is to show how
the new generation of Moroccan women understands feminist activism. The chapter is structured in the following way; it starts with a
discussion of "activism" and how it is theorized. Then, it proceeds by
briefly tracing the history of women's movement in Morocco and the
methods of activism it followed to achieve gender reforms. The
chapter concludes by comparing and understanding the existing differences between two types of activism.

Activism: Types, Goals and Requirements

Women's political agency is witnessing significant changes in the
last five recent years in Morocco. These changes are mainly due to
the space of activism used by the old generation of women activists
and that of 20-Feb Movement. In this regard, a good understanding
and comparison of the two types of activism performed by both
generations entail in the first place investigating and reviewing
the concept of activism and its goals as well as its necessary conditions to make it a viable one and therefore an agent of
democratization. To this effect, the aim of two coming sections is
to investigate this task.

Activism: types and goals

Activism may defined as the different activities conducted by some active citizens to make other citizens aware that something is going wrong and involve them to seek remedies so as to get things in order. A democratic activism is usually achieved by the citizens themselves, or with the help of the constitutional institutions such the parliament, legislative assemblies, executive bodies, administration, and the judiciary. A democratic activist usually sets himself or herself as "a model of citizen virtues" (Young, 2001). He/she is usually "committed to social justice and normative values" (ibid). He/she advocates the "idea that a politically responsible person ought to take positive action to promote these [values]" (ibid). Activism "has played a major role in ending slavery, challenging dictatorships, protecting workers from exploitation, protecting the environment, promoting equality for women, opposing racism, and many other important issues" (Brain, 2007). Yet, it has received relatively little attention from scholars (ibid). Indeed, "most history is written about powerful and prominent people and about official systems and activities, such as governments, elections, militaries, and wars"(ibid).

Activism can take different forms. Some are concert and take place on the ground, others are invisible. Demonstration is the best example in this regard. It is the core and the most visible expression of activism. It usually includes marches, strikes, sit-ins, sleep-ins, and hunger strikes among many others. Grassroots activism is another traditional strategy worth mentioning in this respect. It is based on founding or joining a specific community to express discontent and to demand change. The objective of this activism is to increase the popularity and support for a specific social cause. Later on, groups are usually organized in large scale-movement to defend their cause and achieve their goals. Activists could also opt for lobbying government officials to enact change. They would insist on organizing meetings and engaging in direct contacts with the target officials for the purpose of immediate action and response. Sending letters and petitions to decision makers, legislative bodies and elected officials is another form of activism. However, the latter is the less effective strategy in comparison with the previous methods of activism namely demonstration. The reason may be attributed to the fact that this method usually gives the chance to the target heads to think out solutions that may not be in favor of the aggrieved groups. In the case of the failure of these strategies, litigation remains as the most straightforward tactic to enforce the law against the concerned institutions. In every society, there always are voluntary lawyers that sympathize with the active groups in defending a social cause. They would file lawsuits against institutions and their executives to make justice prevail. Still, for any viable activism to take place, some conditions must be in place. This is the task of the next section.

Activism: its requirements and specificities

Activism as an agent of democratization requires certain variables that would help facilitate the task of the activists and incite them to go forward in their action. These are distributed as follows:

Existence of a Public Sphere

For any activism to take place, the public sphere must be guaranteed as a realm of freedom from the state and by the state itself (Bernhard, 1993). The concept of public sphere refers to the practice of open discussion about matters of common interest. The concept owes much of its academic popularity to Jürgen Habermas and the publication of his pioneer book *The Structural Transformation of the Public Sphere.* In this book, Habermas argues that the public sphere is "made up of private people gathered together as a public and articulating the needs of society with the state" (Habermas, 1991). Habermas' public sphere is formed when citizens, of any state, are able to enjoy fundamental freedoms of thought, opinion and expression. In Morocco, public space, as Habermas envisions it, is still work in progress. Rights and liberties of expression and opinion are still sometimes criminalised. Moroccan authorities make opinions, assemblies and expressions subject to censure and interdiction; when the king and members of the royal family are insulted, criticized or accused of malfeasance publicly, when the legitimacy of Islam as a state religion with the king as its tutelary head is questioned or undermined; when Morocco's territoriality is defied namely regarding sovereignty over Western Sahara (Smith and Loudiyi, 2005). Also, criticizing the surrounding government authorities and the police can result in imprisonment. The best and recent example one could mention in this regard is Rachid Nini – the former editor of *Almasae* daily newspaper and one of the most famous Moroccan journalist nowadays. Nini was imprisoned for more than a year for his courageous discussion of corruption of those who are very close to the palace. This example makes the democratic promises of the 2011 constitutional reforms ink on paper. In fact, the implementation of the reforms such as the press code and the judicial system remain to be seen

On the other hand, the continuous existence of some independent newspapers that indulge in 'ex-taboo issues' and publicly criticize public political figures and enrich the public debates that surround reforms the Moroccan state engages in suggest, though not enough, a positive shift towards the construction of a distinctive Moroccan public sphere. However, this contradiction is taking place very slowly given the pace of changes that occur at the international level.

Autonomy of Institutions

A viable activism encompasses "the existence of autonomous institutions" (Kazemi, 2002). That is, no single institution or agency dominates social or political life or should work as the only legible arbiter of norms. In the drafting of the 2011 reforms, the preoccupying question was how much power the king would exercise in the new constitution. This is because in the previous constitutions, the king garnered absolute power in matters of the state and in the interpretations of what is best for the community (Smith and Loudiyi, 2005). The reforms of 2011 have actually empowered some institutions. They have broadened the role of the parliament allowing it to pass laws on most issues, laid the ground for protecting the independence of the judicial system and increased the role of some independent commissions. The reforms have also given to the head of the government –previously called prime minister-the right to preside over the government council. Interestingly however, the king still has the right to preside over the cabinet when security issues and strategic policy decision are at stake. This is due mainly to the fact the new constitution does not clearly state what constitute a strategic decision (Ottaway, 2011). Indeed, the king's powers are still absolute in matters of religion, security issues and strategic major policy issues (ibid).

Existence of Democracy

The linkage between activism and democratization is symmetrical. Democracy paves the ground for activism and in turn activism enhances democracy promotion. In other words, activism flourishes in democratic political systems and democracy is promoted and enhanced through a committed activism. In Morocco, the nascent civil society that flourished with the political liberalization the state has engaged in since the late 1980s and early 1990s managed in a way or another to pressure and force the government to articulate political reform agendas and remove the 'taboo' aspect from different issues such as human rights violations, poverty and corruption. Still, given the inchoate nature of the Moroccan political system and state's intervention into every single detail make civil society groups activism swirl only within the boundaries it defines and delimits (Yachoulti, 2012). This way, the state manages to keep society in a relative autonomy, while remaining in the positions of control.

Prevalence of Civility

Last but not least, any type of political activism presupposes the existence of civility as a precondition for its survival. That is, political activism flourishes only when individuals are willing to stay concerned with the good and the welfare of society; when they voluntarily relate to each other on the basis of shared interests (Shills, 2002). More specifically, "civility is the conduct of a person whose individual self-consciousness has been partly superseded by the collective of his self-consciousness" (ibid). Also, civility implies tolerance; that is, respect for different point of views and social attitudes and requires regularity of behaviour, rules of conduct, respect of law as well as of individual's autonomy that is based on trust among people who perhaps never met. In Morocco, a large segment of society shies away from any political activism due to the prevailing conviction of its unworthiness. This is the result of the nature of the existing political system on the one hand and the prevalence of political apathy because of the lack of trust between the citizens and political actors and the ideological gap between the political actors on the other hand.

Recently however, the pro-democracy calls that swept the region inspired a number of youngsters to take action and initiate a campaign of struggles through the use of the internet. The unifying demands and claims of these activists were "freedom, equality, an end to corruption, better living conditions, education, labor rights, Amazigh rights and many others" (ibid). Despite the discredit received by the official national media, this virtual campaign managed to stir a number of people and encouraged the creation of multiple Facebook groups at the level of cities (Rabat, Casablanca, Fez , Marrakesh to mention but the main ones). These local groups decided to meet, discuss, prepare and urge citizen to go to demonstrate on February 20th. Interestingly, on February 18th, *Al Adl wa lihsan* [1] published a communiqué stating that its youth section members would join the protest throughout the country, a fact which boosted the courage of all the activists and proved once again that their claims and demands are the demands of all ideologies in Morocco. Actually, all this helped to give birth to the 20-February Movement.

The success of the first protests that swept all Moroccan cities and villages did not only set the ball rolling for subsquent rallies but had immediate response from the king who announced the establishment of a commission to propose amendments to the Constitution. The general aim of the reform was to limit the power of the monarchy and strengthen the roles of the prime minister and parliament.

After the announcement of these reforms, the protests of the movement started to take new directions; the movement's rallies started to decrease in both number and membership because of many reasons. First, the yawning gap between the Islamists and the radical left started to impose itself namely when each group wanted to head over and lead the movement (justice and Charity and the radical left). Second, the victory of the party of Justice and Development (PJD) in the legislative elections gave hope to the protestors that their demands will be responded. Third, the king's strategy or step to call for a constitutional reform helped contain the enthusiasm of the pro-testers. Fourth, *Adl wa lihsan* suspension of involvement in the protests badly influenced the movement as it lost the majority of its protesters. Finally, the bloodshed in Libya, Yemen, Syria and the gloomy picture that surround the future of these countries convinced somehow protesters that change can be achieved peacefully.

Now, despite the persistence of some protests of the movement in some cities, their influence in the political sphere has turned to be very weak. The weakness of the new government performance is dividing the activists into two blocks; the first calls going back to the street while the second one still insists on the "wait and see" strategy. They stress giving the government some more time to see how it would implement its political agenda and promises. In general, the importance of 20-February Movement and its rallies lies in the fact that they have re-thrown all fractions of Moroccan society into the political sphere after years of indifference and political apathy.

In brief, given the nature of the Moroccan political system, the specificity of the Moroccan public sphere, the political apathy that pervades in Morocco because of the lack of trust between the citizens and political actors on the one hand the ideological gap between the political actors on the other, it is safe concluding that activism in Morocco has its own specificities that distinguishes it from the normative activism discussed above. This would be understood more clearly when tracing the history and activism of women's movement organizations before 2011.

Research Method and Approach

The chapter adopts the generational approach to understand the existing difference between types of activism led by two generations of women in Morocco. This approach owes much of its popularity to the Hungarian Sociologist Karl Mannheim and most importantly to his pioneer essay "The Problem of Generations" (Mannheim, 1952: 292). In this essay, Mannheim claims that a ""generation" represents nothing more than a particular kind of identity of location, embracing related "age groups" embedded in a historical-social process" (ibid). For him, the fact of "belonging to the same generation or age group [. . .] endows the individuals sharing in them with a common location in the social and historical process, and thereby limits them to a specific range of potential experience, predisposing them for a certain characteristic mode of thought and experience, and a characteristic type of historically relevant action" (Mannheim, 1952: 291). To put it in very simple terms, the historical-social process usually creates a shared affinity and a collective consciousness among an age group leading therefore to specific modes of thought, feeling and behavior. In fact, this generational differences are "central both to our thinking of historical time and change and the placing of individuals and their agency in those times and processes of social change (Aboim and Vasconcelos 2011)". In this regard, I use the generational approach to refer to the ways or techniques in which each age group negotiates change within a historical context of social transformation. I believe that the importance of this approach lies in the fact it will allow us to grasp wider processes of social and generational change, particularly those massive transformations taking place in Morocco with regard to women's agency. To investigate this, this chapter builds on some of the findings of my doctoral thesis in 2012 on Moroccan women's organizations, and on adopting this new generation of 20-FebMVT on the ground and through media.

Moroccan women's activism before 2011

Indeed, the first discussion of women's issues in the Moroccan public stage was initiated by the national press in 1930s and, interestingly, was largely generated by men (Baker, 1998). The only female voice was that of Malika al-Fassi- coming from one of the great intellectual families of the Fez bourgeoisie (ibid). This voice took girls' education as the first priority for Moroccan women. Malika al-Fassi's articles at that time aimed "to persuade fathers of the necessity of sending their daughters to school" (Baker, 1998: 48). Indeed, access to education and schooling meant a new life and an absolute end to the seclusion of her generation of Moroccan women.

From the middle of 1940s onward, the journey of Moroccan women's movement started to take shape through the instigation of state, political parties and civil society (Sadiqi, 2003). Also, Moroccan women massively joined the armed resistance, taking active militant roles in the fight against colonization; they managed to fulfil important tasks that facilitated men's fighting. In this regard, Alison Baker writes: "Mission for resistance not only brought them (Moroccan women) out of seclusion, but sent them into dangerous situations, traveling long distances by themselves carrying weapons and even setting bombs all the way using their wits to escape (Baker, 1998). In fact, the struggle Moroccan women led had a "two-fold" dimension; they rebelled against colonial occupation and oppression on the one hand and against the restrictive attitude of the Moroccan traditional society on the other.

After independence however, Moroccan women discovered that nothing had changed in the society at large and in regard to their interest or issues and status in particular; the women's question and the women themselves were for the most part relegated to the periphery of the public and private spheres. In simple terms, they found themselves helpless with no power circles willing to speak for them and defend their cause. Actually, different factors came up together during that period to prevent women from participating in the public life namely at the political level. These factors ranged from the rate of illiteracy, lack of interest and the heavy burden of the domestic role. This was reinforced by the political structures which were and are still oppressive and which turned political life into a male–exclusive world. Further, this marginalization was exacerbated by the total absence of women leadership in the political parties and government official institutions, who could have advanced women's status.

By the 1960s and 1970s, namely during what is known as the Years of Lead[2], the political atmosphere negatively impacted the vibrancy and effectiveness of active civil society groups including the female ones. Authoritarianism and political oppression did not help women to take action except for some state-sponsored groups. Added to this, political parties were very reluctant to deal with gender issues and claims very seriously except when they were part of pushing to a national consensus.

Since the late 1980s, the political and economic reforms Morocco has engaged favored and encouraged the rise of a number of associational bodies – under rubric of civil society- . These groups seized the opportunity to proliferate, voice their demands publicly and also contribute to enhancing the reforms. Because of their conviction that only an autonomous activism or struggle would bring changes to their status, women activists seized the new political atmosphere to establish a number of women's organizations as part of the emerging

civil society groups. These organizations coalesced into a new movement pressuring to change many things for Moroccan women. In this
regard, Chafaai (1993) describes the Moroccan women's movement
as "a set of feminine voluntary organizations, whose ideological discourse aims is to defend women in a general framework of struggle
and implement the laws that enlarge public liberties and guarantee
equality between the sexes" (Chafaai, 1993). Using this definition, I
would like to make three remarks. Firstly, women's activism in
Morocco is practiced through women's organizations, a fact which
makes women's movement organizations as the best label of this
brand of feminism. Secondly, Moroccan women's movement fluctu-
ates between a social movement organized and directed by women
and a political movement that struggle for the emancipation of
Moroccan women. Finally, the precedence of the social characteristic
over the political one validates the claim that Moroccan feminism
activism emerged out of real social needs of women and not from an
alien Western concept.

Generally speaking, women's activism within their own organizations helped them gain new presence in society, allowed them
greater visibility and facilitated in infiltrating into the public sphere.
More than this, activism within their own organizations allowed
them the chance to achieve a number of gender reforms and many
victories in the name of democracy and equality. For example in
2004, women's movement organizations managed to help reform
the family, now considered one of the two most advanced family
laws in the Arab and Muslim world. However, it is worth mentioning
in this regard that the activism of these organizations did not conform to the principles of "a democratic activism" defined in the
democratic theory. To put it more succinctly, in the late of 1990s,
after the failure to implement the national Plan for Integrating
Women in Development launched by the government and the
growth of the Islamists as key actors in the political arena, the leading organizations within the women's movement bypassed all the
democratically elected institutions and addressed the king in person to achieve their agenda of reform.The same story of addressing
the king in person repeated itself in 2007 when women's movement
organizations sought the reform of the Nationality Code. During a
royal visit to Europe in 2005, the Moroccan king, Mohammed VI,

met a delegation of Moroccan women living abroad and married to non-Moroccan citizens. The delegation claimed the Moroccan citizenship for their children and pointed to the difficulties their children faced because of some articles of 1958 Nationality code. The king promised to find a solution to the problem. On July 30, 2005, in his throne speech King Mohammed announced that Moroccan women will be able to pass on their nationality to children born to non-Moroccan of fathers and asked the government to submit him the sensible proposals to amend the legislation on citizenship (Yachoulti, 2007). Following the royal decision, both the cabinet and the parliament adopted the draft bill to reform the country Nationality Code that was released in the official bulletin on April 2nd, 2007. The cornerstone of this new code was the amendment to article six which sought to put men and women on equal footing when they are the source of citizenship; it sought to achieve a complete equality regardless of whether it is the mother or the father who is the single Moroccan parent. The Nationality Code is a continuation of the 2004 Family Law reforms. It was indeed 'postponed' for one reason or another.

Taking into account these two examples of reform, we may conclude that the apparent victories of women's movement in the name of democracy promotion are in their content but a reinforcing of the existing system of government. In other words, women's movement organizations direct resort to the king and asking him for his personal intervention or interest made them violate the norms of a democratic activism that would put the whole society on the democratic track. Even worse, their type of activism has had dramatic repercussions on both themselves in particular and the democratic practice in Morocco in general. To explain, the way women's movement organizations have achieved their gender reforms has reinforced the existing political practices and system of government. More than this, this fact has opened the door to other components of society to follow the same trajectory when claiming their rights or expressing their grievances. Nowadays, social media is full of videos in which ordinary citizen address the king in person claiming injustice or specific grievances. For them, the king is only decision-maker to that could end up their sufferings. Secondly, the undemocratic manner in which the changes have been introduced has negative repercussions on the implementation of the legislation on the ground. In other words, despite campaigns being carried out by some governmental departments and civil society associations, the new provisions of the *Mudawana* are in fact largely ignored within the judicial system. This is mainly due to the fact that they are top-down reforms. Finally, there are many reasons for the non-application of the legislation. The best examples of which are the poor training of judges, the isolation of large areas of the country, the widespread of illiteracy, the traditionalism of specific social milieus, the conservative mindsets of officials within the judicial system, and the illiteracy of many Moroccan women. The coming section discusses the emergence of the new women activists in the Moroccan public arena.

Moroccan Women's Movement After 2011: the Rise of a New Generation

The pro-democracy calls that swept the Middle East and North Africa (MENA) region inspired a number of Moroccan youngsters to take action and initiate a campaign of struggles that called for "freedom, equality, and end to corruption, better living conditions, education, labor rights, Amazigh rights and many others" (Benchemsi, 2012). These youngsters organized themselves in small local groups all over the cities of Morocco and decided to meet, discuss, prepare and urge citizens to demonstrate on February 20th. Of course, women were not an exception. They constituted an integral part of the Moroccan uprisings; they were involved in every aspect of these uprisings: they have contributed to create Facebook group pages, contributed to the riseand flourishing of virtual activism through posting their opinions and views on Facebook and twitter pages and blogs, prepared and initiated the demonstrations of the movement (Four of the 14 activists featured in the 20- February Movement's YouTube video announcing its creation are young women, asking not for gender equality, but for a representative democracy), encouraged and urged the citizen to take part in the protest, kept informing when and where the meetings and rallies would take place, wrote slogans, shouted in the rallies and marched alongside men, took the front lines to confront the security forces and served as spokespersons of the movement.

Following these activists on the ground and through social media has shown that these women are young in their age, modern in their visibility, belong to different social strata and educational backgrounds, and come from urban and rural areas. Also, some are economically independent while others are unemployed graduates let alone that some hold different ideologies and political orientation while others engage for the first time in their life in a political activism or social protest. Still, what is worth mentioning in this regard is the fact that though these women have engaged in this movement with the purpose of advancing rights and liberties of all Moroccans, many of them reported that they received threats and were met with opposition because of their activism. Some bitterly said that they received threatening messages via Facebook and phone calls. Others reported that they were warned by their families not to participate in the protest as they would be jailed and beaten by the police. For example, Kamilia Raouyane, an intern at the Moroccan Association of Human Rights, said at the start of the movement she received calls at 3 a.m. from someone calling her a whore and threatening sexual violence[3]. She also said "My grandma, every time I meet her, she says don't protest, you will go to jail, they will beat you, [...] But I'm not afraid. I really believe in it. If I don't do this, no one will do this for me"[4]. However, despite all these challenges and threats, women activists, like Kamilia, continued protesting and be part of the movement core. This way I believe that, the choice to work side by side with men in all the structures, steps and organization of the20- Feb Movement is revealing at different levels. It is practice that shows a new consciousness or understanding of the feminist activism among the young generation of Moroccan women. The coming section explains this claim.

Moroccan Women's Activism Before and After 2011: What differences?

Indeed, the Arab spring has offered a fertile ground for a new generation of women who is both unsatisfied or in disagreement with the activism led by the leaders of women's movement organizations[5] and is suffering from unemployment, poverty, corruption, favoritism discrimination, and political misrepresentation. This generation seized the 20-Feb Movement demonstrations to take efficient actions, voice their demands and pave the ground for a new awareness, more mobilization, and pressure for human rights in general and women's issues in particular. This shift in attitudes, arena of activism and modes of action favored the development and emergence of generational differences among Moroccan women activists worth studying.

To begin with, the new generation of women activists has chosen a new brand of feminist activism. Indeed, by embracing and engaging in the 20-Feb Movement, they have marked a great shift in the feminist understanding of political practice in Morocco. To explain, before 2011, feminism in Morocco has been confined to women's organizations and has been controlled by elite of leaders. Women of 20-Feb Movement have chosen another space activism that abandons any confinement within any political or civil society organizations. They have been very practical in action; they took the street and social media as the main arena of their activism. This is due to the lack of trust in all pervious social and political actors.

Equally important, before 2011, the focus of Moroccan women's movement organizations has been on gender equality that bases itself, in most of the times, on seeking positive discrimination (Yachoulti, 2012). To put it more succinctly, activists within women's movement organizations have asked for a quota system to have political representation of women in the Moroccan parliament and are insisting now on the principle of parity in decision-making bodies. The new generation of 2011, consciously or unconsciously, has shown that gender equality begins through the practice of parity on the ground and through an equal division of labor among men and women protesters in the movement. In other words, women have been key players in the 20-Feb Movement; they involved themselves in all stages of setting up and in the activities of the youth-led democracy movement. This way, they have shown a new feminist understanding of the political practice to change their individual life and their society. In their belief, any reform or change of the political system would undoubtedly in its turn bring change to their status.

Correspondingly, women's movement organizations have, throughout their activism, struggled for specific gender reforms.

They have also involved the king as the main and only 'referee'. On the other side of the line, the new generation of 20-Feb Movement has focused on its activism on calling for the freedom and equality of all Moroccans. Tahani Madad, a nineteen year-old science student who spoke on behalf of 20-Feb Movement during a conference that took place at "Association Marocaine des Droits de l'Homme" (AMDH) in Rabat, concluded here talk that their overall objective is to see the "flag of freedom, equality and social justice reign over Morocco, through peaceful means"[6]. In other words, gender issues and sensibilities are totally ignored in the rhetoric of equality before the law. More importantly, women of 20-Feb Movement aspire is to "see truly representative institutions and a political regime in which the king reigns but doesn't rule"[7]. They also managed, along with their male partners, to trigger and diffuse a culture of protest as a way of keeping the spirit of the movement alive in the future.

Another key point to emphasize is that activism within women's organizations has always favored elitism, sectarianism and fragmentation among the organizations which make up Moroccan women's movement (Yachoulti, 2012). Also, the majority of their activists were or are still members within political parties. Therefore, in their activism within their organizations, they usually reproduce ideologies of their parties[8]. Women of 20-Feb Movement have opted for democratizing their activism by setting it free of political or ideological affiliations. Tahani Madad insisted that "no sectarian, political, or religious slogans are authorized." She insisted that the movement is "secular, modernist (*hadati*), democratic, and independent of all foreign agendas or political affiliations." (ibid)

Last but not least, women's organizations are established on clear rigid hierarchy. A single woman or a small group of women retains control over the organizations (ibid). Some organizations are entirely synonymous with their founders. The working staff is treated as followers of the leader than as equal partners (ibid). In 20-Feb Movement, "the leadership alternates between men and women. The issue of concern including gender [issues], are commonly shared and discussed" (Salime, 2012).

In brief, women of the 20-Feb Movement have shown a new feminist understanding of political practice in Morocco. Their discourse

and action reveal their commitment to institutionalize the democratic process and put up with the elitism, rigid hierarchy,
sectarianism and fragmentation among the organizations that have
made up Moroccan women's movement. Further, their enthusiastic
activism has secured them a number of gains that are significant in
terms of their contents and future action. These gains are distributed as in the following:

–   As a response to the uprisings, King Mohammed called upon five
    women to make up the Consultative Commission to review the
    constitution and deliver recommendations for democratic
    reform. (Commission was made of 18 members)
–   On April 18, 2011, Morocco formally withdrew its reservations
    to CEDAW and its optional protocol. Now, those fighting for
    women's rights and empowerment have authority under the
    national constitution to cite all of CEDAW's provisions as leverage
    to hold the government to its commitment to move toward
    women's full equality[9].
–   October 2011, following reform of the Constitution, two laws
    were adopted containing provisions on the participation of
    women in political.

    •   Law N° 27–11 on the Chamber of Representatives (lower
        house of parliament) establishes a quota of 60 seats reserved
        for women out of a total of 395 seats, representing 15%.
    •   Law N° 29–11 "on political parties" provides that "all politi-
        cal parties work to achieve a proportion of one-third of
        women in their governing bodies" (art. 26). However, the law
        does not make such representation obligatory.

–   The newly approved constitution has brought many significant
    changes to Moroccan women. A new section entitled
    "Fundamental freedoms and Rights " includes the following :

    •   Article 19 makes both men and women equal citizens
        before the law (freedom and equality of all citizens and
        their participation in the political, economic, cultural and
        social spheres).
        –   The state works for the realization of parity[10]

- It creates an Authority for Equality and the Fight Against all Forms of Discrimination for the purpose of achieving equality between men and women[11]
- Article 21 prohibits sexism[12]
- Articles 32 and 34 that state clearly the rights of women, children and the disabled[13].

Later in the constitutional draft/text, we find

- Article 59 safeguards these rights and liberties during states of emergency[14][15].
- Article 175 says that these rights cannot be retracted in future constitutional revisions[16].

In fact, Morocco's official ratification of CEDAW and its optional protocol in addition to the articles of new constitutional will open Moroccan women the doors widely for further legitimate action. They would be used to change the discriminatory laws that still imped Moroccan women to achieve their full citizenship.

Conclusion

Tracing women's activism in Morocco is a fascinating exercise. It has gone through different stages, has adopted different strategies, has taken different shapes and has instigated unprecedented gender reforms namely in the Arab World. Despite its contentious nature, the activism led by women's organizations has enabled them to achieve unprecedented gender reforms in Arab Muslim world. On the other hand, women of the 20 Feb Movement have managed to revolutionize the feminist thinking in Morocco by directing consciously or unconsciously their activism toward putting the whole society on the democracy truck. Their young age, type education, their openness on the regional and international development through media are but some of the factors that explain this incredible shift. Indeed, despite their gains may appear few in number, this shift is very significant in terms of future action. Still, I believe that the survival of this consciousness is conditioned upon the willingness, ability and commitment of all Moroccans to engage in new regional waves of change.

Notes

1   *Al-Adlwallhsan* is the biggest and best-organized Islamist group in Morocco.. It is active mostly in universities and in helping the poor, but it is banned from politics due mostly to what is seen as its hostile rhetoric towards the monarchy.
2   Years of Lead is a term used by the opponents to the rule of King Hassan II to describe a period of his rule which was marked by political unrest and a heavy-handed government response to criticism and opposition.
3   http://womensenews.org/story/leadership/120424/young-moroccans-keep-arab-spring-spirit-alive#. (accessed on May 21, 2014).
4   Ibid.
5   In addition to falling an easy target to many problems, Moroccan women's movement organizations are discredited for a number of reasons: they focus, in their demands, largely on issues important to more elite women of urban areas and fail to address properly the need of poor rural women; they are not homogenous in their "raison d'être" nor in their organization or operating methods; they are trapped by the web of elitism of their leaders and are essentially hierarchal and exclusive.
6   See the press conference, watch this video on YouTube: https://www.youtube.com/watch?v=-i9mEB_sWnw
7   Ibid.
8   Ibid.
9   International women's democracy network. "Women's Rights and the Arab Spring: Middle East/North Africa Overview and Fact". Sheethttp://www.learningpartnership.org/iwdn/2011/11/women%E2%80%99s-rights-and-the-arab-spring-middle-eastnorth-africa-overview-and-fact-sheet/
10 Morocco' new constitution text, 2011 As Promulgated 29 July 2011, translated by Jefri J. Ruchti. Retrieved from http://www.womenonwaves.org/en/media/inline/id.(accessed on May 29, 2014).
11 Morocco' new constitution text, Op,cit.
12 Ibid .
13 Ibid.
14 Ibid.
15 Ibid.
16 Ibid

References

Aboim, Sofia and Vasconcelos, Pedro. 2011. "From Political to Social Generations: A Critical Reappraisal of Mannheim's Classical Approach. Annual Meeting of the American Sociological Association, Caesar's Palace, Las Vegas. ttp://repositorio.ul.pt/bitstream/10451/7742/1/ICS_SAboim_FromPolitical_AI.pdf(Accessed on Feb.21, 2015)

Baker, Alison, 1998. *Voices of Resistance: Oral Histories of Moroccan Women*. New York: State University of New York Press,

Benchemsi, Ahmed Reda 2012. "Feb20's rise and fall: a Moroccan story".Retrieved fromhttp://ahmedbenchemsi.com/feb20s-rise-and-fall-a-moroccan-story (accessed on May 21, 2014).

Bernhard, M. 1993. "Civil Society and Democratic Transition in East Central Europe'" *Political Science Quarterly* 108, 2: 307–22.

Brand, Laurie. 1995. ""in the beginning was the state....": The Quest for Civil Society in Jordan". In Norton, Augustus. Richard (Ed.). *Civil Society in the Middle East,* Vol I. (pp. 148–185). Leiden. New York & Köln: EJ: Brill.

Chafaai, Laila. 1993. "Alharakanisai'yawa alamojtma3 lamadani: moulahadatawalitya". (In Arabic). ["Feminist Movement and Civil Society: Preliminary Observations"]. *Afaq.* 102: 100–108.

Ennaji, Moha. 2004. "Women and Development". In Sadiqi, Fatima (Ed.). *Femmes Méditeranéennes*, pp. 39–46. Mohammadia: Imprimierie Fédala.

Ennaji, Moha. 2005. *Multiculturalism, Cultural Identity and Education in Morocco.* New York: Springer.

Ennaji, Moha. 2008. "Steps to the Integration of Moroccan Women in Development". *British Journal of Middle Eastern Studies, 35, (3): 339–348.*

Habermas, Jürgen. 1991. *The Structural Transformation of the Public Sphere: an Inquiry into a Category of Bourgeois Society.* (Thomas Burger & Frederick Lawrence, trans). Cambridge, MA: MIT Press.

Kazemi, Farah. 2002. "Perspectives on Islam and Civil Society".In Hashimi, Salih (Ed.). *Islamic Political Ethics: Civil Society, Pluralism and Conflict*, Princeton & Oxford: Princeton University Press.

Mannheim, Karl. 1952. 'The Problem of Generations.' In Paul Kecskemeti (Ed.) *Essays on the Sociology of Knowledge*, pp. 276–320. London: Routledge and Kegan Paul.

Martin, Brain. 2007. "Activism, Social and Political." In Gary L. Anderson and Kathryn G. Herr (Eds.). *Encyclopedia of Activism and Social Justice,* , pp. 19–27. Thousand Oaks, CA: Sage. Retrieved from http://www.bmartin.cc/pubs/07Anderson.html (accessed on Feb. 21. 2015).

Pilcher, Jane. 1994. 'Manheim's Sociology of Generations: An Undervalued Legacy.' *British Journal of Sociology* 45(3): 481–95.

Ottaway, Marina. 2011. "The New Moroccan Constitution: Real Change or More of the Same?". http://carnegieendowment.org/2011/06/20/new-moroccan-con-stitution-real-change-or-more-of-same/5l (accessed on May 29, 2014).

Sadiqi, Fatima, et al. (Eds.). (2000). *Feminsit Movement: Origins and Orientations.* Fez: Faculty of Letters Dhar el Mahraz

Sadiqi, Fatima. 2003. *Women. Gender and Language in Morocco.* Leiden: Brill.

Sadiqi, Fatima. 2004. "Civil Society and Feminism in Morocco". In Ennaji, Moha (Ed.). *Société Civil, Genre et Développement Durable*, pp. 52–54. Fez: Fes-Saiss Publications.

Sadiqi, Fatima. And Ennaji. Moha. 2006. "The Feminization of the Public Space: Women's Activism, the Family Law and Social Change in Morocco". *Journal of Middle East Women's Studies, 2,(2):86–114.*

Sadiqi, Fatima. & Valentine, Moghaddam. 2006. 'Women's Activism and the Public Sphere: an Introduction and Overview '. *Journal of Middle East Women's Studies,2,(2): 1–7.*

Sadiqi, Fatima. 2006. "The Impact of Islamization on Moroccan Feminisms". *Signs special issue: Gender and Spirituality. 32, (1),32–39.*

Sadiqi, Fatima. 2008. "Facing Challenges and Pioneering Feminist and Gender Studies: Women in Post-colonial and Today's Maghrib". *African and Asian Studies,7: 447–470.*

Sadiqi, Fatima. 2008. "The Central Role of the Family Law in the Moroccan Feminist Movement". *British Journal of Middle Eastern Studies, 35, (3): 325–337.*

Shils, Edward. 2002. *"The Virtues of Civil Society"*. In Sajoo, Amyn (Ed.). *Civil Society in the Muslim World*, pp. 61–94. New York: St Martin's Press.

Skalli, Loubna H. 2011. "Generational Politics and Renewal of Leadership in the Moroccan Women's Movement". *International Feminist Journal of Politics. 13, (3): 329–848.*

Smith, Andrew. R. And Loudiy, Fadoua. 2005. "Testing the Red Lines: On the Liberalization of Speech in Morocco". *Human Rights Quarterly, 27, (3): 1069–1119.*

Yachouti. Mohammed. (2007)."Women and the Moroccan State: The Struggle over the Issue of Citizenship", a paper presented in Politics and Gender: On Citizenship, Representation and Reform, a panel for the German Congress of Oriental Studies, September 24 – 28, 2007, Freiburg im Breisgau – Germany.

Yachoulti, Mohammed. 2012. *Civil Society, Women's Movement and The Moroccan State: Addressing the Specificities and Assessing the Roles.* Saarbrücken: LAP Lambert Academic Publishing.

Young, Iris Marion. 2001. "Activist Challenges to Deliberative Democracy". *Political Theory* Vol 29, 5: 670–690.

Zakia Salime. 2012. "Signs of New Feminism? Promises of Morocco's February 20". Retrieved from http://www.jadaliyya.com/pages/index/8842/signs-of-new-feminism-promises-of-moroccos-february (accessed on Mar. 29,2014)

Chapter 10

DIVAS, PSYCHOS AND ACTION CHICKS

Depictions of Women's Place and
Space in Moroccan Cinema in
the Age of Globalization

Valérie K. Orlando

Introduction

The contemporary film industry in Morocco reflects the sociopolitical and cultural transitions that have taken place in the country since 1999 and the enthronization of King Mohamed VI. In contrast to King Hassan II's repressive, almost forty-year rule known as *Les Années de plomb* (The Lead Years, 1963–1999), Mohamed VI's tenure thus far has been defined more or less through positive reform. The democratic climate has also fostered progressive legislation and a more open political climate. Encouraged by the augmented democratic transparency, male and female filmmakers have engaged once taboo topics in order to explore pressing sociopolitical and cultural debates in contemporary Morocco. Many of these debates encompass the roles of women in public space.

As feminist scholars have noted, political and legislative reforms as well as the Moroccan feminist movement (gaining momentum certainly since the late 1990s), have led to the "gradual feminization and, hence, democratization of the public sphere in Morocco. This impact has triggered significant social and discourse changes in [society]" in all areas spanning from the political to the cultural (Sadiqi and Ennaji 1987). This essay considers these "discourse changes" through several socio-cultural and political polemics that have taken place in the last decade and how these have influenced the subjects of Moroccan cinema.

Legislative Reforms, Women's Stories and Film

First, the positive outcomes stemming from the 2004 Moroccan legislative reforms to the *Mudawana* (the Moroccan family code), have influenced how women access public space. Second, through discussion and dialogue about past abuse of human rights, fostered through such efforts as the 2005 report handed in to King Mohamed VI by the "Instance Equité et Reconciliation" (Equity and Reconciliation Committee), which documented the imprisonment, torture and the general abuse of thousands during King Hassan II's reign, have also impacted women. Many of the abused were women whose stories were never told until recently. Third, the international movements that have occurred in the guise of the "Arab Spring" have, in part, championed more rights for women across the Arab world, thus generating debates about the roles of women in public space.

Specifically, this essay demonstrates how several Moroccan films made in the last decadehave reflected interesting debates and issues rooted in the legislative reforms, as well as current feminist writing and theory emanating from feminist movements in the country.[1] The winds of change, promoting the political reforms discussed here, have helped inform the roles women play on screen. The films considered in this essay are social-realist texts which often promote "what if scenarios" but also are meant to didactically present to audiences the hurdles women face every day in Moroccan society as they seek equal enfranchisement in the public sphere with men. Film, like traditional forms of print media as well as social media and television, has aided in realizing feminist goals that promote women, more often than not, as strong agents of change. Sexuality, sexual freedom, women's rights to their bodies, have all been subjects brought to the fore in Moroccan cinema.

"Arab new media" has played a role in influencing change in mores pertaining to women on screen. Internet, blogging, social networking through Facebook and Twitter, not only in Morocco, but elsewhere, have contributed to shaping feminist discourse and depictions of feminine identity. Amal Al-Malki, David Kaufer, Suguru Ishizaki and Kira Dreher's (2012) collective study entitled *Arab Women in Arab News: Old Stereotypes and New Media* has offered groundbreaking research that helps contextualize the diverse roles women are playing and shaping across the Arab world through and in media of all forms. The informative value of their study is revealed in its diversity with respect to the countries surveyed and its goal to dissuade stereotypes both in Arab nations and the West. The polysemous nature of the study's framework is captured on the first page where the authors ask the question: "Why are women hard to find" in media generated both in the Arab world and the West?:

> The Arab woman is a flesh-and-blood human being living in twenty-two countries and territories among some 340 million people spanning northern Africa and western Asia.... She is illiterate and lives in abject poverty. She is blessed with unimaginable wealth enjoying near universal literacy. ...She is a sister, wife, mother, daughter, grandmother, aunt, and cousin. She is the vital tissue binding her immediate and extended family together. She is educated, with doctoral and medical degrees. She holds titles in universities and labors on the streets.....The Arab woman is no different from women everywhere. (Al-Malki et al. 2012: 3)

In general, the authors note, both western and Arab media "have muffled, scripted, or staged" women on the screen (Al-Malki et al. ibid: 21). Many scripts rely on stereotypes that have their origins in the mythical, colonial fantasies of the 19th and early 20th centuries. "From the postcard images of Algerian women sold as trinkets to French tourists" to more recent "editorial cartoons mocking women in veils... to staged photography of Western models posing as 'harem women' in the formative days of Hollywood", women of the Middle East/North Africa (MENA) region have not been favorably cast in public space (Al-Malki et al. ibid: 14). Moroccan filmmakers, therefore, more than ever before, are compelled both nationally and internationally to dispel the stereotypes that prevail about women's roles, place and agency in both private and public spheres in society.

Moroccan women's identity, subjecthood, and agency in society (or lack thereof), have been the favorite *sujets du jour* in many films since the early 2000s. Heroines are "action chicks", *femmes fatales*, abused spouses, raped girlfriends, prostitutes, and martyred mothers. For the most part, these films are made solely for Moroccan audiences and rarely screened abroad. They cast women at the heart of some of the most intense culture wars currently taking place in the country. Heroines are depicted as standing at the crossroads of modernity and tradition, asking themselves how best to form identities that are modern but not too westernized, and religiously devout without being too submissive, in a country whose economic development puts its GDP on par with Brazil. Women find themselves ensconced in scenarios which tackle secularism verses religiosity, Western verses Eastern, and French verses Arabic and/or Berber languages. These films also demonstrate that, although many of the roles women play on screen are formidable, and "while presently, the presence of women in the public sphere may be no longer taboo, women's access to positions of power remains so" (Glacier 2013 xv).

Influential Political Reforms Affecting Women's Roles in Moroccan Film

As mentioned above, the themes of Moroccan cultural production, predominantly forms of expression on screen –film and documentaries, social media—, have been significantly influenced by two major events in the last decade: the 2004 *Mudawana* reform, and the 2005 report handed in by the "Instance Equité et Reconciliation" (IER, Truth and Reconciliation Committee).[2]

Many of the egregious human rights violations noted in the IER report were purported against women, as Susan Slyomovics notes in *The Performance of Human Rights in Morocco* (2005). The IER report did not pass judgment on the former regime (indeed, the caveat for the investigative reporting done by the commission was that none of the perpetrators would be prosecuted). Instead, it was meant to aid society as a healing agent for change that would help address inadequacies in the inquisitorial system and to ensure better protection of human rights for all citizens. Particularly with respect to women, the IER contributed to revealing the untold stories of many former victims of torture and imprisonment during the Hassan II era (Slyomovics ibid).

On screen, women victimized during the Lead Years has been a topic of several films made in the last fifteen years, the most notable of which is *Jawhara* (2003, Saâd Chraïbi). This interesting, if not compelling film, focuses on women's prison life, rarely accounted for in official documents or the press prior to the IER report. The film tells the story of a girl born in prison after her mother, Safia, is raped by a prison warden. The young girl is destined to remain in prison as long as the sentence is sustained. Set in the 1970s and subsequently told through flashbacks by the now adult Jawhara, we learn of her mother's militancy and activism in the Communist party and its efforts to present alternative political views during a time that was exceedingly dangerous for those who spoke out against the status quo.[3] Although gleaning mixed reviews at the time of its release, *Jawhara* was one of the first visual depictions of women's imprisonment during the repressive Lead Years. The fact that women are shown imprisoned, when in the official documents from the 1970s women were unnamed and virtually unmentioned, serves to adjust historical memory and inscribe women into the Moroccan past as never before.

The *Mudawana* reform of 2004, as discussed elsewhere in this volume, granted women significant rights under the law (although it is still debatable as to how much the reform has really helped illiterate, rural women). Specifically it raised the marriage age to eighteen (for both men and women), granted women the right to contract their own marriages (no male family member need be involved), granted equal authority in the family to both genders, approved greater financial rights (women have new rights to assets acquired through marriage), established judicial divorce (men must go to court, instead of simply verbally repudiating their wives with no legal intervention), and both men and women have the right to seek divorce through the courts.

Both the *Mudawana* and the IER report have entered the societal debates depicted on screen about women and sexuality in the public sphere. For example, the comical film *Number One* (2008), made by Zakia Tahiri, takes to task the influence of change both in public and private spheres that the *Mudawana* proposed for Moroccan men and women. Although tongue and cheek, Tahiri's film about a macho husband and his reticence to embrace his wife's desire to be something else than "just a housewife", all the while debating in the background the 2004 *Mudawana* reform, takes to task the very real views and fears of men. From the beginning, Tahiri notes, the *Mudawana*, although decreed as law, "has remained insufficiently explained to some, not understood by others and badly interpreted by many who propagate conflicting ideas about it" (Chaâba 2014.) The filmmaker captures these sentiments in a scene where three men discuss what will happen to them when the law becomes a reality in everyday society: "We are dead with this new *Mudawana*", they quip. Perhaps exaggerated, Tahiri's film nevertheless captures a certain male paranoia that is rooted in women's perceived power to corrupt men and cause chaos in society if not managed and controlled. Fatima Mernissi's (1987) now well-known text, *Beyond the Veil*, discusses this topic at length, explaining that women in traditional Muslim societies are viewed as the root of *fitna* –chaos and disorder—and must be contained in order to assure masculine rule and the domination of the evil temptations that women can cause: "The Muslim woman is endowed with a fatal attraction which erodes the male's will to resist her and reduces him to a passive acquiescent role. He has no choice: he can only give in to her attraction, whence her identification with fitna, chaos, and with the anti-divine and the anti-social forces of the universe" (Mernissi, ibid: 41).

As social texts, Moroccan films promote what scholar Margot Badran notes is a "feminist discourse and practice that...[are].. seeking rights and justice within the framework of gender equality for women and men in the totality of their existence" (Badran n.p.). Contemporary filmmakers overwhelmingly promote women as public, active agents in society. Their heroines seek to contribute socio-culturally and politically to the social discourse on and about women in society. While heroines often fail in effectuating their individualism when confronting the hurdles of family and relationships, tradition and established mores, they nevertheless expose for debate some of the most essential, socio-political gendered questions of Morocco's modern times. In the context of the rapidly changing MENA region, women are challenging the "rescue myth" attached to them by the West wherein they are always cast as "unassertive, compliant, and voiceless" (Al-Malki et al. ibid: 14).

While often didactically driven, contemporary films do present to audiences many of the above-mentioned dualisms specific to Morocco that consume women both on and off the screen. Films such as *Pegase* (Pegasus, 2010), for example, prove that male filmmakers are often as astute as their female colleagues in understanding the psychological hurdles and pressures women in Moroccan society face, particularly in rural areas. These filmmakers note that "views on human nature, culture, and society are not neutral when it comes to gender" (Kozlova 2002 15). And, when it is a question of psychology, as *Pegase* demonstrates, culture as well as tradition influence to what extent a woman, who has been determined to be mentally ill, is accepted in society. In Morocco, as psychiatrist Rita El Khayat (2000:45) notes, "mentally ill women" are often caught in a "prison-like system....reductionist and devaluating" from which there is no possibility of escape.

Contemporary Moroccan films symbolically represent the socio-cultural transitions taking place with respect to gender in Morocco and seek to dispel stereotypes purporting women as voiceless and victimized. Films such as Hassan Ben Jelloun's *Jugement d'une femme* (Judgment of a Woman, 2000), Narjis Nejjar's *Les Yeuxsecs* (Dry Eyes, 2002), Leila Marrakchi's *Marock* (2005), Farida Bourquia's Deux*Femmes sur la route* (Two Women on the Road, 2007), and Mohamed Moufkir's *Pegase* (Pegasus, 2010), among many others, cast women in a variety of roles—from a battered wife who, in the end, gets justice (Ben Jelloun), to poor Berber women living in a remote village who must eke out a living through prostitution (Nejjar), to young, rich girls who sleep around, smoke marijuana, and live lives on the edge in Casablanca, seemingly enjoying all the freedom western women have (Marrakchi),to women trapped in mental wards as depicted in the surreal and haunting film *Pegase* (Mouftakir). What these films have in common is their drive to demonstrate that women cannot be viewed as one "homogenous and unchanging social group" wherein they can never hope to attain other alternative identities (Hamil 2009: 86). Also among these multifaceted roles are crime-solving, gun slinging *Nikita*-types as portrayed in NourredineLakhmari's crime drama the first episode of which is entitled *El Khadia*. The series introduced audiences to young and sexy, officer Hajjami.

Although often cast as *femmes fatales,* action chicks, prostitutes or psychos, cinematic roles allow women almost always to harness power-engaging agency that challenges antiquated (both persisting colonial and nationalist) views about them. These roles demonstrate that women must (and can) emerge from not only the yokes of the orientalized colonial past, but also the "gendered nature of various movements—notably nationalist and fundamentalist movements" that have contributed to how they are symbolically viewed in society (Moghadam 2013: 25). Many Moroccan films explore "the centrality of gender and the 'woman question' in constructions of national, cultural, and religious identity" in the postcolonial state, and how these have hampered women's access to individual agency; in short, the right to be themselves in public space (Moghadam, ibid: 25). Valentine Moghadam (ibid: 25) notes that in the MENA region, "women have been socially constructed as symbols of the nation-state, bearers of cultural identity, and repositories of religious values". Thus, film becomes the ultimate media through which to engage audiences to think about these "constructed symbols", unpack them, and imagine a new reality for women. In a country where illiteracy rates in any language are still exceedingly high, film serves an essential role in furnishing a place for debate that is visually driven, while also significantly meaningful in the message that are conveyed. TV miniseries such as *El Khadia* and feature-length films like *Two Women on the Road*, for example, are defiantly representing the conflicted and tenuous places that women, particularly in the MENA region, occupy in the public sphere of the fast-paced global modernity in which they must live.

Of Veils and Action Chicks: Hijab al hob (Veils of Love, 2009) and El Khadia (The Affair, 2006)

The 2009 film *Hijab al hob* (Veils of Love/*Amours voilés*) tells the story of Batoul a 27 –year old successful pediatrician, working in a private hospital, who lives with her family in the upper echelons of Casablanca's elite. She is beautiful, educated, successful, and independent (despite living with her extended family). She owns and drives her own car, and stays out late whenever she likes with her free-thinking, fun-loving girlfriends. While she professes to be religiously devout, religion for her is a private matter.

Out on the town one evening, Batoul meets the dashing divorcé, Hamza, an older, grizzled, man-of-the-world type, who was previously married to a French woman, lived abroad for many years, and has only just returned to Morocco with his young daughter to take care of his ailing mother. He is secular, loves women, but does not want to make any further lasting commitments. His desire for Batoul is carnal. Batoul, on the other hand, is still a virgin who is conflicted and caught in the middle of her own desire to be a free, independent woman, embracing all facets of her sexuality, and the taboos of traditional Moroccan culture. These traditions dictate that women are to remain pious and virgins until marriage. While her immediate family places few demands on her (other than her mother continually asks her to think about getting married), the larger Moroccan cultural taboos prove to be daunting. However for a time, her individualism and her own desire for Hamza do win out. She takes risks and breaks all normative cultural conventions. Batoul begins frequently visiting Hamza's bachelor pad alone where they have sex. Their love making becomes more arduous throughout the film as they become more daring in their love-making. Batoul's naked breasts and the sexually explicit scenes of the film are some of the most risqué ever to be seen on Moroccan movie screens.

Although he professes to be infatuated with Batoul, Hamza refuses to discuss marriage. She gives him an ultimatum, telling him that he can think about not having her during Ramadan. If, in one month, he still wants to see her, then he must propose. Out of respect for her family and the traditions associated with the holiday, Batoul started wearing the traditional Islamic headscarf, the *hijab*. First, just at family gatherings, then slowly its presence becomes more of her daily routine as she begins to wear it to her office at the hospital. She declares that during Ramadan, thinking about religion is a duty. Her fragile personality, which seems to be her reason for wearing the veil, is due to the earlier stresses in her life caused by the death of her father, her mother's marriage to another man, the death of a young boyfriend, as well all the sacrifices she made for her medical studies. These all result in deep soul searching.

At the time of the film's release, filmmaker Aziz Salmy insisted that his film was not only about the conflicted views that often surround wearing the *hijab*, but about women who desire to live independently and who, at a certain age, wrestle with the misconceived notion that the veil will help them catch a husband. This assumption is discussed among Batoul and her friends in several scenes. Although all independent women, they are worried that not veiling will make them seem "loose and wild" to men. When *Hijab al Hob* was released, it sparked heated debates on blogs and the internet for months about the value of veiling to impede sin. These internet exchanges were primarily written by young people; both male and female, veiled and unveiled, and religious and secular.

Salmy insists that his film was not conceived to provoke, but rather to ground meaningful discussion about what the veil represents in modern Moroccan society where women do have choices, particularly those who are educated. Morocco "is not Iran", he emphasizes. Yet, the PJD –Parti de la justice et du développement – the Islamic political party represented in the Moroccan parliament, sought to censure the film immediately after its release; even though its leaders professed they hadn't seen it. Their calls fell on deaf ears. Salmy's film was endorsed by the CCM (Centre Cinématographique Marocain), the national film institute of Morocco, and not banned. Defending his film, Salmy noted: "I seek to provoke debate and to draw attention to these young women in their thirties who have made it socially, but who still are pulled between their professional ambitions and the temptation of a family life *bien rangée* (well taken care of), and the tutelage of a protecting and kindly man" (Ziraoui, 2012).Batoul represents the general desires and frailties expressed by many Moroccan women as she tries to navigate between her professional life, love for Hamza, and religious piety. In one scene, when Hamza takes her shopping, she tantalizes him in sleeveless short dresses while also wearing the veil. In another, more daring scene (one which particularly rankled the cockles of the PJD, leading to their calls for censorship), Batoul and Hamza make love as he slowly removes her veil all the while the muezzin's call to prayer at the local mosque is heard in the background.

In the concluding scenes of *Hijab al Hob*, Batoul finds herself pregnant with still no commitment from Hamza; in fact, they are now estranged. She decides to "raise her child on her own." The veil and man are jettisoned in favor of Salmy's version of the Moroccan modern woman. Batoul is a woman who uses the agency in public and private spheres that the *Mudawana* reforms have promised her. She decides to tackle the daunting obstacles presented by the traditional, socio-cultural hurdles of raising a child out of wedlock. She exercises her reproductive power, disrupting the social order as rarely depicted on Moroccan screens. A few years ago, the very notion would have been taboo and unthinkable.

Batoul's fragility is starkly contrasted when compared to gun-slinging, crime solving Inspector Hajjami. In 2006, Moroccan filmmaker Nourredine Lakhmari was asked by 2M, the principal state run TV network of Morocco, to write and direct nine episodes of a crime series called *El Khadia* (The Affair) to be aired during Ramadan. The series was influenced by American TV crime dramas such as *CSI, Bones, Cold Case, Prime Suspect* and *Body of Proof.* Its hardboiled plots –although simplistic, violent and extremely graphic– touch upon a host of social messages in addition to the overarching one which states that women can be tough police officers and have a place in the fast-paced modernity that characterizes the Morocco of this millennium. Inspector Hajjami is sent to investigate a young woman's murder in the remote village of Aïn Leuh in the Atlas Mountains. She is the quintessential "Action Chick," recognizable by all contemporary audiences the world over (Inness 2004:7). As a woman forensic science police officer, she profiles murderers through the latest technical innovations and scientific inquiry in order to solve heinous crimes. Hajjami, beautiful, feminine, analytical and intellectual, represents a new generation of law enforcement, as well as a "new" brand of Moroccan woman; both of which aspire to exist in modern, 21st century Morocco. Like generic Action Chicks (particularly those on American TV screens—Temperance Brennen in *Bones*, Beckett in *Castle*, etc), Hajjami "reinscribes notions of Western and white heteronormative superiority....[evoking] 'West-is-best'" narratives (Tung 2004: 106). Her looks are a composite of cosmopolitan whiteness and urban-savvy that remind audiences of *La Femme Nikita*, the universal, globally recognized standard model (even in Morocco) for the modern Action Chick. Another overarching theme is that women's roles and places within urban culture, as found in Casablanca, are associated with the most modern aspects of Moroccan society. Filmed entirely in Moroccan Arabic, the series offers audiences an overview of past history and present socio-cultural and political hurdles as well as reflects the IER Committee's influence on judicial and police procedures (certainly with respect to cleaning up corruption and police brutality).What is most interesting about the series is that it projects what Morocco is and what it aspires to be on many fronts; ranging from women's emancipation to uncorrupted, just police procedure. In the first episode, Hajjami is sent to investigate a murder by the police commissioner in Casablanca because she is considered "the best man for the job". Upon her arrival in the mountain village, she is cross-examined by the local *sheik*. Sidi Abbas, who has come to meet the "detective from the city" at the bus stop, has no idea that the "he" is, in fact, a "she".

Abbas:	Hi.
Hajjami:	Hi.
Abbas:	Did the bus come by?
Hajjami:	Yes.
Abbas:	Damn.
Abbas:	I always miss the bus. Did a man get off the bus?
Hajjami:	No, nobody.
Abbas:	He didn't come. I came for nothing. Those people in Rabat spend all their time criticizing and are never efficient. You, my daughter, you seem like you're waiting for someone. Can I take you to the village?
Hajjami:	Yes. Thanks, Mr...
Abbas:	My name's Abbas. I'm the sheik of the region.
Hajjami:	Mr. Abbas, Officer Hajjami.
Abbas:	And the other...man?
Hajjami:	Mr. Abbas, there is no other *man*. I'm the man you're waiting on.
Abbas:	But,here we're not used to women police officers.....
Hajjami:	Mr. Abbas, times have changed......

This particular episode, like all the others which follow, ends with Hajjami solving the crime. More symbolically it also entreats contemporary audiences to think about Morocco's socio-cultural schizophrenia and the division between genders, urban/rural, and rich/poor as the above exchange reveals.

Psycho-social-political Dis/Enfranchisement: Agency and Power in *Deux femmes sur la route* and *Pegase*

No two films made in the last decade so accurately depict the wide range of roles envisioned for women on the screen as do *Deux femmes sur la route* (Two Women on the Road, 2007) directed by one of the first Moroccan female directors, Farida Bourquia, and the more recent *Pegase* (Pegasus, 2010) by Mohamed Mouftakir.

Two Women on the Road reminds audiences (certainly American) of the iconic film, *Thelma and Louise* (1991, Ridley Scott), which made a statement about women's lack of enfranchisement in American society in the early 1990s. Faced with few options at the end of the film, suicide is perceived as the only viable solution for Thelma and Louise. Although reminiscent of the American film, Bourquia's rendition is divergent in its messages. It not only entreats audiences to think about women's enfranchisement (or lack thereof) in contemporary society, it also draws out interesting debates about class, urban vs. rural, and generational divides that also contribute to women's conflicted roles in public space.

The film opens with Amina driving alone on a desolate road on the way to Tetouan in the northeastern part of Morocco. Her car overheats and she is stranded on the barren highway. She is helped by a goatherd who promises to go to a nearby village to find a new radiator. Once in the village, she realizes after waiting hours for the new part, that the goatherd has absconded with her 300 dirhams and her radiator.

While waiting, smoking a cigarette, Amina is approached by middle-aged traditionally dressed Rahma, who declares "that the young woman owes her money for the blankets she has brought her from the market." Amina tells her she has ordered no blankets and that Rahma has mistaken her for someone else. Rahma will not budge and asks her pryingly where she is going. Amina replies, "to Tetouan" but tells her that her car has broken down and she is waiting on a part. The older woman tells her to forget it, that "the men are dishonest around here; you'll never see your radiator or the money again." She convinces Amina to spend the night with her and wait until the next day to confront the dishonest mechanics.

As she walks through the hot, dusty village, Amina, skimpily clad in tight-fitting jeans, tank top with bared shoulders, sporting stiletto heels, wearing lots of makeup and openly chain-smoking (something women, up to a few years ago, would never have been seen doing in public in Morocco), is an oddity. The young urban woman of the millennium generation, juxtaposed to the traditional, middle-aged Rahma of the country, who wears a headscarf and long dress, is a symbol for the socio-gendered schizophrenia women confront every day as they are caught between the conventional past and the uncertainties of the present.

Rahma is fat, dowdy, and walks clumsily behind the brazen Amina as they traverse the village. Yet, one thing both women have in common is that their husbands have deserted them. They recognize that their differences are only in physical appearance. Rhama states that her husband "went back to his village and left me for a younger woman as soon as he retired." Amina reveals that she is trying to find money to pay off a judge to get her husband out of jail. Despite the young woman's emancipated ways and independence, she divulges that she, too, has been betrayed by her husband, who told her after their marriage that he "already had a wife." When Rahma asks Amina how she could marry a married man, she replies: "for money." The young woman later admits that her husband has been jailed for drug trafficking in Tetouan.

Rahma also must go to Tetouan, a city to which she has never been. She, like many mothers before her, is summoned to identify the body of her son who has allegedly washed up onshore after he embarked in a small boat for Italy. Without a car, Amina agrees to accompany Rahma on the bus to Tetouan. Both women's stories end on a conflicted note. Amina decides that she will never be free of the life of crime she has led if she stays with her dubious husband, so she leaves him. And, Rahma's son who, in the end, is not dead in the morgue, is perhaps safe in Europe "somewhere." As they stand on the cliffs overlooking the sea, Amina asks Rahma what she thinks of the ocean. The older woman replies: "It's the first time I've seen it. I like it, except it is monstrous". Accompanying the universality of her message, Bourquia symbolically uses the majestic cliffs on which the women are standing to represent their newfound, unfettered freedom.

Bourquia's film exposes the everyday hurdles women face because of the whims and broken promises of men. The overtly "chick flick" quality of the filmmaker's story casts men as inept and made fragile by unemployment, alcohol, and poverty. In general, *Two Women on the Road* offers audiences a pessimistic depiction of contemporary women's lives, no matter their class, education, or social standing. Whether they are rural or urban, educated or illiterate, rich or poor, women all face a particular kind of feminine misery that can be caused only by men. However, the film also instructs audiences that in contemporary Morocco women can also persevere and survive on their own. In the end, Amina and Rahma climb into their car and drive away. Unlike Thelma and Louise, they do not choose to drive over the cliffs, but to tackle the obstacles before them.

Mohamed Mouftakir's *Pegase*, in part, exposes the psychological instability and physical abuse of women in rural areas. At the same time, the film presents an interesting intersection of myth, dreams, and modernity contextualized in a story about female mental illness. It is a story that alludes to the dark vestiges of Morocco's brutal past (imprisonment and torture), scrutinizes the mythical ideologies associated with mental illness, and wrestles with the taboos of sexual abuse. Mouftakir's dream-like script, demonstrates the power of symbolism while also exploring taboo subjects such as rape, incest, and the marginalization of rural societies in Morocco.

The story, located perhaps in the past or the present (this remains unclear throughout the film), focuses on two women, Zineb and Rhianna. Zineb is a mentally and emotionally unstable psychiatrist working for a male doctor, somberly dressed in black, who walks with a limp. He seems to be the head psychiatrist whose only aide in the asylum, besides Zineb, is a nurse (whose headdress resembles a nun's), also dressed in black. All three spend their time in the prison-asylum with one young female prisoner/patient named Rhianna. The young girl was mysteriously found abandoned in the streets, thus like many Moroccan films, her story alludes to the modern problem of child abandonment, street children, poverty and abjection. These social ills affect the most vulnerable – women and girls – , as Soshana Felman notes:"Madness is the impasse confronting those whom cultural conditioning has deprived of the very means of protest or self-affirmation" (7).

Rhianna is traumatized and pregnant, claiming to have been impregnated by "The Lord of the Horse." During multiple flashbacks, audiences are taken back to Rhianna's childhood, where she is brutally abused by a tyrannical father who is a skilled horseman and also the head of the tribe. Due to the lack of a male heir, the father raises Rhianna, whom he now calls Mehdi, as a boy so that she may continue the tradition of breeding and racing horses (duties reserved only for men) and, thus, maintain the power and prestige of the tribe. He tells Rhianna: "When you're a man, you can have everything...when you are a woman, you have nothing....The world is at your feet, take advantage of it....manhood is earned, no one is born a man". The tribe lives under the patriarchal tale of the powerful "Lord of the Horse", a mythical warrior who remained single all his life, had no heirs, and was only powerful as long as he ruled all horses and men.

Interestingly, this mythical, orientalized past of Mehdi is depicted in vivid color, whereas the tortured, imprisonment in the asylum, where Rhianna finds herself in the present, is shot in drab grays, blues and blacks. The present is haunted by the patriarchy and masculine domination of prison and mental institutions which psychiatrist Rita El Khayat (2000: 45) explains are systems of incarceration, "un univers concentrationnaire" (concentration universe).

The "universe of incarceration"manifests on Rhianna's body as her breasts are bound in cloth to hide them, her hair cut short in order to make her believable in the identity of Mehdi who will insure her/his father's prestige in the village as "The Lord of the Horse". The fortune that the father has amassed must be passed down to his heir and the heir can only be male. Thus, Rhianna's body must be abstracted and refashioned in order to play a role in a political field of power over which she has no control as a woman.

When Rhianna is brought to the asylum, she has suppressed all memories of being raped by her father, claiming instead that the baby is Zayd's, her lover and friend who has taught her secretly how to write. Her story, slowly told to Zineb, becomes a tale of Freudian transference as psychiatrist becomes patient, delving into her own haunted past. Both women have been abused, escaped the overbearing patriarchy of rural life, and are now seeking to find their true identities as free women. "Open your eyes", is a resounding, repeated phrase as the momentum of the film increases. Eyes (male, female, and equine), looking, gazing and penetrating are catalysts which propel both women to unlock the keys to suppressed pasts. Yet seeing the truth through the walls of so many prisons – symbolic, metaphoric and real – is seemingly impossible, since they are both enclosed by the physical prison/asylum and their troubled minds. The message that these women have been repressed by male domination, a hyper-patriarchal structure wrapped in traditional belief systems, is not lost on audiences. "Le système patriarcal tout entier a besoin de l'asile et de la prison, des gardiens et des chaînes" (the total patriarcal system needs the asylum, the prison, the guards and the chains) (El Khayat 2000: 50).

In the concluding scenes of the film, it is Zineb the psychiatrist who is told to "open her eyes". In reality it is she who finds herself in the asylum cell with her grown daughter, Rhianna, the psychiatrist at her bedside. "She's your daughter", the doctor tells the patient, "you left her twenty years ago." "I'm your daughter," Rhianna emphasizes. Zineb's closing remark is one that she sings: "Please father take me to see my ancestors". This phrase she sings as she closes her eyes, thus symbolically locking her in a prison from which she cannot escape.

Conclusion

Morocco, as elsewhere in the Arab world, is undergoing extreme transitions both social and political. Positive political and social reforms have influenced how women engage their agency in public space. In the last decade, filmmakers have attempted to capture this agency on screen. It remains to be seen, however, where the positive gains will ultimately lead women. One thing is sure, though, women in Morocco as elsewhere in the world will eventually reach political and social parity with men even if they have no help from anyone else but each other.

Notes

1 Women's movements in Morocco include: L'Union de l'action feminine (Union of Women's Action), which in 1992 "collected one million signatures in three months to demand that the *Mudawana*....be reformed" (Glacier xv-xvi). The ADFM (Association des femmes au Maroc) has also been instrumental in fostering lasting socio-political change in the country. See: http://www.adfm.ma/index.php?lang=fr (last accessed 1/18/15)

2 The reforms have most noticeably influenced urban women who are educated and who are middle and upper class. There is still much to be done in rural areas where women are 80% illiterate and often victims of acute poverty and lack of political enfranchisement in local communities (see Moghadam 2013).
3 It is estimated that during the Lead Years over 13 thousand people were "disappeared" under the Hassan II regime (see Slyomovics 2005).

Bibliography

Al-Malki, A. Kaufer, D., Ishizaki, S. & Dreher, K. 2012. *Arab Women in Arab News: Old Stereotypes and New Media.* London : Bloomsbury.

Chaâba, Q. 2014. *Le SoirEchos.* <http://www.yabiladi.com/article-culture-744.html>. (accessed on Jan. 18, 2–15).

El-Guindi, F. 1999. *Veil: Modesty, Privacy, and Resistance.* Oxford. : Berg Press.

El-Khayat, R. 2000. *La Folie: El Hank-Casablanca.* Casablanca : Eddif.

Felman, S. 1991. "Women and Madness" In R. Warhol et al (Eds.) *Feminisms*, pp.6–19 New Brunswick: Rutgers University Press.

Glacier, O. 2013. *Political Women in Morocco: Then and Now.* Trenton: The Red Sea Press.

Hamil, M. 2009. "Itineraries of Revival and Ambivalence in Postcolonial North African Cinema: From Benlyazid's 'Door to the Sky' to Meknèche's 'Viva Lalgérie,'" *African Studies Review*, vol. 52, no. 3, pp. 73–87.

Inness, S. 2004. "Boxing Gloves and Bustiers". In S. Inness (Ed.). *Action Chicks: New Images of Tough Women in Popular Culture*, pp. 1–17. New York: Palgrave.

Kozzlova, N.N. 2002. "Gender and the Advent of Modernity: Gender Analysis and the Methodology of Social Knowledge," *Russia Social Science Review*, vol. 43, no. 4, pp. 13–29.

Mernissi, F. 1987. *Beyond the Veil: Male-Female Dynamics in Modern Muslim Society*, Bloomington: Indiana University Press.

Moghadam, V. 2013. *Modernizing Women: Gender and Social Change in the Middle East*, 3rd edn. Boulder: Lynn Rienner Publishers.

Sadiqi, F. & Ennaji, M. 2006. "The Feminization of Public Space: Women's Activism, the Family Law, and Social Change in Morocco," *Journal of Middle East Women's Studies*, vol.2, no. 2, Spring, pp. 86–114.

Slyomovics, S. 2005. *The Performance of Human Rights in Morocco.* Philadelphia: Pennsylvania University Press.

Tung, C. 2004. "Gender, Race, and Sexuality in La Femme Nikita," In S. Inness (Ed.). *Action Chicks: New Images of Tough Women in Popular Culture,* pp. 95–121. New York: Palgrave.

Ziraoui, Y. 2014. "Amour et voile sont compatibles: Interview with Aziz Salmy." *TelQuel* (February 14–20). <http://www.telquel-online.com/360/interrogatoire360.shtml>. (accessed on Jan. 18, 2–15).

Chapter 11

THE EMPOWERING LEGACY OF WOMEN SAINTS

Venerators and Islamist Feminists

Aziza Ouguir

Introduction

This chapter investigates women saints' construction of sainthood within the context of Sufism and the significance of this construction to broader discourses on gender and feminism in Morocco[1]. The importance of women saints in Moroccan history is evident from the extensive contemporary, but also historical literature on them. Contemporary scholars have studied women saints and the rituals concerning their veneration.[2]These researchers relied on oral primary sources and fieldwork methodologies to study saints and their veneration. Other contemporary researchers have focussed on the study of the archives to highlight the role women saints played in history.[3] What has been overlooked in these two approaches is a combination of both written and oral sources that could highlight historical and contemporary instances of women's religious participation and serve to fill the gap in the scholarly literature on Moroccan women's religious practices. Despite women saints' historical significance and the enduring impact of their legacy on women throughout Morocco today, little is known about them.

I will start discussing my methodology in relation to the relevant scholarly literature, and introduce my concepts of Sufism and agency, that are important parts of the conceptual framework of my study on women saints and their construction of saintly personalities. Drawing on hagiographies[4] and other historical works, as well as oral histories, the chapter examines the self-formation process undertaken by exemplary women saints in Moroccan history to construct saintly personalities and achieve empowerment and their reception by their venerators and by Islamist feminist activist today. It places this process within the broader context of ethical freedom practices and ethical self-transformation techniques[5] and investigates the reception of these exemplary women by their venerators and the Islamists feminist activists, discussing the extent to which their legacy inspires contemporary women's empowerment.

Ethical self-formation, Freedom Practices and Agency

The concept of agency has received considerable scholarly attention in recent years. In her study of Egyptian mosque movement, Saba Mahmood (2005) bases her approach to agency on Michel Foucault's work, in particular his theory on ethical self-formation. In her view the participants of the women's mosque movement she interviewed are agents, who practiced ethical self-formation, without however challenging the patriarchal order. Instead, their actions conform to the male dominant system. Mahmood therefore questions the concept of agency as meaning free action, opposed to domination. People can also actively inhabit dominant norms, as agents, that is. Feminists should stop wanting all women to be free from domination, women can choose as agents to conform to their subordinated position.

According to Dutch scholar Karen Vintges, Mahmood reads Foucault selectively, where it concerns the concept ethical self-formation. Foucault did come up with a normative perspective which Mahmood totally obliterates, namely with the concept of ethical self formation as a freedom practice, working on the limits of patterns of domination.[6]

Foucault referred to Greek and Roman antiquity, where he found ethical self practices which were designed to cultivate ethical self-improvement. In his view, these techniques were characterized by a relative autonomy from moral rules or moral codes. The adherents to the philosophical schools and religious groups where these techniques were implemented freely undertook to transform themselves by cultivating a personal 'ethos' or ethical life. He therefore speaks in terms of ethical freedom practices.

Furthermore, Foucault asserts that ethical self-formation techniques are to be found in many moral systems, which entail an ethical relationship of the self to the self one aspires to be, and which one tries to realize by so called self-techniques involving all kinds of exercises. This ethical relationship of the self to the self has four dimensions, according to Foucault. First, *what* should be cultivated or transformed through the techniques. Second, *why* is the cultivation or transformation process necessary? Third, *how* is this process to be undertaken, and finally, *for what* purpose should it be undertaken[7]. Foucault in this way delivers analytical tools to analyze ethical self formation in other moral systems besides the ancient Greek one.

But he made it clear that his preference was that ethical self-practices were rather autonomous from moral rules, and he pointed to several strands of Islam and Buddhism to argue that this was also the case in other moral systems. This perspective of Foucault is totally obliterated by Mahmood.

And it is this perspective of Foucault which informed my research, where I was looking at women's religious agency in the past and present of Morocco. Do we deal here with ethical self-formation in the way Mahmood found in her study, namely do the religious women merely oblige and conform to the dominant moral system, or do we find here agents that transgress dominant patriarchal patterns, and do we deal here with ethical self formation in the sense of freedom practices? Similarly, I question whether their venerators do this, and the feminists that I interviewed. But let's first have a look at the women saints themselves.

Sufism and Female Sainthood

Sufism is gender neutral in principle and does not make any distinctions between men and women in as far as both can enter the Sufi path and acquire sainthood.[8] From the written hagiographies and oral stories in Moroccan contexts we indeed find that there are basically no differences between men and women where it concerns the main self-formation techniques that they undertook in order to become saints. This will become clear in the following sub-sections, which discuss exemplary cases of female saints.

Some main self-techniques used by Sufis are the practicing of piety, acquiring learnedness, the performing of miracles, and practicing *jadhb* (Divine attraction), as will be discussed respectively. The practicing of piety begins with some first steps of initiation into the Sufi path. One of the most important actions a Sufi performs in the beginning of her Sufi path is repentance (*tawba*), a word that describes the person's desire to change his or her life. *Tawba* signifies not only turning away from sin and worldliness, but it also conveys a person's total transformation of selfhood.[9] As comes forward from hagiography, Sufi women, like men, experienced an internal desire to radically change their material existence and to lead a pious life.

One enlightening example of this initiation is found in al-Tādilī's hagiographic entry of the female saint 'Umayya bint Yaghrusin (12th century), one of the greatest spiritual masters of' Aghmāt. One day when she visited 'Abd Salām Tunusī (12th century), she asked him to pray to God for her, then she left him and went to her house. She confined herself in retreat in a cave, where she led a lonely mystical life until she died.[10] She thus entered in a Sufi life, leaving behind worldliness to pursue piety and spirituality.

As narrated, Muniyya bint Mimūn al-Dukkalī (12th century) recorded with amazement the presence of large numbers of Sufi women in the gatherings in a *ribāt* (Sufi order). She said: "'One thousand women saints visited *ribāt Shākir* this year.'"[11] Moroccan women's strong desire to become religious and Sufis, impelled them to seek spiritual guidance offered by Sufi orders. They participated in religious meetings and ritual gatherings to learn about, and undertake, the stages of initiation and piety. Women, like men, adhered to a *ribāt* to undergo initiation and to develop their spirituality.

In hagiographic and oral narratives, the Sufi body comes forward as being subjected to certain rules and conditions for developing piety. Women Sufis are described as similarly purifying their bodies and constraining their needs against material desires. They are also presented as training their bodies to adapt to the hard ways of Sufi life in order to cultivate a pious personality. Through asceticism, prayer, remembrance, fasting, nightly invocations and austerity both men and women became pious. Through *mujāhada* (self-denial), women's bodies became inhibited and damaged. Muniyya bint Mimūn al-Dukālī (12 Century) when old became so thin that her skin stuck to her bones.[12]

Women saints chose other ways to destroy the physical properties of their bodies. They experienced biological crises such as *jadhb* (divine attraction) and *junūn* (foolishness) which made them behave freely and without social constraints. *Jadhb* is mad mysticism that Sufis sometimes chose as a medium for becoming saints. Al-Kattānī refers to Ṣafiya Lubāda (19th century). She was called Lubāda because she fabricated *Lubbād* (traditional woolen carpets). She spent entire nights weaving carpets and remembering the Divine until she was attracted to God. As a *majdhūba*, she left her family and roamed the streets of the medina of Fes.[13]

During the Sufi's journey to the Divine, his/her eyes often did not stop shedding tears. Crying expresses the Sufis' internal feelings such as *taqwā* (piety) and *khushū'* (submissiveness). Women used crying as an utterance to express their desire for God and for His salvation. Ibn Qunfud (1965) refers to an unanimous pious woman who never stopped weeping such that her eyes were stricken by blindness.[14]

The Sufi, on his/her Sufi path, also engages in celibacy and avoids marriage to preserve himself/herself exclusively for God. Marriage is not much praiseworthy in Sufism. It is a worldly life that hinders the spiritual life.[15] Al-Tādilī refers to anonymous female saints who led celibate lives in caves so as to live their spirituality freely.[16] Ibn Qunfud also presents the urban woman saint Mu'mina al-Tilimsāniya (14th century) as a celibate.[17] Her strong mysticism attracted the attentions of orthodox religious scholars who came to her door seeking her friendship and love. Instead, she chose to remain faithful to God. These Sufi women found in their celibacy a refuge for living their spirituality peacefully.

Sufi women, like their male counterparts, also marked their personalities within orthodoxy through the quest for knowledge. They engaged in learning different sciences. Narratives are pregnant with examples of women mystics who were interested in education and learning. There are some who founded educational centers and built schools and universities from their own money. This is the case of Fatima al-Fihriya (8th century) who built in Fes al-Qarawiyyīn, the first mosque and religious educational center in North Africa. Zaynab al-Nafzāwiya (12th century) also built many schools in Morocco to teach women about Islam and the Islamic sciences.[18] The woman saint, Saida Tiṭīliya (12th century) studied the Qur'an, hadith and other Islamic sciences. Her desire to propagate her knowledge to students and other people enhanced her to become "*nāsikha*" (copier of books).

Lalla Mḥilla (12th century) also dedicated her life to the quest for religious knowledge and the study of the Islamic sciences. She rejected the marriage her father arranged for her. She consulted with al-Qāḍī 'Ayāḍ, one of the greatest seven spiritual masters of Marrakesh, about her desire of knowledge. Al-Qāḍī 'Ayāḍ trained her in religion and Islamic sciences. Mḥilla soon acquired the status of a scholar and knowledgeable woman.[19]

Women Sufis in the Middle East like their counterparts in Morocco, also constructed educated personalities that challenged conventional norms. Dhu Nūn al-Miṣrī acknowledged Fatima Nishapur's high educational level and considered her to be his teacher ('ustādī).[20] Muḥi al-Dīn ibn 'Arabī was a disciple of another female spiritual master called Fāṭima bint al-Mutanā. She was his teacher and spiritual guide. Ibn 'Arabī served her as a *murīd* serves his *shaykh*. He learned from her the Islamic sciences and Sufi secrets.[21] These women were religious scholars whose strong knowledgeable personalities greatly impacted their communities.

This impact is clear in women saints' abilities to play political roles in their times. When Safiya Lubāda and Amina bint Khawā went deeply into ecstasy, they rebuked publically the unjust and corrupt people of their times. Aziza al-Sksāwiyya (14th century) is another example of this opposing of the political elite. As the political leader of her tribe, Lalla Aziza faced abi 'amir al-Hantati, the governor of Marrakech, who came with his army to invade Sksāwa region. She ordered him to retire from his plan and leave her Sksawā tribe in peace.[22] Zaynab Nafzāwiya (12th century) and Khnata bint Bakār (17th century) were Sufi women who helped their husbands, the Sultan Yūsuf ibn Tāshafīn and Mulay Isma'īl to rule their empires and secure peace in most of the Moroccan territories.[23] Their sainthood empowered these *majdhūbāts* to impose their power on the common people and the elite and to command them to submit to their demands. Thus, the construction of sainthood comes forward from these stories as basically gender-neutral. From the above, which types of agency do we come across among these women?

Women Saints' Agencies

The next section discusses the various types of agency which these women saints, from the narratives, display.

Ethical Self-Formation

As we saw from the previous section, the female saints applied basically the same self-techniques as their male counterparts. Women saints and Sufis engaged in the Sufi life and practiced self-techniques to achieve sainthood. Their work on themselves, i.e. their applying of all kinds of self-techniques, thus took place in the context of a project of ethical-spiritual self-formation. They trained their bodies as well as their souls, these being the ethical substance of their ethical spiritual self-formation. They did so on behalf of (their veneration for) God, which is another characteristic of their project of ethical self-formation. It is this type of agency that we find among Sufi saints, be they male or female. Moroccan orthodox religious spaces marginalized women. For this reason, women sought a space where they as persons could live their religion. Sufism became a means by which women developed their own spirituality and realized themselves as saintly personalities.

The women saints' religious lives, as narrated in the discourses on them, convey gender equality effects, with sometimes even egalitarian conditions and treatment.[24] The gender-neutral self-techniques often implied the breaking of conventional rules and values. The hagiographic accounts about women saints mentioned above are pregnant with instances of their non-conventional behavior. Their choice for Islamic mysticism as a strategy to live their piety and to construct saintly personalities differed in many ways from the standards that their local traditional culture imposed on them. Another strategy women employed in constructing saintly personalities is spiritual marriage with a saintly male figure, which consequently entailed rejecting conventional marital relations. Fatima al-Andalusiya left behind her family in *al-Andalus* and came to Morocco to meet her spiritual master Abu al-Madyan al-Ghut (12th century),[25] one of the greatest spiritual masters of the Maghreb. Amina bint al-Qāḍī (14th century) left behind her family and roamed the streets of Fes with her spiritual master Ali Sanhāji *al-Majdhūb*.[26] *Al-jadb* makes women able to give up their gender roles. Finally, intellectual forthrightness constitutes another way through which women achieved independence.

Ethical Freedom Practices

The ethical self-techniques applied by women saints are (mostly) similar to the ones of male saints. This conveys equality effects, as I argued above. Moreover, in the context of the patriarchal patterns in which they lived we can conclude that their ethical self-practices, can be called freedom practices. Ethical freedom practices invent positive ethical ways of life, which implicitly or explicitly oppose domination. From what we have seen above we can conclude that Moroccan female saints invented alternative – publicly visible – ethical ways of life for women, alternative to the dominant patterns. They as such worked on the limits of the patriarchal patterns they lived in. Through the vocabulary of Sufism, they challenged the dominant orthodox religious system and cultivated an independent and personal spirituality. It is in that sense that we can speak in terms of freedom practices.

Women's independence is evident not only in their choice to lead a mystical life but also in the definition of the type of relationship with God that they chose to establish. Sufi women loved God so intensely that they chose to express publicly their sense of intimate proximity to Him. The power of this feeling of proximity empowered them to reject their conventional roles (wives, mothers, and daughters) and to live a mystical life. The women saints discussed above as well as other Moroccan women saints proved themselves able to re-orient their religiosity and to cultivate their piety in their own way. They sought and acquired the power to refuse to be led by the conventional patriarchal norms and values.

From the narratives, women saints who engaged in the Sufi path were rewarded for their strong piety and hard spiritual work by God, who bestowed them with *baraka*. *Baraka* is the quality of sacred grace and salvation that saints could transmit to others. It enables saints to meet the hardships of lives and to get God's answers to their prayers. *Baraka* empowered saints to become spiritual leaders and to exercise power over others.

Women saints' powerful personalities are recorded in oral and written sources. Through attaining strong saintly personalities they had – and still have – an impact on people. It was this impact that inspired hagiographers to preserve their life stories. As we already saw in the previous section, they not only developed into spiritual leaders, but into political and social leaders as well.

Equality, and even egalitarian effects of their ways of life as spiritual and political and social leaders once more come to the fore, to such a degree that we can affirm Leila Ahmed's conclusion that 'the beliefs on which feminism rests are an endemic part of Islamic civilization.[27] This conclusion seems particularly applicable in the context of Moroccan history. The question that emerges is: How do women today receive these historical women saints?

The Venerators' Reception of Historical Women Saints

Saints venerators believe that female saints are able to offer them concrete help and assistance. To them the saints are intermediaries between the believers and God, who have curative powers themselves. In their pursuit of healing, pilgrims find moral assistance and refuge at a sanctuary. How does this work in practice?

A visit to a sanctuary is called a *ziyāra*. Pilgrims undertake daily, weekly, monthly and annual visits to saints' shrines. People visit saints to seek their *baraka*. It is a force that endows women and men with capacities to meet their daily troubles and to protect themselves against misfortunes such as evil eye, bad luck, illnesses and accidents. Their regular visits to the shrines and performance of different rituals display their strong relationship with the saints. Moroccan women actively participate in these rituals. In shrines, their religious agency becomes highly visible.

In all the shrines I visited, the women performed similar rituals, including trance rituals, *dhikr*-rituals, sacrifice rituals, marriage and fertility rituals, next to the celebration of mainstream religious activities. Venerators are free to choose the ways to pay respect to their women saints and to perform the rituals they need.

The women I focus on in this section are functionaries at shrines and women venerators. The functionaries are important to fulfill the needs of pilgrims. They are *muqaddamāt* (custodians), *fqirāt* or *ḥeddarāt* (pious and/or Sufi women in charge of trance dances) and healers. All functionaries display women's leadership and mediation in rituals and the centrality of women's active religious agency.

The *moqaddamāt* are crucial. Whether or not they are descendants of their women saints' and inheritors of their *baraka*, they are all empowered to behave as the overall leaders of most of the shrines' activities, and as the guides of the venerators' rituals and worship, and the teachers of women. They help women in crises and satisfy their needs, and see to it that the instructions of religion are respected.

Women venerators of female saints cover a wide range of categories: young and old, illiterate and literate, sick and healthy. Most of them are in the midst of an emotional or social crisis; many have failed to meet the requirements of the conventional roles. All these women's problems and inabilities to live up to the cultural norms urge them to search for spiritual comfort, peace of mind, and relief from daily-life pressures. Many rural, illiterate women with no financial means find in the veneration of women saints a budget solution to their health problems.

Mernissi (1978) and Bartels (1994) stress the functional goal of women's visits to the shrines. They conclude that Moroccan women's religious rituals around women saints only serve practical goals. However, from my research I found that women venerators gain more from their strong attachment to pious women.

While venerators of women saints visit a shrine to strengthen themselves so as to cope with daily life issues, they also use the cults for spiritual self-development. They may learn a lot from the functionaries in the shrines, who in many cases experienced a period of growth and learning themselves. The *baraka* that Rqiya, the *moqaddama* of the Lalla 'Azīza Saksāwiyya (13th Century)'s shrine in the Atlas, passively inherited from her saintly foremother empowered her to actively search for more knowledge and to have other women profit from it.

From my fieldwork I heard Rqiya focused on the notion of good intention (*niyya*) as the primary condition of saint veneration. I heard her advising a woman to venerate 'Aziza's shrine with good intention. She says: "*diri niyya, temshi b-hajt-ek maqḍiyya*" "Maintain positive intention and your request will be accomplished." Here *niyya* is a standard of saint veneration and the achievement of a desired religious life-style and of a strong spiritual personality. The *moqaddama* encourages women venerators to cultivate *niyya* while venerating the woman saint. That is why the women feel free to express their love to God in the way they want: by words, songs or ecstatic dancing.

Most Moroccan women venerators stressed that their female are *qudwa*'s (examples) to them in religion and piety. They argued that they perceived them as role models because they succeeded to achieve a level of piety, which was even stronger than that of male saints.

Many women venerators who praise women saints' religious lives in their rituals actually follow their path of piety. Devotees of Lalla Fatima Muhdūz (19th century) prayed and fasted over long periods of time. They also distributed food and gave charity to poor people because, as some older ladies put it, Lalla Fatima used to do so during her lifetime. The venerators contended that their frequent visits to women saints empowered them to perfect their spirituality and to achieve their women saints' perfect spiritual and social status. Their visits to women saints' shrines didn't have therapeutic purposes; they just aimed at improving themselves by creating a moral person-hood, in other words, an ethical self-formation.

Venerators not only seek help but also gain power to overcome gender injustice and discrimination. But the women venerators vice versa empower the historical women saints. This is evident from their continuous visits to their tombs, the rituals that they perform within shrines and the chanting of stories about their lives. One might notice here that venerators unconsciously revive the memory of these historical women saints and keep their legacy alive within their contemporary society. This conclusion is similar to that of Jansen and Notermans (2009), who also acknowledges the mutual relationship of empowerment existing between women saints and venerators.

Moroccan women within both the historical and the contempo-rary religious space display strong desires and commitments to shape themselves in a way that does not necessarily conform to the politics of the patriarchal local culture. Their agency displays their desires to re-shape the religious sphere that was (once) reserved exclusively for males. They also aspire to render themselves active agents within private and public religious institutions. Other than Mahmood (2005) concluded regarding the women of the Egyptian Mosque movement, from my research that Moroccan women's reli-gious agency either in the past or the present entails freedom practices that display a challenge to the patriarchal order. Finally, we can ask ourselves if historical women saints arouse the interest of the Moroccan female Islamist activists.

The Islamist Activists' Reception of Women Saints

My research shows that Morocco's current Islamist women organizations as well receive historical women saints as a means of empowerment and as role models.

Although the Islamist interviewees disapprove of saint veneration because it is not permissible in orthodox Islam, from my interviews it turns out that they approve of the use of Moroccan history and women saints as original sources to inform their debate on women's rights. Basima al-Haqqaoui, a member of *al'Adala wa al-Tanmiyya* (Justice and Development), argues that women saints who attained spiritual and political leadership are *"marji'iyya"* (a reference), that emanates from Islamic and Moroccan ethnic backgrounds. She acknowledged the importance of understanding the historical roles of women saints. According to her, modern women should employ this understanding to face the future and to build strong personalities.

However, the Islamist activists refuse to visit the shrines of women saints. Their understanding of *Baraka* is different from that of the saint venerators. The Islamists, however, do not believe in women saints as holders of *baraka* in the sense of blessing power but define it in terms of the wisdom and knowledge that a woman saint acquired through which she gained fame and sometimes authority.

The Islamist activists are interested in some of the spiritual aspects of historical women's sainthood. They value women saints' abilities to achieve strong piety that enabled them to reach God's closeness. Attaining Divine proximity is not an easy task, al-Haqqaoui asserts. She calls women saints 'educators of piety and religion,' and acknowledges women saints as spiritual masters who taught Sufis how to reach the Divine.

The Islamists of *al-'Adl wa al-Iḥsān* (Justice and Faith) are also very interested in women saints. They organize monthly meetings to discuss women saints' life stories. Their aim is, as Nadia Yassine (the leader of women section of *al-'Adl wa al-Iḥsān*) puts it, to understand the way these historical women created saintly personalities that challenged patriarchy and impacted their communities.

The Islamists do, however, appreciate women saints' style of achieving great social and knowledgeable personalities. Their self-techniques of attaining greatness through education are the most important reasons why activists consider women saints role models. They refer to knowledgeable and educated women saints as a source of their empowerment in these fields. They are conscious of the phenomenon of illiteracy, which is still particularly high among Moroccan women (40% of the women in urban spaces and around 60% in rural areas are illiterate).[28] For this reason, feminist activists keep stressing in their discourses the way historical women challenged patriarchal norms to achieve educated personalities.

The Islamists as well contend that female saints by their self-transformation into knowledgeable, spiritual leaders challenged the conventional roles and created personalities that impacted their communities. From my interviews, the Islamist activists' positive feelings toward female saints were fed because these historical women created personalities that impacted their communities. In their opinion, these historical women used Sufism as a technique to resist their local patriarchal ideologies that privileged men and discriminated women. To most of the Islamists I interviewed propagating women saints' historical role is useful out of its challenging to the dominant system.

We can conclude that Islamists are inspired by women saints, especially by their self-formation techniques involved in their development into socially and politically active women. They emphasize women saints' social role in the public sphere as a strategy to impact other women to be participants in activism and voluntary associations.

But how does this relate to their views on gender equity and complementarity as normative ideals, instead of as equality? During my interviews I explicitly asked for their opinion on these issues. The Islamists' ideas about complementary roles for the sexes are based on the conviction that men and women are different by nature. They argue that women's hormonal constitution and bodily roles as mothers predispose them to certain emotions and, therefore, to certain preferences in terms of types of work. These are connected to a natural tendency to be passive and in need to be protected by men, who, as a result of their own hormonal constitution, tend to be physically stronger and more aggressive and inclined to take on the role of the protectors of women.

But from my interviews, I found that most of them support gender equality in the public sphere and limit complementarity to the private sphere. The Islamists argue that, in spite of their natural constitution and dispositions, women are able to realize what they need in various situations. They can work toward, insist on, and even fight for the right to fulfill these needs and wants. Some of them see no contradiction between women's natural dispositions and the desire to pursue higher education and employment in a variety of areas and at multiple levels. Some believe that women are free to take care of her house and to participate in activism and public life at the same time.

Moroccan feminist activists are impressed by the women saints' strong and ethical personalities, and by their abilities to challenge patriarchy. They esteem them as role models and a source of empowerment and are determined to follow these historical women's footsteps by carrying on their religious, social and political activities.

While Islamist women's organizations are usually described as traditional and conservative with regard to women's issues, I more or less found the opposite to be the case, asking female activists about their stances concerning female saints.

Conclusion

In this chapter, I have discussed hagiographic and oral life stories of women saints and Sufis, and the self-formation techniques that they used to construct ethical saintly personalities that enabled them to challenge the dominant order and to continue to serve as model both for the venerators and the feminist activists. I approached the women saints as agents, discussing the way they actively sought and pursued paths to sainthood, while simultaneously transgressing patriarchy.

I discussed the concept of agency by making reference to scholarly contributions by Foucault and Mahmood. Like Mahmood, this chapter builds on Foucault's approach to ethics and the conceptual tools he presents (ethical self-formation and ethical self-techniques) both of which refer to embodied ways of advancing on one's life path. But unlike Mahmood's work, this chapter employs Foucault's ethical concept of freedom practices, which constitute means of ethical self-formation that challenge forms of domination. The life stories of women saints found in the archives and the oral literature show that these women employed self-techniques that empowered them to become saints with power and authority and enjoy equality and egalitarianism. The chapter has discussed the way women saints are received by their venerators. The latter express their strong devotion to and veneration of their favorite women saints through practices aimed at acquiring *baraka* from them, developing their own pious selves, and constructing their own spiritual personalities. They define the women saints they venerate as role models and moral exemplars. Similarly, the Islamist activists show a positive attitude towards women saints in their agendas and discourses. They respect the historical women saints as sources of empowerment in the context of their own self-techniques and efforts in the pursuit of ethical self-formation.

As is evident from the data and analysis elucidated in this chapter, my research results challenge the conventional image of Moroccan Muslim women as passive victims of patriarchal religious ideologies. Through my research, I constructed an alternative discourse that presents women, in the past and in the present, as active religious agents who are actively engaged in creating and transforming their religious roles both in the private and the public spheres. The future development and success of research on Moroccan religious women that resurrects feminist voices, while still in its early phases, is tied to the overarching discourses on Moroccan democratic development that pave the way for women to gain access to more democratic, religious, and political positions.

Notes

1 Sufism is broadly defined as the mystical dimension of Islam.
2 Bartels 1993; Dwyer 1978; Jansen 1987; Mernissi 1977; Rausch 2004
3 Ferḥat 1986; Mahmāh 1978; Qattān 1998; Zwanat 2009
4 Hagiography comprises writings about holy people and saints
5 Foucault 1997a; 1997b
6 Vintges 2004
7 Foucault 1997b, 263
8 Shaikh 2009
9 Ibn Manzūr 1955
10 al-Tādilī 1997, 112
11 Ibid.
12 al-Tādilī 1997, 316
13 al-Kattanī 1900, V. 2, 10
14 Ibn Qunfud 1965, 115
15 al-Ṣahrurdī 1999, 340
16 al-Tadilī 1997, 94
17 Ibn Qunfud 1965, 115

18 al-Tāzī 1992, 24
19 Janbūbi 2008, 172
20 al-Sulāmī 1993, 144
21 Ibn 'Arabi 1985, V. 2, 364–65
22 Ibn Qunfud 1965, 115
23 al-Tāzī 1992, 24. See also Ibn Khaldūn al-Amranī 2009
24 Stuurman 2004a. Egalitarianism favors equality. People should be treated the
    same or be treated as equals (see Arneson 2013)
25 al-Tādilī 1997, 319
26 al-Kattanī 1900
27 Ahmed 1989, 144
28 Sadiqi 2008, 13

Bibliography

Arabic Sources

al-Kattānī, Muḥammad ibn Ja'far b. Idrī s.1900. *Salwat al-Anfās wa Muḥādathāt al-Akyās bi-man Uqbira min al-'Ulamā' wa Ṣulaḥā' bi-Fās*. Casablanca: Maṭba'at al-Jadīda, Vol. 2 wa 3.

al-Ṣahrurdī, Shihāb al-Dīn. 1999. *'Awārif al-Ma'ārif*, Baghdad: Dār al-Ma'ārif.

al-Sulāmī, 'Abd al-Raḥmān. 1993. *Al-Niswa al-Muta'abbidāt al-Ṣūfiyyāt*. Mahmūd al-ṭanjī, (ed.). Cairo: Maktabat al-Khanjī.

al-Tādilī, Abū Ya'qūb Yūsufi bin Yayḥa. 1997. *Al-Tashawwuf ilā Rijāl al-Taṣawwuf wa Akhbār Abī al-'Abbās al-Sabtī*. Aḥmad Tawfīq, (ed.). Casablanca: al-Najāḥ.

al-Tāzī, 'Abd al-Hādī. 1992. *Al-Mar'a fī Tārīkh al-Gharb al-Islāmī*. Casablanca: Nashr Finik.

Ibn 'Arabī, Muḥyī al-Dīn. 1985. *Al-Futūḥāt al-Makkiyya*, vols. 2. 3. Beirut: Dār al-Ṣādir.

Ibn Khaldūn al-Amranī, Muhammad al-Salḥi. 2009. *Sab' Sayyidāt Marrakishiyyāt bi Istiḥqāq*. Marrakech: Jarīdat al-Afaq al-Maghribiya.

Ibn Manẓūr, Abū 'l-Faḍl al-Dīn Muḥammad ibn Muhammad. (No date). *Lisān al-'Arab*. Beirut: Dār Ṣādir.

Ibn Qunfudh al-Qusṭanṭinī, Abū l-'Abbās Aḥmad al-Khaṭīb. 1965. *Uns al-Faqīr wa 'Izzu al-ḥaqīr*. M. Fasi wa A. Faure, (eds.). Rabat: Manshurāt al-Markaz al-Jāmi'ī li al-Baḥth al-'Ilmī.

Janbūbi, Muḥammad. 2008. *Al-Awliyā' fī al-Maghrib*. Casablanca: Maṭba'at Dār al-Qarawiyyīn.

Mahmah, Mustafā 'Abdassalām. 1978. *Al-Mar'a al-Maghribiyya wa al-Taṣawwuf fī al-Qarn al-ḥādī 'Ashar al-Hijri*. Casablanca: Matba'at al-Dār al-Bayḍā'.

Qaṭṭān, Rashīd. 1998. 'Al-Mar'a al-Maghribiyya fī Adab al-Manāqib: al-Tashawwuf ilā Rijāl al-Taṣawwuf Namūdhajān'. *Majallat Amal* 13, no. 1:129–138.

English and French Sources

Ahmed, Leila. 1989. 'Feminism and Cross-Cultural Inquiry: The Terms of the Discourse in Islam'. In: E. Weed (ed.), *Coming to Terms.* New York and London: Routledge, 143–151.

Arneson, Richard. (2013). 'Egalitarianism'. In Edward N, Zulta (ed.), *The Standard Encyclopedia of Philosophy*. Available at the website:http://plato.standard-edu:archives:sum2013/entries/egalitarianism/

Bartels, Edien. 1993. *Eén dochter is beter dan duizend zonen* (One daughter is better than a thousand sons). Utrecht: Van Arkel.

Chodkiewicz, Michel. 1993. 'La sainteté féminine dans l'hagiographie Islamique'. In: D. Aigle (ed.), *Saints orientaux*. Paris: De Boccard, 99–115.

Coon, Linda. 1986. *Sacred Fictions: Holy Women and Hagiography in Late Antiquity*. Philadelphia: University of Pennsylvania Press

Dwyer, Daisy Hilse. 1978. 'Women, Sufism and Decision Making in Moroccan Islam'. In: L. Beck and N. Keddie (eds.), *Women in the Muslim World*. Cambridge: Harvard University Press, 585–598.

Ferḥat, Halima and Hamid Triki. 1986. 'Hagiographie et Religion au Maroc Médiéval'. In: *Hespéres*, 24, 17–51.

Foucault, Michel. 1997a. 'On the Genealogy of Ethics: An Overview of Work in Progress'. In: P. Rabinow (ed.), *Ethics, Subjectivity and Truth: The Essential Works of Michel Foucault 1954–1984*, vol. I. New York: The New Press, 253–280.

Foucault, Michel. 1997b. 'The Ethics of the Concern for Self as a Practice of Freedom'. In: P. Rabinow (ed.), *Ethics, Subjectivity and Truth: The Essential Works of Michel Foucault 1954–1984*, vol. I. New York: The New Press, 281–301.

Jansen, Willy, Anna-Karina Hermkens, and Catrien Notermans. 2009. *Moved by Mary: The Power of Pilgrimage in the Modern World*. Farnham and Burlington: Ashgate

Mahmood, Saba. 2005. *Politics of Piety: The Islamic Revival and the Feminist Subject*. Princeton and Oxford: Princeton University Press.

Mernissi, Fatima. 1977. 'Women, Saints and Sanctuaries'. *Signs*. 3, 1, 101–112.

Rausch, Margaret. 2004. 'Ishlhin Women's Rituals in Southwestern Morocco: Celebrating Religio-Cultural and Ethno-Linguistic Identity'. In: *Minority Matters: Society, Theory, Literature*. Oujda: Publications de le Faculté des Lettres. Série: Colloques et Séminaires, 32, 199–224.

Sadiqi, Faṭima. 2008. 'Facing Challenges and Pioneering Feminist and Gender Studies: Women in Post-colonial and today's Maghrib'. *African and Asian Studies*, Vol. 7, 4, 447–470.

Sadiqi, Fatima. 2006. 'The Impact of Islamization on Moroccan Feminisms'. *Signs*, vol. 32, 1, 32–40.

Shaikh, Sa'diyya. 2009. 'In Search of *Al-Insān*: Sufism, Islamic Law, and Gender'. *Journal of the American Academy of Religion*, vol. 77, 4, 781–822.

Stuurman, Siep. 2004a. 'How to Write a History of Equality?' *Leidschrift*, 19, 3, 40–62.

Vintges, Karen. 2004. 'Endorsing Practices of Freedom: Feminism in a Global Perspective.' In: D. Taylor and K. Vintges (eds.), *Feminism and the Final Foucault*. Urbana and Chicago: University of Illinois Press, 275–299.

Zouanat, Zakia. 2009. *Le Royaume des Saints*. Graz: éd. ADEVA

Chapter 12

THE IMPLICATIONS OF HAVING DRUNK THE WATER OF THE NETHERLANDS

Narrations on Agency and Communion in the Life Story of a Moroccan-Dutch Woman

Marjo Buitelaar

Introduction

"My mom often states: 'You have drunk the water of the Netherlands'." This is how Boushra, a thirty years old Moroccan-Dutch medical specialist, concluded a number of stories in an interview with me about growing up in the Netherlands as the daughter of a Moroccan *gastarbeider*.[1] The Dutch term *gastarbeider* (guest worker) designates the Turkish and Moroccan men who migrated to the Netherlands in the 1960s. The euphemistic label *gast* referred to the expectation that these poorly paid laborers would only stay temporarily. Despite an enormous increase of family reunification migration in the 1970s, all parties involved took it for granted that eventually the migrant families would return home. This, however, has not occurred, although many of the original migrants who are now in their late sixties and seventies, alternate living in Morocco and in the Netherlands every few months.

While the term *gastarbeider* was initially employed exclusively by native Dutch speakers to designate the migrant "other", it has been appropriated by the descendants of Moroccan migrants to pay tribute to their fathers. By evoking the prototypical rural migrant with little or no formal education and lack knowledge about the country of settlement where he performed heavy and often dirty labour for very low wages, they emphasize the great sacrifices their fathers and later their mothers made to provide their families with a better future. The connotation of "othering" in the term *gastarbeider,* however, lingers on. Characterizing their fathers as *gastarbeiders,* the descendants of these migrants equally draw attention to the enormous social mobility that they themselves have accomplished in comparison to their parents.

Boushra belongs to the category of first children of Moroccan background who entered the higher echelons of the Dutch educational system and labor market. She is one of twenty five female "pioneers" who were willing to share their life stories with me for a longitudinal research project concerning the narrative construction of multiple identifications of highly educated women of Moroccan descent in the Netherlands. While a few quotes from her lengthy interview transcript (±68.000 words) featured in previous publications (cf. Buitelaar 2007; 2009; 2014), so far I have not yet discussed her life story as such. Since it lends itself *par excellence* to reflect on the agency of female descendants of Moroccan background in the Netherlands, I will remedy this previous omission by putting Boushra center stage here.

I will briefly sketch her "life chapters" and then zoom in on various modalities of agency that come to the fore in her life story. In variation to the title of Kiran Desai's brilliant novel *The Inheritance of Loss*, my particular focus is on how the inheritance of loss and aspirations that comes with migration informs Boushra's quest for a satisfactory balance between agency and relatedness as she pursues self-realization in Dutch society as the daughter of a Moroccan "guest worker". Before turning to Boushra's story, however, I will present the theoretical and methodological framework of the biographic research project in which she participated.

Agency and life storytelling in a diaspora context

The research project was launched in 1998. Its aim was to examine representations in the interviewees' life stories of intersecting social identifications. In 2008 I revisited fifteen of the twenty-five women for a follow-up interview, among whom Boushra. In the meantime, besides 9/11, the subsequent "War on Terror", and several serious local incidents had had a great impact on the Dutch discourse on Muslims.[2] The aim of the follow-up interview was to study the interplay between changes in the Dutch societal climate and developments in the personal life course in my interlocutors' narrative construction of multiple identity.

Two theoretical strands were used to analyze the life stories: Dan McAdams' theory on the narrative construction of identity over the life course, and Hubert Hermans' Dialogical Self Theory. The work of the psychologist McAdams focuses on the continuously evolving life stories or what he calls "personal myths" that people tell themselves and others to formulate answers to the question "Who am I?". McAdams argues that two basic human desires are the motor behind the development of the "plot" in any life story: agency and communion (McAdams 1993). Slightly adapting McAdams' use of the term agency for reasons I will explain later, I use agency here to refer to the capacity of individuals to make well-informed biographical choices in order to lead what to they conceive of the "good life". Besides the competence to formulate and pursue life plans, in my use of the term agency also refers to coping strategies: one's response to challenges and threats that may jeopardize one's life plans (cf. Skinner & Edge 2002). McAdams' concept of communion refers to meaningful personal relationships such as love, friendship, companionship, and to secure social embeddedness.

Both the choices that people make in formulating and pursuing life plans, and the scope of their agency are shaped by the cultural, socio-economic and historical factors that impact their life worlds on the one hand, and their personal dispositions, ideals and beliefs about desirable self-realization on the other (cf. Mahmood 2005). Although the life goals that groups and individuals formulate may diverge widely, each can be classified in terms of a specific combination of the universal human motivational needs summarized by McAdams as agency and communion.

While I would argue that it certainly takes agency to develop and maintain meaningful personal relationships, McAdams tends to focus on the potential contradictory nature of agency and communion. This can be explained by the fact that he thinks of agency predominantly in terms of personal autonomy and achievements. To conceive of agents as independent and bounded individuals is in line with a typology that has permeated popular discourses on "Western" and "other" cultures. According to this typology, self-determination and independence is valued most highly in so-called "individualist" cultures, and communion or relatedness in so-called "collective" cultures where group interests have precedence over personal interests gives rise to "interdependent" subjects (cf. Hofstede 1991, p. 261).

Cultural models of the self should, however, not be mistaken for actual experiences of individualism and relatedness (cf. Spiro 1993). Moreover, cultural discourses and practices are distributed dispro-portionately among the members of a society rather than being shared equally by all. Factors such as age, education and social class inform the interplay between the psychological make-up of individuals and their internalization of cultural discourses (cf. Frank 2006). Therefore, cultures and selves should not be viewed as either inde-pendent or interdependent, but as animated by tensions between group loyalties and personal ambitions (cf. Gregg 2007).[3]

In a rapidly globalizing world people everywhere are confronted with different cultural models of the self. This is particularly the case for migrants and their descendants, who are faced with a large variety of possible self-presentations. This is where Dialogical Self Theory (DST) comes in. According to DST the self is dialogically constructed in two ways: we can look at ourselves through the eyes of significant others, and comment on ourselves as we switch between different temporally and spatially specific positions that we inhabit as embodied actors. Hermans calls these positions "I-positions" (Hermans 2001, pp. 248–249).

From each particular I-position, we enter into dialogues with the selves we are in different I-positions and with significant others to whom we relate in these positions. Such dialogues can be internal, taking place in our minds, and external, as in conversations with others. The statement 'You have drunk the water of the Netherlands' for example, features not only in actual dialogues between Boushra and her mother, but also in internal dialogues that Boushra engages in as she looks at herself through her mom's eyes. More specifically, Boushra's life story contains many instances in which she responds to the internalized voice of her mother in internal dialogues between her I-position as the daughter of low educated Moroccan migrants on the one hand and her I-position as a higher middle class medical specialist on the other.

Strictly speaking, in terms of DST as first developed by Hermans, for analytical purposes this description of these two I-positions of Boushra should actually be broken down into a larger number of I-positions: I as a daughter; I as a lower class kid; I as a migrant; I as Moroccan; I as Muslim; versus I as a doctor and I as a member of the Dutch higher middle class. I would argue, however, that it is exactly the dialogical nature of self-constructions which prevents I-positions to be so neatly divided. For Boushra, being a daughter only comes in the modality of being a daughter in a lower class Muslim migrant family in the Netherlands. Her social and personal identifications mutually co-constitute each other rather than add up in the various I-positions she inhabits.

At first sight, by inviting an analysis of self-constructions in terms of different I-positions DST seems to go against the "intersectionality" approach to the study social identity; the core feature of the "intersectionality" approach is its critique on the view that social inequalities based on the categories of class, gender, and race multiply, as is, for example, suggested in statements about the "double burden" of black women who are being oppressed both as women and as blacks. Instead, an intersectionality approach takes into account that identity construction takes place at the cross-roads of such categories in specific historical and socio-cultural contexts. Dependent on how these categories intersect in a particular situation, the different categories co-construct each other in different ways. While in a more systematic analysis of intersectionality the emphasis is on how people are positioned by the interplay of various categorizations, in a more constructionist analysis the emphasis is on how scripts of gender, race, ethnicity and class are appropriated by individuals in creative ways in the specific circumstances in which they "perform" such scripts (Prins 2006).

The usefulness of DST to study intersectionality is that I-positions do not coincide with dominant cultural scripts for social positions. Rather, they pertain to the ways in which such scripts are creatively appropriated by individuals as they inhabit or perform social positions in their "own" way. The quotation marks are added here because in line with a more constructionist approach to intersectionality, DST foregrounds the relational nature of identity; the "voices" of others that address the self in various I-positions are an intrinsic part of dialogical self-construction (Hermans 2001). It is precisely because DST addresses the simultaneity of various kinds of "voices" in the construction of identity that it provides useful tools to analyze how the performance of and dialogues between different I-positions are informed by the various power structures that people are embedded in on the basis of cultural categorizations.

Individuals internalize both personal voices of significant others in their lives, as well as the collective voices of the groups to which they belong. These voices represent the rules, conventions and established worldviews of those groups. The dialogical self is developed by "orchestrating" both factual and internalized or imagined "voices" that address people in the different I-positions between which they shift. These voices, in other words, represent different "sites of self" (cf. Holland et al. 1998, p. 29–30). Some voices that address the "dialogical self" are more hegemonic or penetrating than others. The ways that our social positions are embedded in discourses representing different power structures, for instance, create dispositions to voice opinions or to silence oneself, to enter into activities or to refrain from doing so (Holland et al. 1998, p. 136). Thus, the various personal and collective voices that inform our sense of self shape our specific desires for agency and communion. Conversely, we use our agency to orchestrate and appropriate these voices to inhabit our various I-positions in accordance with our own intentions.

This comes particularly to the fore in self-narratives, in which different experiences and cultural discourses are integrated. Self-narration both demands and stimulates self-reflection and self-regulation. In this respect life storytelling is an agentic act in itself: it consists of a discursive negotiation of the self in relation to others. Also, producing an account of how one has become the person one is today involves the articulation of past, present and future plans and the creation of more or less meaningful links between accomplishments and disappointments.

In order to stimulate this agentic dimension of storytelling in the research-project in which Boushra participated, the metaphor was used of the life story as a book. The interviewees were invited to produce narrations about different "life chapters", "characters", "key events", "dilemmas", "future plans" and "story lines" in their life stories (cf. McAdams 1993). In this way, they themselves could select the topics that they judged to be of interest.

However: narratives are always shaped by the audiences that each participant in the interview situation has in mind (cf. Olson and Shopes 1991, p.193). Therefore, the responses of my interviewees were inevitably influenced by their knowledge that I had approached them because of their Moroccan backgrounds. Also, Islam has become a dominant marker of identity in popular Dutch discourse, Moreover, it is an identity marker that is highly charged with negative connotations. Much of what the interviewees told me was therefore organized around the purpose to challenge assumed misconceptions of presumed readers about Islam and Moroccans.[4] Proving to be "no less competent" than native Dutch citizens, for example, is a recurring topic in Boushra's life chapters.

Boushra's life chapters

Participants in the research project who were old enough at the moment of migration to have childhood recollections of their lives in Morocco, all organized their life stories in terms of "before" and "after" migration (cf. Buitelaar 2009). Boushra is no exception: she designates her childhood years in Morocco as the first of her life chapters. She lived with her siblings and mother in one of the larger towns in the Rif, to which her parents had moved from the Riffian countryside a few years after they had married. Her father had migrated to the Netherlands several years before Boushra was born as the fourth surviving child in her family. There are sixteen years between her and her oldest brother, fifteen and seven years between her and her older sisters. A younger sibling was born two months before the family moved to the Netherlands in the winter of 1974. Boushra was 4,5 years old then. Another child would be born a few years later.

Although Boushra states that she does not have many memories about life in Morocco and her family's migration to the Netherlands, she depicts the constrast between Morocco and her new home in the Netherlands in vivid detail: "In Morocco you find many of these pastel-colored houses, and I faintly remember a light green house...What I remember is warmth, colors, bustling streets." Her first impression of her new home in the Netherlands is quite different. She recollects being struck by what she calls the "functional architecture" of the 1950s that characterized the houses in the part of the town where the family settled: "Everything was straight, the stairs were dead straight. In Morocco things are not as straight. There things are crumbling and curved. [...] I also remember that it was snowing when we arrived, so it was white and cold."

Life at school dominates Boushra's narrations about her post-migration childhood. The first recollection she presents concerns an incident that took place during her first week in school: she badly needed to go to the toilet, but did not know how to ask in Dutch for permission to go. Eventually, she wet her pants. Boushra is quick to frame this narration in terms of firm resolution. Recalling her embarrassment about the situation, she states: "I decided then and there that something like this would not happen again".

Indeed, most of Boushra's narrations concern her determination to make the most of what Dutch society had to offer and prove her competence. She proudly relates how, in elementary school, she soon discovered the public library and became an avid reader: "I taught myself Dutch thanks to the books in the library. That's how I tried to tackle my language deficiency in comparison to my Dutch class-mates." The library also offered her a place to escape the family's cramped housing conditions. Moreover, the library books intro-duced her to a world hitherto unknown and provided her with knowledge that helped her familiarize with Dutch society.

Boushra repeatedly points to the advantage of having been the only Moroccan girl in her class: she easily struck up friendships with Dutch girls, some of whom are still close friends. She mentions in passing how embarrassed she had felt when having to handle fork and knife on one of those rare occasions that she had been invited to stay over for dinner at a Dutch friend's house. Again, she presents this experi-ence as reaffirming her determination to develop strategies to become a competent participant in Dutch society: "If I detect something that might be a handicap, I turn it into a motive for self-improvement".

After completing elementary school, it went without saying that Boushra would go to the same school that her sister attended, rather than the high school where her Dutch friends enrolled. While she accepted this decision of her parents, many stories about her high school years concern strategically selected negotiations with them over her restricted freedom of movement: "I chose my battles: I did not bother to fight over a school dance, but I kept nagging them about permission to take driving lessons." What bothered her more than the fun that she missed out on by not attending extra-curricular school activities, was being set apart from her Dutch classmates. Boushra considers herself lucky, however, that her older sister had struggled with her parents over the same kind of issues, thus paving the way to a considerable extent for her younger sister.

The same goes for continuing her education after high school; while Boushra's parents had always stimulated their daughters to get the highest education possible and pursue a good career, in practice it proved difficult not to succumb to the pressure exerted by the wider family and Moroccan community to marry off their daughters at a young age. By the time the first suitor asked for Boushra's hand, her older sister had already successfully negotiated postponing marriage until completing her studies. The girls' parents accepted Boushra's wish to do the same without much persuasion: "I told my parents I would not give up my university training for any man. My mom thought that was nonsense, but my dad understood, so he kept potential suitors at bay."

Boushra met her future husband on the commuter train between her hometown and the city where she studied medicine. On their frequently shared journeys to the university he also attended, they began to compare notes about growing up as a Moroccan in Dutch society. The sense of bonding with a Moroccan young man as an equal was not something Boushra had expected to be possible, and for the first time she began to consider a future married life. Still, it took quite some time before she would admit to her travel companion that the feelings he had expressed towards her were reciprocated: "I was like: you're always worse off with a Moroccan man, so you'd better make very sure that you know extremely well who you are dealing with before you marry one".

Gradually, the young man managed to win over Boushra, and after some years of secret courtship the couple decided to marry. They felt they owed it to their parents to let them organize the marriage in line with Moroccan traditions: "I find the institution of dower completely nonsense. But I knew that in the eyes of my parents not asking one would be like throwing away their daughter. So we decided to let our parents negotiate the marriage in line with what they thought proper." Out of respect to their parents, the couple kept silent about that fact that they had known each other already several years and asked their sisters to act as go-betweens for the families.

At the time of the first interview in 1998, Boushra had been married for four years and was struggling to combine being a devoted mother to her one year old daughter and doing her first residency in a regional hospital. Her husband, family and in-laws were all of great help in taking turns attending to the little girl during Boushra's long shifts in the hospital. Rationally, Boushra knew that things were going fine, but emotionally she worried whether she was failing her daughter by pursuing a career as a doctor: "I know she is in good hands, that she is fine with her father. But I can't stop wondering: should a small girl not be with her mother?" Contrary to narrations about previous life chapters, the stories about this phase in her life are characterized by expressing ambivalent feelings and uncertainty about her future plans.

By the time we met again ten years later, Boushra had given birth to two more children. She no longer worked full time, but had been promoted to a better position. She therefore had more control over her own calendar and earned a salary that had enabled her to buy a large house in an up-market neighborhood. Her husband had recently started his own business, thus allowing the couple flexibility in arranging the care for their children. Boushra was more relaxed and confident about her situation than she had been during the first interview: "We've got it all worked out. Sometimes I even miss these earlier hectic days!" Her stories indicated that by 2008, she had obviously proven to herself and others that she was both a competent mom and doctor.

Central to the 2008 interview was a "new project" that she had recently embarked upon: joining the board of a local Moroccan women's association. During the 1998 interview Boushra had stated not to be interested in getting involved in Moroccan networks in the Netherlands. When in 2008 I reminded her of her former stance, she explained that the increasingly negative public discourse about

Muslims in the Netherlands both worried and grieved her. As a highly educated woman she had come to see it as her responsibility to contribute to the empowerment of Moroccan women who, like her mother, find themselves in a more vulnerable position. Also, becoming a mother had made her realize the importance of teaching her children that their cultural heritage is something that they can feel proud of: "Morocco is much less prominent in our everyday lives than in the family I grew up in. But I feel it is my obligation to pass on that Moroccan connection to my children. Rooting is very important." Bourshra expressed the hope that a positive relation with their Moroccan roots would help her children cope with the stigmatization she fears they might be confronted with. Simultaneously, she wants to teach them that they were *Dutch* Moroccans and that their future lies in the Netherlands. In the remainder of this chapter I will address the issue how this wish relates to her inheritance of the loss and aspirations of her own migrant parents.

Upward mobility and its costs

While the topics in Boushra's life story are highly personal, variations to them often feature in the narratives of other participants in the life story project: e.g, a poor, but happy childhood in Morocco, the determination to catch up with – if not outperform – Dutch classmates, the negotiations with parents over more freedom of movement, struggles to combine a career with building a family, and ambivalent feelings about indebtedness towards parents. Even some details in Boushra's story refer to common topoi: many of the life stories contain narrations about falling snow upon arrival in the Netherlands, discovering public libraries, and "testing" potential husbands for their degree of emancipation (cf. Buitelaar 2009). On a more general level, the most striking feature that the narratives of these pioneers share is the preponderance of highly agentic voices. Much like Boushra, most women present themselves first and foremost as resolute actors, determined to grasp every opportunity to get ahead in life and prove themselves as equal to Dutch class mates in school, and to Moroccan brothers in the family home.

Considering my interviewees' migrant background, their emphasis on agency should not come as a surprise. Migration is a very agentic act per se; its prime goal is to improve one's standards of living. For most migrants, upward mobility constitutes the most important desired outcome of migration, if not for themselves then for the next generation. This explains why most descendants of migrants, much like Boushra, tend to pursue high status careers in medicine and law, or at least white collar jobs (cf. Coenen 2001).

This drive for agency and the accomplishment of upward mobility, however, come at a cost. Besides inheriting parental aspirations, the descendants of migrants also have to accommodate an inheritance of loss: in a post-migration context, former feelings of home and belonging are no longer self-evident and new forms of relatedness have to be negotiated both in the country of settlement and in the country of origin.[5] This tends to work out differently for subsequent generations, as a closer look at the quotation in the opening sentence of this chapter will reveal.

"You have drunk the water of the Netherlands" was something that Boushra's mother would state to reproach her children for being too direct in addressing their parents; for dressing in ways that she considered in appropriate; or for otherwise behaving in ways that proved to her that they had "dutchified". Alternatively, it was her way to express admiration for the accomplishments of her children and the apparent ease with which they navigate their course in Dutch society.

Although she did not state so herself, I surmise that quoting her mother's remark expresses Boushra's ambivalent feelings about her achievements as a highly educated migrant daughter.[6] In terms of DST, the quotation represents the dominance of the internalized voice of her mother in Boushra's "orchestration" of voices that inform her dialogical construction of self. Moreover, it becomes particularly loud in self-evaluations of I-positions that are informed by a Dutch cultural repertoire that her mother is not familiar with.

Why this may be the case becomes clear by analyzing the ambivalent appreciation that Boushra's mother's metaphorical reference to the effects on her daughter of growing up in the Netherlands bespeaks. The remark "You have drunk the water of the Netherlands" points to the inherent paradox that children whose migrant parents have enjoyed little or now formal education are confronted with as they strive to realize the family migration project; in order to live up to their parents' expectations concerning upward mobility, they must adopt an outward orientation and explore the avenues that the society of settlement has to offer. To their parents, however, the family home is the only remaining true comfort zone and connection to the home land, often resulting in an inward orientation and a focus on familial closeness. Thus moving in different directions, children and parents inevitably grow apart somewhat.

Put differently: inheriting their parents' strong desire for agency in terms of high achievements, the children of migrants cannot but simultaneously contribute to the sense of loss of communion that their parents experience in their own diasporic lives. Moreover, as the children expand their position repertoire and acquire new "I-positions" and new "voices" that accompany these I-positions, they also develop desires for agency and communion that diverge from those of their parents. This is the process of "dutchification" that Boushra's mother both admires and resents, and that Boushra both takes pride in and feels guilty about. Many narrations in Boushra's life story refer to this process of dutchification and to coming to terms with it. Sometimes such references are explicit and concrete, at other times I only recognized them when pondering on the similarities between her story and those of other participants in the life story project.

An example of such similarities concerns Boushra's comparison between Moroccan childhood recollections and those from the Netherlands. The contrasts she describes between Morocco's rich colors, warm climate and close social relationships versus bleakness, straightness and reserved relationships in the Netherlands, recur in many life stories of Dutch-Moroccans. Taking into account that most women only visit their country of origin in summer, it is self-evident that differences in temperatures stand out. There is, however, more to these contrasts than just different weather conditions. I would argue that besides echoes of a European orientalist discourse through which my interviewees have learned to reflect on their cultural background, internalized parental voices also resonate in such contrasts.

An indication of this can be found Boushra's recollections of family life during the first years in the Netherlands. Boushra remembers that while she and her siblings quickly learned to find their way in the new environment, her parents would never get used to it. Even after having lived over thirty years in the Netherlands, they still feel insecure. Particularly her mother tries to avoid the outside world as much as possible. Reflecting on her parents' attitude, Boushra stated:

Probably in reaction to the cold climate and the unreal outside world, at home they created a warm and close atmosphere; telling us lots of stories for example.... I guess they tried to continue life as in Morocco.

Contrasting Moroccan and Dutch society in terms of warm versus bleak features echoes Boushra's parents' appreciation of the family's two life worlds. As Stock (2014, p. 112) argues, in the narratives of the descendants of Moroccan migrants such oppositions are not static and do not operate as clear-cut positive or negative evalua-tions. This also goes for Boushra. After having described the contrasts between her "warm" and familiar Moroccan home and her new "cold" Dutch home, she was quick to point out the convenience about the straight street that her new Dutch home was situated in: it took her directly to her new school, so that she would not have to be afraid to get lost and walk there herself. Dutch society would soon become much more to her than a puzzling new environment. Moreover, going to school would soon be related to desires for both agency and communion.

Not so to her parents. While encouraging their children to venture beyond the safe family home to get a good education, according to Boushra they did so purely for instrumental reasons:

In the reasoning of my parents, school is where you go to learn. If you wanted something else, then they'd ask '*wash nâfiᶜ?*' [Is is useful?, mb] That word *nâfiᶜ* would always enter the con-versation. Attending school parties and making friends was one thing, going to school to learn another. To them these were sepa-rate things... very instrumental, you know. They just could not understand arguments like: 'it is fun', or: 'I would like it so much'.

As the last sentence in this excerpt shows, Boushra's wishes for com-munion with classmates put a strain on the same close family relations that her parents sought to preserve: as their daughter's life world expanded, they were falling out of touch with it. This comes even more to the fore in an excerpt about the misunderstandings that occasionally arose as Boushra mediated between the "outside" world of school, and the "inside" world of the family home:

> I had to explain about 'parents' evenings'. Of course I did not really know myself. My mom would say. 'Why do your father and I have to show up in school? Have you been up to something bad?' 'No, I haven't done anything. They only want...' 'You must have done something!'... Or the Christmas dinner: 'Why should you eat in school? Do they think that we don't feed you well at home?' 'No, no, it's just something they do for Christmas.' That's how things went.[. . .] Looking back I can laugh about it, but it must have been quite frustrating for a young girl.

A sense of resentment might be read into Boushra's observation that her parents "could not understand" arguments relating to their daughter's desire for communion at school in the previous excerpt. Her formulation in the last sentence of this last excerpt, however, illustrates how she carefully avoids voicing such feelings explicitly: after presenting the dialogues with her parents from her past I-position as Boushra the young school girl, she shifts to her present I-position as Boushra the adult woman to comment distantly that "it must have been quite frustrating for *a* young girl" [my italics, mb].

As was already mentioned in the overview of her life chapters, what Boushra regretted most about not being allowed to participate in extra-curricular school activities was that it set her apart in class. Note how, in the next excerpt she again chooses to quote her parents in Moroccan-Arabic rather than in the Dutch language that she used throughout most of the interview. Her switching to Moroccan-Arabic exemplifies the gap between the speech genres and expectations that characterized her life at home and those that reigned at school:

> When I asked: 'Why am I not allowed to go on a schooltrip?' my parents would respond: 'Because you are Moroccan: *Nti magrebîya.*' That's how it got drilled into me that I am different [...]. What I would say to myself to deal with that was – quite arrogant in a way – something like: 'They don't know any better.' That's how I could live with it without getting into a conflict with them.

Excusing the restrictive behavior of her parents by telling herself that "They don't know any better" is a coping strategy that allows Boushra to accommodate the increasing lack of understanding between herself and her parents. Again we can see her switch between different I-positions as she does so: "They don't know any better" is uttered by Boushra the higly educated and independent daughter. By calling this "quite arrogant in a way" she shifts to another I-position: as the loving and respectful daughter she excuses and denounces her own stance simultaneously.

The statement "They don't know any better" also indicates that family relations not only changed because of the new desires for communion that Boushra and her siblings acquired by participating in Dutch society; her parents also depended heavily on the very agency that they encouraged their children to develop. Boushra summarized her narrations on the impact of migration on power relations within the family as follows:

At a certain stage you outpace your parents, particularly in terms of language. Within a few months my sisters and I got by fairly well in Dutch. But my parents didn't. They still don't, but at the time the difference was painfully large. So we had to go shopping, make inquiries for them, do their administration and all that. That's when the parent-child relation actually gets inverted.

Although Boushra formulates the effect of migration on her relationship with her parents in terms of a neutral observation here, her self-critical interjection "quite arrogant in a way" in the earlier excerpt bespeaks a sense of guilt towards her parents for having outgrown them.

In fact, when asked about an absolute low "key event" in her life, Boushra mentioned the depression her father slid into once he realized that his dream about the family's return to Morocco had collapsed. For years, he had been preoccupied with a project to build seven houses in Morocco; one for himself and his wife, and one for each of his children. The land was bought, the bricks delivered, but the houses never materialized. By the time the walls demarcating their contours had been built, the lack of enthusiasm and even unease he noted in his children about the prospect of returning to Morocco confronted him with the fact that they had settled firmly in the Netherlands and would never return to the country of origin permanently. Once he realized this, Boushra's father lost interest not only in his building project, but in life in general. Although he eventually recovered from his depression, he never managed to shake off the apathy that had gotten hold on him.

It both grieves and frustrates Boushra that no matter how hard she and her siblings have worked to realize her parents' aspirations for the family's upward mobility, she has failed in helping them procure a happier life:

> There is always this sense of having to pay off debts to your parents. Not financially – well, it does take a financial form also – but it's more a sense of emotional debt; owing them for something that they missed out on by leaving in Morocco but that they never found here [...] And *never* having the feeling that it has been enough, that you *have* paid off your debts to them [italics indicating Boushra's strong emphasis, mb].

Particularly becoming a mother herself has increased the burden of Boushra's feelings of guilt towards her parents. Having firmly established herself as a doctor, by the time of the 2008 interview, she had finally found the mental space and time to address the issue. This time, she decided to turn feelings of impotence into positive action by getting involved in community work to support the empowerment of Moroccan women who find themselves in a similar vulnerable position as her mother.

Hearing herself encourage the women to take their lives in their own hands, however, she came to realize that she ultimately failed to do so herself as long as she allowed the internalized voice of her mother who reproached her for having drunk the water of the Netherlands dominate her life. It bothered her, for example, that although being a grown up woman who is free to make her own choices, she still refrains from doing certain things that her parents used to forbid when she was a child:

> Take, for example, this nice coat that I came across in a shop. I looked at it, liked it, but then I said to myself: 'Actually it's too short' [...] It would have been different had I thought: 'I don't like the color' rather than 'It's too short'. I mean: too short for whom

> or for what? This is the kind of situation in which I realize: 'Wait a minute! This is a very schizophrenic conversation I am having with myself.' Things like that happen to me time and again and it bothers me a lot. I mean: I am no longer part of that kind of family, I am entitled to decide for myself now. But somehow I can't seem to manage to get rid of this kind of thinking.

Boushra's inner dialogue illustrates that in developing our selves we cannot but make use of the meanings of words within the contexts in which they were articulated. Each word "tastes" of previous contexts in which it has lived its socially charged life. The words – or clothes – we choose are therefore "populated" with the intentions of others (Bakhtin 1981, p. 293). Therefore, the influence of others on our self-evaluations can be big.

Since selves are always dialogically constructed and therefore relational, I would argue that agency should not only be looked for in fully independent choices of autonomous individuals as McAdams tends to focus on in his understanding of the concept, but also in the capacity to develop strategies to cope with the limitations inherent to social embeddedness. Boushra will probably not be able to resolve completely the ambivalent evaluation in her mother's remark that she has drunk the water of the Netherlands. She has come to realize, however, that she does have the agency to diminish its impact on her and to create more space for other voices in her position repertoire:

> This kind of issue is not only something that affects me, but also many of my friends. I guess that has to do with our becoming mothers ourselves. You reach a point where you begin to detach yourself from your own mom, while simultaneously feeling closer to her by being a mother yourself.

In terms of DST, one could argue that becoming a mother herself has created a "third position" for Boushra; a new I-position that reduces the tension between two other, incongruous positions (cf. Hermans & Hermans-Konopka 2010, p. 70). By having become a mother Boushra has contributed to the realization of her parents' desire for familial communion by adding a new generation to the family. Like her mother, she wishes to pass on to her children both the ambition to make the best of what The Netherlands has to offer and the significance of the family's Moroccan cultural heritage. To accomplish this, she draws on the multiplicity of voices that have informed her sense of self as the daughter of Moroccan migrants in the Netherlands: while in her parents' view Moroccanness stood for communion and Dutchness for agency, Boushra has integrated "agentic" and "communal" voices in providing her children with the skills to become rooted as resilient Dutch citizens of Moroccan background.

Conclusion

In this contribution I have reflected on the impact of migration on the quest for a satisfactory balance between agency and communion in Boushra's life story. I have done so by discussing how this highly educated daughter of Moroccan descent has accommodated the inheritance of loss and aspirations inherent to family migration in her self-narrative. More specifically, my focus was on the implications of Boushra's impressive upward mobility on her desires for agency and communion and on her efforts to realize these desires. I have demonstrated that Boushra's main biographic challenge in this respect is based on an intrinsic tension in the assignment the descendants of migrants face in their endeavors to realize the aims of family migration project: living up to the expectations of parents to make the most of what the country of settlement has to offer on the one hand, and complying with the wishes of the same parents to preserve family closeness on the other hand.

For Boushra, coping with this paradox entails coming to terms with the ambivalent meanings of her mother's remark "You have drunk the water of the Netherlands". In the narrations that I have presented here, we have seen Boushra the highly educated doctor engage in dialogues with the internalized voice of her mother that addresses her I-position as a loyal, grateful daughter. Eventually, she appears to have found a satisfactory balance between her desires for agency and those for communion. She has accomplished this not by silencing the voice of her mother completely; having internalized it, this would amount to denying a part of herself. Rather, she has come to realize that she can deal with her "dutchification" by bringing the internalized voice of her mother in closer harmony with the other voices that she has appropriated over the course of her life.

Indeed, Boushra gives the floor to many other voices in her life story besides those informing her I-position as the daughter of migrants. She explicitly states, for example, that in everyday life, she is often not aware of her multiple identity:

> In my car on the way to my job, I am not Moroccan or Dutch or anything; that is just me! It's only when you stumble on something and reflect on it afterwards that you realize 'this is related to this, and that to that'.

While I have tried to do justice to Boushra's agency as the director of the voices that populate her life story, it is, of course, impossible to reproduce the richness of her story here. Zooming in on narrations about the impact of migration on her quest to balance agency and communion in a satisfactory way, inevitably implies reduction. Therefore, in conclusion, I will zoom out again and put these narrations in a larger context by pointing to similarities that Boushra's story shares with more general features in life stories of narrators who have grown up in the West.

First of all, one does not have to be of Moroccan background to observe that one's relations to parents change as one grows older. Also, the sense of guilt or even betrayal regarding parents one has outgrown is not unique to migrants, but can equally be recognized in the life stories of other categories of highly educated individuals with lower class backgrounds (cf. Higginbothom & Weber 1992; Matthys 2010; Roberts & Rosenwald 2001). Furthermore, the gradual shift in Boushra's life chapters from narrations that focus on personal achievements to those that focus on generativity, that is, the passing on of skills, wisdom and love to others, is a frequent pattern in the life stories of people as they grow older (cf. McAdams 1993, pp. 223–250). Last of all, specific gender-related dimensions of storytelling should be taken into account. In general, the life stories of women tend to focus more frequently on relatedness, and those of men on personal achievements (Diehl et al 2004). One could therefore wonder if the narrations that touch upon Boushra's sense of guilt for not having been able to make her parents happy would have been as prominent in her life story had she been a man. Similarly, taking into account that women tend to be more strongly conceived of as the "gatekeepers" of culture (cf. Dion & Dion 2001), one could wonder whether the tone of resentment in Boushra's mother's remark about the "dutchification" of her daughter would have been quite as strong had Boushra, in fact, been a man.

These observations demonstrate that while for the sake of analysis it can be productive to focus on I-positions that are closely linked to a particular social position, social identifications always intersect: we cannot understand Boushra's life story by reducing it to the self-narrative of a migrant daughter: her narrations about being a migrant daughter are the result of her creative appropriation of the various voices that inform her sense of self as a highly educated Muslim daughter of Moroccan descent in the Netherlands.

Notes

1 To protect my interviewee's privacy, she appears under a pseudonym in this article. For the same reason, no specification is given about her medical specialism, nor of any other personal or contextual details that might reveal her identity.

2 In 2002 the liberal-rightist politician Pim Fortuyn was assassinated by a radical environmentalist of Dutch background. Since Fortuyn spoke very negatively about Muslims, his death is often associated with a perceived danger posed by the presence of Muslims in Dutch society. In 2004, Theo van Gogh, the producer of a film which contains shots of Koranic texts written on a naked female body was murdered by a young man of Moroccan descent who motivated his act in religious terms. The screenplay for the film had been written by Ayaan Hirsi Ali, at the time a member of the Dutch parliament. The film was part of what this Somali-born politician called her "*jihad* against Islam's oppression of women". Particularly during her years in parliament, Hirsi Ali's views had a high impact on the public debate on Islam in the Netherlands. Currently, the flagrantly anti-Islamic statements of Geert Wilders, a rightist member of the Dutch parliament receive much media attention.

3 To disentangle notions of agency, autonomy and relatedness from views in which independence and autonomy or separateness are conflated, Kagitçibasi (2005) distinguishes between a *behavioral* and a *relational* dimension that underlie the construction of selves. Behavioral autonomy, for instance, is not exclusively compatible with separateness from others, but may also occur in combination with relatedness (cf. Buitelaar 2013).

4 Towards the end the interview, all participants were asked for their motivations to cooperate. Most frequently mentioned motivations pertained to the importance of "positive stories" to counterbalance misconceptions about Islam and the wish to provide Moroccan youth with positive role models.

5 for two recent most insightful dissertations on the "homing" of descendants of Moroccan and Turkish background in the Netherlands, see Eijberts (2013) and Stock (2014).

6 The suggestion that her mother's remark is of great significance to Boushra is confirmed by the fact fact that she quoted it not only to me, but also in an interview in a Dutch newspaper. I cannot provide further details, as this would reveal Boushra's true identity.

Bibliography

Buitelaar, M. 2007. "Staying Close by Moving Out. The Contextual Meanings of Personal Autonomy in the Life Stories of Women of Moroccan Descent in the Netherlands", *Contemporary Islam Dynamics of Muslim Life,* vol. 1, no. 2: pp. 2–23.

Buitelaar, M. 2009. *Van Huis uit Marokkaans. Over verweven loyaliteiten van hoogopgeleide migrantendochters.* Bulaaq: Amsterdam.

Buitelaar, M. 2013. "Constructing a Muslim Self in a Post-migration Context. Continuity and Discontinuity with Parental Voices". In M Buitelaar & H Zock (Eds.). *Religious Voices in Self-Narratives. In Making Sense of Life in Times of Transition,* pp. 241–274. De Gruyter: Berlin,

Buitelaar, M. 2014. "Dialogical Constructions of a Muslim self through life storytelling" In R. Ganzevoort, M. de Haardt & M. Scherer-Rath (Eds.). *Religious Stories We Live By. Narrative Approaches in Theology and Religious Studies,* pp. 143–155 Brill: Leiden.

Coenen, L. 2001. *'Word niet zoals wij!' De veranderende betekenis van onderwijs bij Turkse gezinnen in Nederland,* Het Spinhuis: Amsterdam.

Desai, K. 2006. *The Inheritance of Loss.* Hamish Hamilton, London.

Diehl, M, Owen, S. & Younblade M. 2004. "Agency and Communion Attributes in Adults"Spontaneous Self-representations', *International Journal of Behavioral Development,* vol. 28, no. 1: 1–15.

Dion, K. & Dion K. 2001. 'Gender and Cultural Adaptation in Immigrant Families', *Journal of Social Issues,* Vol. 57, 3: 511–521.

Eijberts, M. 2013. *Migrant Women Shout it Out Aloud. the Integration/Participation Strategies and Sense of Home of First- & Second-generation Women of Moroccan and Turkish Descent in the Netherlands.* PhD Thesis, Free University.

Frank, K. 2006. 'Agency', *Anthropological Theory,* Vol. 6, 3: 281–302.

Gregg, G. 2007. *Culture and Identity in a Muslim Society,* Oxford University Press, Oxford.

Hermans, H. 2001. 'The Dialogical Self. Towards a Theory of Personal and Cultural Positioning', *Culture & Psychology,* Vol. 7, 3: 243–281.

Hermans, H. & Hermans-Konopka, A. 2010. *The Dialogical Self: Positioning and Counter-positioning in a Globalizing World.* Cambridge: Cambridge University Press.

Higginbothom, E. & Weber, L. 1992. 'Moving up with Kin and Community', *Gender & Society,* Vol. 6, 3: 416–440.

Hofstede, G. 1991. *Cultures and Organizations: Software of the Mind,* McGraw-Hill, London.

Holland, D. Lachicotte, W, Skinner, D. & Cain, C 1998. *Identity and Agency in Cultural Worlds.* London & Cambridge, MA: Harvard University Press.

Kagitçibasi, C. 2005. "Autonomy and Relatedness in Cultural Context. Implications for Self and Family". *Journal of Cross-Cultural Psychology,* Vol. 36, 4: 403–422.

Mahmood, S. 2005. *Politics of Piety. The Islamic Revival and the Feminist Subject,* Princeton U.P: Princeton, NJ.

Matthys, M. 2010. *Doorzetters. Een onderzoek naar de betekenis van de arbeidersafkomst voor de levensloop en loopbaan van universitair afgestudeerden,* Aksant, Amsterdam.

McAdams, D. 1993. *The Stories We Live By. Personal Myths and the Making of the Self,* The Guildford Press: New York & London.

Olson, K. & Shopes, L. 1991. "Crossing Boundaries, Building Bridges; Doing Oral History among Working-Class Women and Men" In S Berger Gluck & D Patai (Eds.). *Women's Words. The Feminist Practice of Oral History,* pp. 189–204. London: Routledge.

Prins, B. 2006. "Narrative Accounts of Origins: A Blind Spot in the Intersectional Approach?", *European Journal of Women's Studies*, Vol. 13, 3: 277–290.

Roberts, S. & Rosenwald G. 2001. 'Ever Upward and no Turning Back: Social Mobility and Identity Formation among First-generation College Students". In D. McAdams, R Josselson & A Lieblich (Eds.). *Turns in the Road. Narrative Studies of Lives in Transition,* pp. 91–119. American Psychological Association, Washington, DC.

Skinner, E. & Edge, K. 2002. 'Parenting, Motivation, and the Development of Children's Coping'. In L. Crockett (Ed.). *Agency, Motivation, and the Life Course,* pp.77–143 , Lincoln : University of Nebraska Press.

Spiro, M. 1993. 'Is the Western Conception of the Self 'Peculiar' within the Context of the World Cultures?', *Ethos,* Vol. 21, 2: 107–153.

Stock, F. 2014. *Speaking of Home. Home and Identity in the Multivoiced Narratives of Descendants of Moroccan and Turkish Migrants in the Netherlands.* PhD. Thesis, University of Groningen.

BIOGRAPHIES OF CONTRIBUTORS

Soumaya Belhabib is an associate professor of English Literature and Gender Studies at the Department of English Language and Literature, School of Human Sciences, IbnTofail University, Kenitra, Morocco. She is a researcher and author of several articles on gender and women's issues. She has directed the publication of a collective book, entitled "Gender, Power and Society" (Okad, 2012). She has been the coordinator of the 'Gender Studies' Research group within the university since 2007. Besides, she is a women's rights activist, being engaged in fieldwork and advocacy on a wide range of issues relating to women, the law and human rights. She is Vice-President and founding member of the Association Chaml for Women and Family since its creation in 1998.

Sara Borrillo holds a PhD in Middle East Studies from University L'Orientale in Naples, where she is currently a post-doctoral research fellow at Asia, Africa and Mediterranean Department (since 2015). In 2014 she was researcher in the project "Which gender of citizenship? Voices from the South shore of Mediterranean", at University of Florence, for the case study of Morocco. She is associated researcher at Centre Jacques Berque for social sciences (CNRS) in Rabat (Morocco) and at WUNRN (Women of United Nations Research Network). She is Expert in Gender Equality and Women's Empowerment in Public Administration (GEPA) at United Nations

Development Program (UNDP). Her main research topic is about secular feminism, Islamic feminism, social and cultural movements and female religious authorities in Islam, gender politics in MENA region, with particular attention to Morocco. For her articles see: https://unior.academia.edu/SaraBorrillo

Marjo Buitelaar (1958) is senior lecturer Anthropology of Muslim Societies at the University of Groningen. She is an area specialist of Morocco and Muslims in the Netherlands. Her research interests concern the practice of Islam in daily life and the construction of identity of Muslims. Besides several Dutch books, she has published one English book: *Fasting and Feasting in Morocco. Women's participation in Ramadan* (1993), Oxford/Providence: Berg Publishers. Buitelaar is currently working on a revised, English edition of her most recent book on life stories by highly educated Moroccan Dutch women.

Souad Eddouada holds a PhD in cultural and gender studies from Mohammed V University in Rabat, Morocco. She has been affiliated to Ibn Tofail University in Kenitra, Morocco, for about 11years. In 2007, she was a postdoctoral research associate at Lund University in Sweden. From 2008 to 2009, Eddouada was a Fulbright Fellow at the Institute for Advanced Study in Princeton, New Jersey, where she took part in various workshops and conferences on gender, Islam, and women's rights in the Middle East and North Africa. In 2010, she served as an advisor for Freedom House's MENA regional committee's report on women's rights in North Africa. Since 2011, she has been the academic director of the Migration and Transnational Identity program. She has published several articles on women's issues in Morocco and Tunisia.

Moha Ennaji is professor of linguistics and cultural studies at Fez University. His most recent publications are: *Minorities, Women and the State in North Africa* (Red Sea Press, 2015), *Muslim Moroccan Migrants in Europe* (Palgrave, 2014), *Multiculturalism and Democracy in North Africa* (Routledge, 2014), *Gender and Violence in the Middle East*, co-edited with F. Sadiqi (Routledge, 2011), *Women as Agents of Change in the Middle East and North Africa*, co-edited with F.Sadiqi (Routledge, 2010), *Multilingualism, Cultural*

Identity, and Education in Morocco (Springer, 2005), *Language and Gender in the Mediterranean Region, IJSL Issue 190, Editor (2008), Migration and Gender in Morocco*, co-authored with F. Sadiqi (Red Sea Press, 2008), *Women Writing Africa, the Northern Region,* co-edited with F.Sadiqi et al (The Feminist Press, 2009). Moha Ennaji is the President of the South North Center for Intercultural Dialogue.

Valérie K. Orlando is Professor of French & Francophone Literatures in the Department of French & Italian at the University of Maryland, College Park. She is the author of four books: *Screening Morocco: Contemporary Film in a Changing Society* (Ohio UP, 2011), *Francophone Voices of the 'New Morocco' in Film and Print: (Re)presenting a Society in Transition* (Palgrave-Macmillan, 2009),*Of Suffocated Hearts and Tortured Souls: Seeking Subjecthood Through Madness in Francophone Women's Writing of Africa and the Caribbean* (Lexington Books, 2003) and *Nomadic Voices of Exile: Feminine Identity in Francophone Literature of the Maghreb,* (Ohio University Press, 1999). She has co-edited the forthcoming volume *Re-imagining the Caribbean: Conversations among the Creole, English, French and Spanish Caribbean* (Lexington Books 2014) and written numerous articles on Francophone women's writing from the African diaspora, African Cinema, and French literature and culture.

Aziza Ouguir obtained her BA degree in linguistics at Ibn Tofail University in Kenitra. She also holds a postgraduate degree in linguistics and gender studies from Sidi Mohammed ben Abdallah in Fes. In 2013, she obtained her PhD degree from the University of Amsterdam, school of humanities the Netherlands. Her PhD thesis is titled "Female Religious Agents: Old Practices and New Perspectives". It is a research project which studies Moroccan female religious women, in particular historical women saints and their reception by women venerators and feminist activists of Morocco today. Her field of study focuses on Moroccan feminine Sufism, women in Islamic History, gender issues and feminism. At present she is an employee at the municipal council of Khemisset city.

Raja Rhouni is Professor at Chouaib Doukkali University at El Jadida. She studied English Literature and Cultural Studies in Rabat, earning her Doctorate in 2005 from the Cultural and Development Studies program at Mohammad V University. During the 2006–2007 academic year, she was a Fellow in the multi-disciplinary research program "Europe in the Middle East: the Middle East in Europe" of the Institute of Advanced Study in Berlin. Her project dealt with "Islamic feminist hermeneutics of the Qur'an." She is the author of *Secular and Islamic Feminist Critiques in the Work of Fatima Mernissi* (Leiden and Boston: Brill, 2010).

Fatima Sadiqi is Professor of linguistics and gender studies. She has written extensively on Moroccan languages and Moroccan women's issues. She is the author of *Women, Gender, and Language in Morocco* (Brill, 2003), acclaimed by many critics as the first book on feminist linguistics in the Arab-Islamic world. Her Harvard Fellowship allowed her to start her new book *Berber Women's Religious Expressions*. Fatima Sadiqi has also co-authored, co-edited, and co-translated a number of books and articles. She is Editor-in-Chief of *Languages and Linguistics*, an international journal, and serves on the editorial board of the *Language and Gender*, the first international journal in the discipline. Her recent interest in gender and migration is part of her concerns with how language, gender and mobility interact with culture in a fast-changing planet.

Susan Schaefer Davis is an anthropologist with extensive research experience with women and adolescents, and much development work in North Africa. She has held teaching or research positions at several institutions including Haverford College, the University of Pennsylvania, Trenton State College (now College of New Jersey), and Al Akhawayn University (AUI) in Morocco. Her work focuses on Moroccan women, adolescence, and changing gender roles. She has written numerous articles on these topics and two books, *Patience and Power: Women's Lives in a Moroccan Village*, and *Adolescence in a Moroccan Town*. She is currently working on a book of photos and interviews with Moroccan women textile artisans. She has a Ph.D. in anthropology from the University of Michigan and did post-doctoral work at Harvard University.

Karen Vintges is a Senior Lecturer in Social and Political Philosophy in the Department of Philosophy at the University of Amsterdam.

She has published *Philosophy as Passion. The Thinking of Simone de Beauvoir* (Bloomington: Indiana University Press, 1996 [originally in Dutch, 1992]); *Feminism and the Final Foucault* (D.Taylor/K.Vintges, Eds., Illinois University Press, 2004), *Women, Feminism and Fundamentalism* (I.Dubel/K.Vintges, Eds. SWP Publishing Company, 2007) and several other books in Dutch. She is currently composing a book entitled *A New Dawn for The second sex.* She coordinated a research project funded by the Netherlands Organisation for Scientific Research (NWO) entitled 'Women and Islam: New Perspectives' (2008–2013).

Mohammed Yachoulti graduated from Mohammed Ben Abdellah University, Faculty of Arts & Human Sciences, Fez- Morocco with a BA degree in English literature, an MA in Gender Studies and a Doctorate in Linguistics & Gender Studies. Currently, he is an assistant professor at the Faculty of Arts & Human Sciences, Moulay Ismail University- Mekness. He is interested in gender and politics, social movement studies and migration. His recent publication is Civil Society, Women's Movement and the Moroccan State: Addressing the specificities and Assessing the roles (2012, Lamber Academic Publishing). He has also participated in many national and international conferences and workshops on gender, civil society, and migration.

Merieme Yafout is a researcher at the Institute of Political, International and Historical Studies (IEPHI) at the Faculty of Political Sciences/University of Lausanne. In 2012, she obtained a PhD in political science (Hassan II University/Casablanca). Her thesis subject was entitled: "The status of women within the Islamist movements in Morocco: between feminine exegesis and political participation". She is author of several articles on "Islamic feminism in Morocco", "female ijtihad", "the status of women in Moroccan political parties", "Islamist movements in Morocco," "elections in Morocco "," field research in Morocco ", etc.

INDEX